Children's Mathematics

Making Marks, Making Meaning

Maulfry Worthington and
Elizabeth Carruthers

P·C·P
Paul Chapman
Publishing

Paul Chapman Publishing
A SAGE Publications Company
6 Bonhill Street
London EC2A 4PU

SAGE Publications Inc
2455 Teller Road
Thousand Oaks, California 91320

SAGE Publications India Pvt Ltd
B-42, Panchsheel Enclave
Post Box 4109
New Delhi 100 017

Library of Congress Control Number: 2002107133

A catalogue record for this book is available from the British
Library

ISBN 0 7619 4069 3
ISBN 0 7619 4070 7 (pbk)

Typeset by Dorwyn Ltd, Rowlands Castle, Hants
Printed in Great Britain by Cromwell Press, Trowbridge

www.childrens-mathematics.co.uk

Children's Mathematics

Contents

Dedication

We dedicate this book to our own creative children: Mhairi, Sovay, Laura and Louise, and to the memory of two strong women – our mothers Elizabeth Gillon Carruthers and Muriel Marianne Worthington.

Acknowledgements

We should like to pay tribute to all the adults and children who contributed to our thinking about children's mathematics.

Our sincere thanks go in particular to Chris Athey who, through her writing, really helped us observe and understand young children's thinking and cognitive behaviour. It was our close analysis of children's mathematical graphics that alerted us to the significance of their marks. It is the meaning in their mathematical marks that enables children to make connections between their own mathematics and abstract mathematical symbolism.

Our thanks go to the other members of the Emergent Mathematics Teachers' group, especially to Mary Wilkinson who founded the group and who believed in the importance of teachers writing – for teachers. Our thanks to all the brilliant women teachers in the group who together shared excitement in mathematics education through numerous discussions: Petrie Murchison, Alison Meechan, Alison Kenney, Bernie Davis, Wendy Lancaster, Chryssa Turner, Sue Malloy, Maggie Reeves, Robin Connett and Julie Humphries.

We would like to thank the staff and children of the following Early Years settings for allowing us to include samples of children's mathematics: Chestnut Avenue Nursery; Littleham Nursery (Fiona Priest) and Walter Daw Nursery. Ide First School, Exeter (Maggie Skeet, Barbara Haddon and Edwina Hill); Stoke Hill First School, Exeter (Steve Greenhaigh); St Nicholas' Combined School, Exeter; Honeywell Infants School, London (Karen Pearson); Weston Mill Primary School, Plymouth (Ann Williams); Hooe Primary School, Plymouth; Bramble Hedge Pre-School, Plymouth (Julie Mills); Uffculm Primary School, Devon; Willand Primary School, Devon; Redhills Combined School, Exeter (Petrie Murchison) and St David's First School, Exeter (Wendy Lancaster).

Our special thanks go to the following people who influenced our thinking over the years and empowered us through their unstinting support: Maggie Skeet; Karen Pearson; Sheila and Michael Rowberry; Heather Tozer; Petrie Murchison; Jean-Anne Clyde, University of Louisville; and the Plymouth Numeracy Team – Chris Clarke, Kathy Jarrett, Liz Walmsley and Rob Pyner.

Thanks go to our families including Steve Worthington and Jane Mulkewich and to all of our friends for their tremendous encouragement. Above all, special thanks must go to the children who have helped us understand, and to Tom Bass who made dinners when deadlines loomed.

Foreword

This is a very important book not least because of its range. The authors have gathered evidence from children over a 12-year period. They analysed almost 700 samples of children's graphics showing how powerful patterns if cognition (schemas) in the early years of development gradually evolve into recognisable forms of writing and mathematics. Their aim, and unique achievement, has been to chart the progress of children's thinking through their mark-making from age 3 to 8. They have bridged the gap between Early Years and primary education.

When seen across such an age range, the children's explanations of the meanings of their own marks represent an exciting intellectual journey through childhood which will provide new insights for parents and professionals into the developing relationship between language and thought. The representations show a gradual emergence of more complex relationships between mathematical language and mathematical thought.

Evolving co-ordinations are vividly illustrated by children's own graphics and speech representations. In each case specific and appropriate references from the literature are given. These aid comprehension of complex material. The references are extensive and illuminative and specific page numbers are given at the end of quotations. This scholarly practice will be much appreciated by readers who may wish to pursue sub-themes in the book of which there are many: variations in pedagogy in different countries, working with parents and creating a mathematically stimulating environment are just a few.

The authors are vigorously in favour of school procedures which encourage children to be more participatory, and have greater autonomy, in their own learning. Many useful references are given in support of this constructivist pedagogical position.

One aspect of the enquiry shows that the majority of teachers still rely on mathematics worksheets where subject matter is neatly divided into discrete steps. Some of the children's cognitive confusions arising from these tasks are discussed. These confusions have to be seen against the clear conceptual understandings of children discussing their own invented symbolic systems.

There is nothing sentimental about the child-centred orientation of the attitude held and evidence gathered by these two authors. They are tough teachers making a case for improving children's thinking, and mathematical thinking in particular. Their central thesis is that the gap in children's mathematical understanding is bridged through supporting the development of children's own mathematical graphics. At present there is a wide, conceptually dangerous gap.

Teachers, hopefully working with parents, can develop their own knowledge of early spontaneous patterns of thought in young children. Where adults learn the language and thought of young children they become better translators for the children into the language and thought of more formal mathematics. Adults are assisted by the children themselves who want to embrace more formal aspects of mathematics just as they wish to acquire more advanced strategies and skills in other areas of the curriculum. In translating between their informal and formal mathematical graphics children can exploit both. They will move with ease between their spontaneous ways of working things out, and their more newly acquired, more formal concepts. This is not a one-way movement: children move in an infinite loop as their translation supports them in becoming bi-numerate. Confidence will be maintained as competence increases.

The book is interestingly written and will strengthen professional knowledge on the development of meaning in children aged from 3 to 8.

Chris Athey
7 October 2002

1

Who Takes Notice of Children's Own Written Mathematics?

Once when I was six years old I saw a magnificent picture in a book, called *True Stories from Nature*, about the primeval forest. It was a picture of a boa constrictor in the act of swallowing an animal ... I pondered deeply, then, over the adventures of the jungle. And after some work with a coloured pencil I succeeded in making my first drawing. My Drawing Number One. It looked like this:

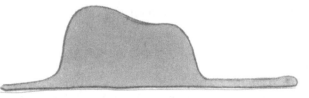

Figure 1.1 Drawing Number One

I showed my masterpiece to the grown-ups, and asked them whether the drawing frightened them. But they answered: 'Frighten? Why should any one be frightened by a hat?'

My drawing was not a picture of a hat. It was a picture of a boa constrictor digesting an elephant. But since the grown-ups were not able to understand it, I made another drawing: I drew the inside of the boa constrictor, so that the grown-ups could see it clearly.

Elles ont toujours besoin d'explications.

They always needed to have things explained ...

I had been disheartened by the failure of my Drawing Number One and my Drawing Number Two. Grown-ups never understand anything by themselves, and it is tiresome for children to be always and forever explaining things to them. (Saint-Exupéry, 1958, pp.5–6).

In the spirit of Antoine de Saint-Exupéry's touching fable, we have written this book to help 'the grown-ups' understand the meanings of young children's mathematical images.

Illustration of the boa constrictor reproduced with the kind permission of the publisher of the original French edition: © Editions Gallimard, Paris, 1944. Text from *The Little Prince* © Gallimard 1944. First English Edition published in 1945 by William Heinemann Ltd and used with permission of Egmont Books Limited, London.

Children's mathematical graphics

This book is a study of young children's mathematical graphics and the way in which, through using their own marks and making their own meaning, children can more readily translate between their informal 'home mathematics' and the abstract symbolism of 'school mathematics'. We argue that by doing this allows children to become bi-numerate.

Why write about children's mathematical graphics?

For 12 years we have developed our practice and explored the theories that underpin this book. Because we were teaching for a greater part of this period we were able to trial ideas, hypothesise and generate our philosophies and pedagogy in our own settings. As our excitement in the development of children's own mathematical marks and their meanings grew, we focused on a number of research projects that have helped inform and guide us. Where they have relevance for the subject of this book, we refer to our findings (see Appendix for a list of our research topics).

On numerous occasions we have been invited to share our practice, understanding and some of the hundreds of children's examples we have collected – with students where we have lectured and with teachers on professional development courses and at Early Years conferences. Students' and teachers' responses are almost always of surprise and great interest – that it makes sense to encourage this, that working in this way offers a real alternative to the use of worksheets and, above all, that it offers tremendous insight into children's understanding and development. But the benefits are greatest for the children.

We had come to children's early mathematical mark-making through our own interest and following many years of experience in supporting emergent writing in our classrooms. We had seen wonderful progress in children's early writing and began to make comparisons with children's early recorded mathematics. A significant element in our development as teachers was the period in which we were members of the 'Emergent Mathematics Teachers' group' (see this chapter).

As we developed our practice and theory we collected samples of children's mathematical marks during a period of 12 years. For a greater part of this period we taught mainly in nursery and First Schools, and also through the primary age range to 11 years. Although we concentrate on the 3–8 age range in this book we feel the development of children's own mathematics through the school is important.

It took time to develop our practice in order to support children's mathematical graphics. Working with local groups of teachers encouraged us to question assumptions and consider different perspectives on teaching mathematics in the Early Years. As we slowly developed our practice we also traced the pattern of children's early development of numerals and established some pathways that led to early calculations on paper. This development did not reveal itself to us as readily as children's early writing had done.

Evidence-based study

The examples of children's mathematics have come from our own teaching either in our own classrooms or when we were invited to teach in other class-rooms. It is this strong teaching background, coupled with our work as consult-ants, advisers and lecturers, that has made us focus on what we believe is important in the Early Years. It has also sharpened our knowledge of underpin-ning theories – of mathematics and mark-making and of all the complexity of teaching and learning in the 3–8 years age range.

International findings

Our search for literature on children's own written mathematics in the 3–8 age range did not reap any major findings. There were individual studies in the USA, for example Whitin, Mills and O'Keefe, (1990); in Australia, Stoessinger and Edmunds (1992) and in England teachers' stories of their work (Atkinson, 1992). There was the beginning of a movement in the direction of advocating what we term a bi-numerate approach to the teaching of mathematics (see Chapter 5). However, Alexander's significant study of five nations – France, Russia, India, the USA and England – found that the teaching of mathematics worldwide is heavily influenced by textbooks and worksheets. India was the exception, not only because of funding difficulties, but due to significant historical and cultural factors (Alexander, 2000). In 1998 and again in 1999 I was fortunate to have two periods of voluntary work with a children's charity in Tamil Nadu, in southern India. At first hand I was able to see children taught in nursery and primary schools.

State-run nursery schools are found in many larger villages, including those in which I worked. The nursery teacher may have completed primary education, though her assistants have often had little or no schooling, and in this rural area there was very little training for nursery teachers. In many of the villages I visited there are few literate adults and this, combined with often extreme levels of poverty, means that perhaps only a handful of homes in the community have any printed matter, pens or paper in their homes. Of the ten nursery schools I visited, nine were totally empty rooms: apart from the adults and children, there were no toys, resources, books or pictures. Discipline was strict with commands to 'sit up straight', 'fold your arms' and 'sit still and be quiet' frequent. The chil-dren attend nursery school until they are 6 years old.

In only one of the nursery schools I visited were there any visual aids. The teacher proudly showed me some small posters she had made – an alphabet with pictures and a small number frieze of numbers 1–10 with pictures. Questions were fired at these 2–6-year-olds and a rapid response was demanded. The math-ematics teaching was a transmission model with an emphasis on correct answers. In the nursery schools I visited there were no opportunities for mark-making or drawing since there were no resources. During a period of several months I did not once see a child make marks on the sandy ground outside, even in play.

Teaching in primary schools was of a very similar style, although funding permitted children in some classes to use slates and older children to use exercise books. They copied standard algorithms from the blackboard and filled in the answers. Alexander includes a transcription of one spelling lesson (in a Hindi-speaking area) with children aged 5-6 years: this is typical of what I saw in every nursery and primary school I visited:

> four children come to the blackboard at the teacher's invitation, to write 'A'. Teacher then writes 'A' herself and asks the class to recite the sound, over and over again. Teacher writes, *ana, Anamika, aachi* (pomegranate; a girl's name; good) on the board. Three pupils come forward to circle the 'A' in these words. Class applauds. Teacher asks questions to recapitulate and children chant in response. (Alexander, 2000, p. 282)

Alexander reported that lessons he had observed in England in 1998 were as tied to textbooks and published schemes as those in Russian schools. Teachers in France and the USA were moving away from the domain of textbooks. Alexander emphasised the tension in the USA between the schools wanting to move away from the dominance of standard textbooks, and the concern of the school board and government of raising standards. The change noted was that instead of using workbooks exclusively, teachers created their own worksheets for children to record their mathematics set by the teacher. This finding is mirrored by our study (see Chapter 5).

In Holland the main influence in mathematics education has been 'Realistic Mathematics Education'. This was initiated by Freudenthal who professed that mathematics must be connected to society and children should learn mathematics by a process of 'progressive mathematisation' (Freudenthal, 1968). Treffers built on this idea and describes two types of processes, horizontal and vertical (Treffers, 1978). 'Horizontal mathematisation' is Freudenthal's term to explain the way in which the gap between informal mathematics and formal mathematics is bridged. Horizontal mathematisation helps children move from the world of real life into the world of symbols. In teaching terms, for example, a picture of a real-life problem is given to the children, perhaps people getting on and off a bus. This would later be shown with symbols and then again, after a period of time, shown without any picture cues (Heuvel-Panhuizen, 2001). The term 'vertical mathematisation' refers to the children working within the world of symbols. Children move on to models such as the empty number line which the National Numeracy Strategy in England has adopted (QCA, 1999).

In Holland mental arithmetic is at the 'heart of the curriculum' (Buys, 2001). Children try to do every calculation mentally. They are also encouraged to write their thinking down on scrap paper so that they remember the steps for more difficult calculations where it is impossible, sometimes, to keep track. Children's own ways of thinking are encouraged through their mental work, and informal recordings through the empty number line have a high priority. We have not found any reference to imply that children's informal and early mathematical thinking on paper is acknowledged or developed in Holland. However, studies by Oers have highlighted the very considerable insights that young children have, in terms of marks that can contribute to their mathematical understanding (for example, Oers, 1994; 1997).

Zevenbergen raises concerns about the philosophy that underpins mathematics curricula in Australia and many other western countries. Comparing the Dutch approach to that of Queensland in Australia, she argues that 'while there are tokenistic references made to children's informal understandings, these are not central to curriculum design' (Zevenbergen, 2002, p. 4).

In 1999, England introduced the National Numeracy Strategy which is a framework of objectives for teaching mathematics for 5–11-year-olds (QCA, 1999). Like the Dutch model, this document also has a heavy emphasis on mental calculation but introduces standard and expanded written forms of mathematics much earlier. England, unlike other countries we have mentioned, has recognised the importance of young children's own mathematical marks and their own choice of written methods have been highlighted in official documentation. Guidance for teachers emphasises: 'children will need to have plenty of experience of using their own individual ways of recording addition and subtraction activities before they begin to record more formally' (QCA, 1999 p. 19). The documents also advise that 'at first, children's recordings may not be easy for someone else to interpret, but they form an important stage in developing fluency' (QCA, 1999, p. 12).

Further support for children's own mathematical graphic representations can be seen in the English *Curriculum Guidance for the Foundation Stage* for teachers of children from 3 to 5 years of age. Teachers are recommended to promote confidence in children when they begin to record their mathematics: 'asking children to "put something on paper" about what they have done or have found out will allow them to choose how to record or whether to, for example, use a picture, some kind of tally or write a number' (QCA, 2000, pp. 71–2).

Our findings – teachers' questionnaire

We wanted to find out the extent to which recommendations in the National Numeracy Strategy had influenced classroom practice, in terms of children's own marks and written methods.

Our questionnaire focused on two key aspects. We asked:

- Do you give children worksheets for mathematics?
- Do you give children blank paper for mathematics?

We also asked teachers to give examples of the sort of things the children might do either on worksheets or on blank paper (see Chapter 5).

When planning our questionnaire we hoped that the findings would provide us with information about adults' expectations and the opportunities that children had to represent their mathematics. In doing this we made a mistaken assumption: we thought that using blank paper would provide children with the sort of open opportunities that we believed would help them make their own meanings. When we analysed the responses we were very surprised by the results (see Chapter 5).

Our responses were gathered during a one-year period, from 273 teachers in four areas of England. Three areas were large cities: one in the north of England; one in the west and one in the south-west. The remaining area was a largely rural county in the south of the country. We had been interested to discover if teachers' practice was different in large, inner-city areas when compared with the largely rural county, but this was not the case.

Worksheet use

Use in research

What was evident was the large difference in use of worksheets when comparing different types of Early Years settings and classes with different ages of children (Table 1.1).

Table 1.1   Results of the questionnaires

Type of setting	Percentage using worksheets
Maintained nursery classes	20
Private nurseries	63
Pre-schools (voluntary)	72
School classes with 4/5-year-olds	89
School classes with 4–6-year-olds	100
School classes with 7-year-olds	100
School classes with 8-year-olds	100

Children in maintained (state-run) nursery classes appeared to be freer in terms of their mathematics, whilst voluntary run pre-schools made the greatest use of these published materials for children under 5 years. Once children arrived in school – in England this is generally at the very early age of 4 years old – almost 90 per cent of teachers use worksheets and by the following year every one of the teachers in our study used worksheets. Four-year-olds who were in mixed-age classes with 5–6-year-olds were more likely to use worksheets than children in classes of only 4- and 5-year-olds. Our findings are consistent with what Millet and Johnson observe is a 'world-wide trend'; 'typical teaching is assumed to be the total or significant use of a commercial mathematics scheme'

(Millet and Johnson, cited in Maclellan, 2001, p. 76).

The recommendations for teachers in the Foundation Stage (QCA, 2000) and for primary teachers (QCA,1999) is not reflected in our research findings. Currently teachers are unsure how they might put recommendations about children's written methods – particularly for children between the ages of 3 and 7 years – into practice. This is comparable to Zevenbergen's (2002) concerns.

Studies that relate to mathematical literacy

We had been thrilled to trace the development of young children's early literacy in our own classrooms for many years. A growing body of literature had supported our teaching and our understanding of children's development. Some of these studies explored children's writing and reading from a teaching perspective, linking theory and practice; for example, Holdaway's *The Foundations of Literacy* (1979), Cambourne's *The Whole Story* (1988), Smith's *Writing and the Writer* (1982) and Hall's *The Emergence of Literacy* (1987). Others such as Bissex's (1980) mother–child study explored a child's natural development in the home. Whilst there are too many to mention here, an earlier and very influential book that stands out for many teachers is Clay's *What did I Write?* (1975) in which she documented the development in 'understanding written codes'. Bringing the subject up to date is Barratt-Pugh and Rohl's book *Literacy Learning in the Early Years* (2000) which includes chapters from different authors on the sociocultural aspect of literacy learning and critical literacies. It was this powerful range of texts that provided the foundation for us to consider an additional 'literacy' – of mathematics.

When in 1990 we began to explore children's development of their mathematical literacy, there was very little published on this aspect of teaching and learning, compared with the wealth of books and articles on children's early writing. Only one text explored this question in depth. In his study, *Children and Number: Difficulties in Learning Mathematics*, Hughes (1986) highlighted the gap that exists between children's home and the abstract symbolism and language of school mathematics: this difficulty had earlier been noted by Ginsberg (1977) and Allardice 1977. In an experiment that is now familiar to many teachers as 'the tins game', Hughes demonstrated the way in which 3- and 4-year-olds could represent numerals in personal ways and which they could later 'read'. He also included a small number of graphical responses of addition and subtraction calculations from children of 5–8 years. Hughes's research appears to have influenced the writers of official curriculum documents in England (see for example QCA, 1999; 2000). However, as our study shows, Hughes's influence on teaching has, sadly, been sparse.

Whitin, Mills and O'Keefe argue that a 'true mathematical literacy must originate not from a methodology, but from a theory of learning: one that views mathematics not as a series of formulas, calculations, or even problem-solving techniques, but as a way of knowing and learning about the world' (Whitin, Mills and O'Keefe, 1990, p. 170).

In 1995 in a chapter entitled 'Emergent mathematics or how to help young children become confident mathematicians', Whitebread discussed Hughes's work, asserting 'what is clear is that children cannot be encouraged to use new strategies very effectively by simply being taught them as an abstract procedure' (Whitebread, 1995, p. 35). Whitebread contends that within this (emergent) approach 'it is clearly important ... that children are encouraged to be reflective about their own processing and to adopt strategies in ways which put them in control' (Whitebread, 1995, p. 26).

In 1997 Gifford discussed the theory underpinning emergent mathematics approaches and compared what she termed the 'British' and 'Australian' models, concluding 'the Australian model of emergent mathematics (therefore) provides a clearer image of the teacher's role in terms of activities and support for children's learning' (Gifford, 1997, p. 79). What Gifford did not know, however, was that the 'Australian model' was not quite so far away: Stoessinger and Wilkinson (1991) had written an article on emergent mathematics. Stoessinger was a researcher visiting England from the Centre for Advanced Teaching Studies in Tasmania, and Wilkinson one of the founder members of the Emergent Mathematics Teachers' group based in Devon, to which we belonged (see pp. 9 and 10).

Gifford argues that one benefit of encouraging children to represent their own mathematics, is the way in which the teacher 'makes links between different aspects of an operation. She does this by showing children that the same words and signs relate to a variety of contexts, thus preventing children giving limited meanings to signs' (Gifford, 1997, p. 85). Gifford reasons that the 'advantage of an emergent approach in encouraging children's own representations, is that it allows children to make sense of ideas by representing them in their own way' (Gifford, 1997, p. 86).

In the same year that Gifford wrote of the 'importance of making links', the authors of the *Effective Teachers of Numeracy* report recognised the value of a 'connectionist orientation': characterised by teachers who believe that being numerate involves being efficient, effective and 'having the ability to choose an appropriate method' (Askew et al., 1997, p. 27). Askew et al.'s study documents some of the most significant features of a connectionist orientation of teaching.

Discovering Athey's (1990) inspirational study of children's schemas, *Extending Thought in Young Children*, we found we gained huge insights into children's cognitive behaviour or schemas. By closely observing, assessing and supporting children's schemas we added considerably to what we knew about their mathematical concerns.

One means of understanding children's mathematical graphics is to view them from joint perspectives – from the mathematics and from the wider subject of all their marks, including writing and drawing. In his recent and important study of the evolution of children's art *The Art of Childhood and Adolescence: The Construction of Meaning* Matthews traces the development of children's early marks. He writes:

the subject domain is important only insofar as it contains instruments, processes and experiences which will promote human development and learning (Blenkin & Kelly, 1996).What needs to be added to our understanding of the subject discipline, is how this interacts with the learner. Only then will we be in a position to provide the kind of interaction and provision necessary to promote intellectual and emotional growth (Matthews, 1999, p. 163).

In recent years several studies have explored the rich variety of ways in which children make meaning in 'multi-modal ways' through their play and with a variety of resources and media. Kress argues that such ways form the pre-history of writing for young children and deserve to be taken seriously by adults (Kress, 1997). Developing the same argument in her book *Transformations: Meaning Making in Nursery Education*, Pahl uses detailed observations to provide powerful evidence and challenge our ideas about communication and literacy. These studies make an enormous contribution to teachers' understanding of the complex ways in which young children make meaning (Pahl, 1999a).

In the Froebel Block Play Project directed by Tina Bruce, Gura analysed children's use of block play at a deep level (Gura, 1992). Through observing children in their block play, Gura presents ways that they represent their mathematics in three-dimensional space. Children discover mathematical relationships as they 'doodle' in their block play, which they use in more challenging structures. Gura states that when children engage in block play that makes sense to them, and in partnerships with adults, they can make relationships between practical mathematics and the disembedded symbolism of formal mathematics. When children in the study voluntarily drew their structures they used a variety of responses from pictographic to iconic. It was noted that children as young as 3 were moving towards less embedded representations. The Froebel Block Play Project illustrates many similar pedagogical issues that we found important in supporting children's own mathematical recordings. For example, Gura advocates an interactionist approach which includes negotiation, and respecting and enabling children and understanding the variety and diversity of children's own representations.

In a recent study of play entitled *Teaching through Play*, Bennett, Wood and Rogers explore teachers' thinking and classroom practice, and highlight the teaching of another member of our Emergent Mathematics Teachers' group, 'Jenny'. In their final chapter the authors consider implications for teachers' professional development, advocating that teachers become proactive and 'use informed awareness and deliberative thought processes' (Bennett, Wood and Rogers, 1997). Such a proactive stance is outlined by Manning and Payne (1993) who recommend a social-constructivist approach which 'involves the processes of social interaction with knowledgeable others, scaffolding procedures, the acquisition and application of knowledge about teaching in general and one's own teaching in particular' (cited in Bennett, Wood and Rogers, 1997, p. 131). In the following section we outline our enquiry into children's mathematics as members of the Emergent Mathematics Teachers' group, where, as proactive teachers, we did just this.

Enquiring into children's mathematics

Whilst he was visiting England in 1990, Rex Stoessinger, a researcher from New Zealand, arranged to meet a county mathematics adviser, Mary Wilkinson. Rex was interested in 'flipping over' the concept of emergent writing into mathematics and asked Mary to invite some local teachers who understood and used this approach in their classrooms. The authors of this book were two of the first few teachers who met to explore this idea. From our initial meeting we met regularly, discussing, reading and challenging each other's thinking and our own. We were anxious to see mathematics in its broadest sense and within the context of Early Years and primary education. During the period in which we met together we explored many aspects of mathematics teaching and learning.

We have worked extensively with teachers and students and developed our classroom practice as our emerging theories evolved. For some years we also held a series of annual conferences with nationally known speakers from the field of Early Years education. The speaker at our first conference posed the following question: 'what is it you believe you must do *deliberately*, to support children's mathematical understanding?' (Gulliver, 1992). This question was to be a key influence on our developing pedagogy.

In Chapter 2 we explore the way in which young children begin to assign mathematical meaning to their marks and introduce a range of mathematical graphics from 3- and 4-year-olds. We look at some theories of learning and show how these different theories have influenced teachers' beliefs and practice regarding their expectations of children's mathematical graphics.

2

Making Marks, Making Meaning

'Goodbye,' said the fox. 'And now here is my secret, a very simple secret: It is only with the heart that one can see rightly; what is essential is invisible to the eye.' (Saint-Exupéry, 1958, p. 68).

Children making meaning with marks

During the past 30 years there has been a growing interest among teachers and educators, in the meaning children make in a variety of contexts through their explorations in the world. Studies have focused on emergent writing (Bissex, 1980; Clay, 1975; Hall, 1989); children's schemas (Athey, 1990); drawings, model making and play with objects (Kress, 1997; Pahl, 1999b); early mark-making, drawing and painting (Matthews, 1999). Early representations of scientific concepts have also been explored from this perspective (Driver, Guesne and Tiberghien, 1985).

These aspects have been considered both from the child's current perspective and in the context of their developing understanding. In other words, as they make actions, marks, draw, model and play, children make personal meaning. It is the child's own meanings that have been the focus of this developing interest, rather than the child's outcome of an adult's planned piece of work, such as copied writing or representing a person 'correctly'.

In his long-term study of children at home and at school, Wells (1986) concluded that children were constantly trying to make sense of their world. Tizard and Hughes's (1984) study of 4-year-olds again emphasised the child as a powerful learner, struggling to make sense of all around him/her. In their studies, Donaldson (1978) and Hughes (1986), both concluded that children responded to situations that make 'human sense': these studies used clinical tasks rather than evidence from natural contexts. Both of these studies are well recognised as contributing to our understanding of children's learning but the tasks were not immediately purposeful or natural to the children.

Carruthers suggests that 'now we have to jump from the idea of "human sense" to observing children's learning in terms of "child sense". Allowing the child to lead gives a deeper indication of their natural development, indicating ways to support their growing knowledge' (Carruthers, 1997a, p. 13). When we observe children's own mathematical marks on paper, then it is this 'child sense' that we see and that is vital to the child's thinking about mathematics. Their own marks make meaning to them and through these, children can further their mathematical thinking. At the same time, the teacher gains insights into the child's current and developing understanding.

Different literacies: mathematical literacy

Marks on paper (and other media) can be used to represent languages and meaning, and can be shaped to form specific symbols of that language. The Centre for Literacy of Quebec (1999) defines literacy in the following way: 'literacy encompasses a set of abilities to understand and use the dominant symbol systems of a culture for personal and community development. In a technological society, the concept of literacy is expanding to include the media and electronic text, in addition to alphabetic and number systems'. To this definition we would add play with objects, model-making, art, music and science. This broader perspective is in tune with Malaguzzi's 'hundred languages', the theme of a poem that refers to the diverse ways children can express themselves and that recognises children's amazing potential in making sense of their experiences and abstract symbol systems (Malaguzzi, 1996, p. 3).

Barratt-Pugh and Rohl (2000, p. 25) argue that 'literacy is a complex and multi-faceted process which is continually evolving'. For young learners, representing mathematics on paper through the use of their own marks, approximations of symbols, numbers and graphics is also 'literacy'. This definition of literacy provides a much broader perspective for supporting early mathematics than seeing writing, art, mathematics, music and science as having distinctive and unrelated systems of symbols and representation.

In this book we use the term 'literacy' to include mathematics: we see the terms 'mathematical literacy', 'emergent mathematics' and 'mathematical graphics' as sharing the same meaning.

Children represent their mathematical actions and understanding on paper

The following examples are a selection of children's mathematical marks on paper: they are from children in our families and Early Years settings in which we have worked.

At home – Matt's numbers

Matt 'read' his spontaneous scribble, 'I spell 80354' (Figure 2.1).

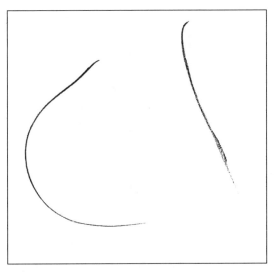

Figure 2.1. Matt's numbers

Matt was 3 years and 1 month old at the time he made these marks. At home with his older brother, Matt said he was 'drawing'. I was sitting writing postcards at the table nearby and Matt's 4-year-old brother was playing computer games. Matt rapidly covered a number of pieces of paper with a range of marks (see Figure 2.6). He showed this example to me and I asked him to tell me about it.

- Matt knows that marks carry meaning and that they can sometimes represent numbers.
- Perhaps he was using a phone number as a reference point for the numbers he talked about.
- It is possible he drew on previous talk within his family, about how to spell either his own or his brother's name, and has linked this with the marks he made on paper.

Whilst he talked about numbers in relation to his marks, it is unclear that he set out to represent them. However, my interest may have encouraged him to attach some meaning to what he had done. Matt is growing up in a family in which his marks and early representations are encouraged and valued. It is also a family in which reading books, using a computer and writing at home are daily events: talk about these tools and the contents of books and written texts are also part of the family's daily experience.

Nursery: Charlotte's 'hundreds and pounds'

Charlotte chose some different coloured felt-tip pens and shouted out, 'Look! I'm doing hundreds and pounds!' (Figure 2.2).

Figure 2.2 Hundreds and pounds

These marks were made excitedly by Charlotte while she was with her friend, Jessica, in the nursery. They each selected a piece of paper and decided to choose different coloured pens, dotting the whole piece of paper. Charlotte's reference to 'hundreds and pounds' meant that she was making connections with the quantity of dots: this seems a lot to her and a hundred fits into her thinking about a lot. 'Pounds' also fits into her sense of a large quantity. Charlotte is using spoken language to express her actions and marks on paper.

Charlotte knows that:

- a hundred is a large quantity
- 'pounds' also have something to do with quantity
- you can represent quantity through action and pictures and attach spoken numbers to this representation.

Nursery: 'the spider'

Joe has made a drawing of a spider (Figure 2.3). He told the teacher, 'My spider's got eight legs.'

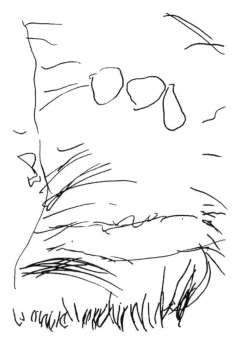

Figure 2.3. Joe's spider

Joe had been looking at and playing with toy spiders in the nursery and had chosen to draw this picture. He has drawn the spider with many more than eight legs. Looking at the spider he saw lots of legs and has represented that idea in his drawing. Joe is showing a growing awareness of number and quantity and is able to describe it. Joe knows that:

- a spider has eight legs
- you can represent that idea in your drawing
- you can attach meaning to numbers.

Reception: role-play – 'the baby clinic'

The marks in this example (Figure 2.4) were made jointly by several children. They include the '4' of their age; the first letters of two of the children's names; approximations of letters in the English alphabet and numerals.

The children's interest arose from a visit to a local baby-weighing clinic. The children had watched babies being weighed, and listened as health visitors talked with parents. The health visitors discussed the babies' progress and recorded current weights on charts and in record books. On their return to school, some rich symbolic play developed spontaneously and the children were very enthusiastic when, a few days later, we were able to borrow a real set of baby-weighing scales.

Figure 2.4 The baby clinic

On one piece of paper this spontaneous example combines marks and symbols from several children in the role-play area. During their play the children integrated their recent experiences with their growing knowledge of symbols. Their marks show that:

- they recognise that adults use marks in specific contexts (e.g. when weighing babies) and for specific purposes – in this instance to record babies' weights
- they are drawing on their knowledge of symbols, including some approximations of letters and numerals
- some children used the initial letter of their names or their age number to stand for what they are saying.

Talking to each other and to themselves, they used language relating to measurement such as 'heavy', 'this big', 'three long' and 'getting bigger', with general questions such as 'how's your baby doing?' as they weighed dolls and teddies. The talk between health professionals and mothers had made an impression on the children and they were able to integrate some of this specific language and make records on paper as they had seen during their visit.

Reception: 'Catherine's fractions'

Catherine wrote '2' (reversed) followed by part of a numeral 2 to represent '2½' for her sister's age (Figure 2.5). The following day she represented her own age in a similar way. She used an approximation of part of each numeral to represent a 'half'.

Figure 2.5 Catherine's fractions

This example is from Catherine on her first day at school. Although she already knew the school from many visits and activities arranged through our 'home/ school' programme, this was Catherine's first 'real' (whole) day at school as a pupil. A quiet, reserved child, she was initially hesitant about deciding what to do during a period of child-initiated play. Catherine quietly told me that her sister was 2½ years old, and after chatting a little more about her sister, she went to draw a picture of her.

Catherine showed me the drawing: she had written a 'C' in the top left-hand corner of the paper, to represent her own name. When I saw the drawing, I asked if she was going to put her sister's age. Catherine then added the symbol next to the picture that looks like either a 'C' underlined or a reversed numeral '2'. Catherine read it out loud as 'two'. At this point I wondered if she was using the initial letter of her name now to stand for 'two'. Smiling, I remarked, 'Oh! I thought your sister was two and a *half*!' Catherine turned to reach for a pen and added the 'C' symbol to the right. Was this her way of representing, approximately, a *half* of a numeral 2?

The following day Catherine confidently walked over to the writing area and soon brought some more marks to me saying, 'I'm 4½ years old'. She had written a numeral '4' followed by the vertical and horizontal bars of another numeral 4 but had omitted the short vertical line at the bottom.

- From these examples we can see that Catherine knows that various marks and ways of representing are used for different conventions.
- She decided to use a drawing that can be used to stand for her sister and a letter 'C' for her own name.
- She knows the conventional number symbols that on paper stand for the ages 'two' and 'four'.
- Her approximations of a 'half' is an ingenious solution and shows considerable insight: she has defined 'a half' by representing only (approximately) a half of the preceding numeral.

Learning theories

It is valuable to look at learning theories past and present, and reflect on the many views of learning, to determine the extent to which we have developed in our thinking of mathematical learning and teaching. For many people, including many teachers and Early Years practitioners, mathematics teaching is synonymous with traditional teaching, based on the behaviourist theory: mathematics has a reputation for being that kind of subject. Ernest (1991) has challenged such a view of mathematics, opening mathematics up to the fallibilistic viewpoint that this subject can be challenged. Mathematics teaching does not need to be a straitjacket for teachers or children.

Table 2.1 gives an account of the development of some theories of learning and teaching mathematics throughout the last century to the time of writing. Although this book centres on the current theory of socioculturalism, one can safely assume that it is not a well-known theory among teachers. Even theories to which we espouse often lie in our heads for some time fermenting, before we actually put them into practice in our Early Years settings.

Behaviourism

The theory of behaviourism has had considerable influence on the teaching of mathematics and beliefs about young learners. Each child was believed to learn best at their own pace through direct teaching and through carefully sequenced steps. Teachers emphasised the need to practise skills and children were encouraged to 'try and try again'. Learning was viewed as a mechanical result following rewards such as praise or a smile, and children were considered to be passively storing information.

These principles led to the idea of sequenced and individualised subject material broken down into discrete steps and, subsequently, to 'programmed learning'. However, there were a number of disadvantages to a behaviourist approach:

- The experience of working with sequenced learning materials could be repetitive and may not have motivated children.
- The child's personal understanding was ignored as they worked through a series of pre-written cards or tasks.

use in
3rth
Assignment.

Table 2.1 Four views of learning mathematics

Theory	*Behaviourism*	*Constuctivism*	*Social-constructivism*	*Sociocultural*
Theory based on work of:	*Thorndike and Skinner*	*Piaget*	*Vygotsky*	*Bakhtin and Bourdieu*
View of children as learners	Children were seen as 'empty vessels' for the teacher to fill with prescribed facts	Children construct knowledge of the world through active involvement with meaningful problem-solving	Children construct understanding through interactions with peers and adults who are more knowledgeable	Children learn about the world through sociocultural practices in which children and adults are involved (Barratt-Pugh and Rohl, 2000)
Implications for teaching mathematics	Skills-based teaching with learning programmed in a planned sequence	Emphasis on autonomy and active 'learning by doing'	Value of discussion with peers and teacher to take the child's understanding further	Children and adults co-construct mathematical understanding. Critical analysis of texts and practices (Barratt-Pugh and Rohl, 2000)
Role of Early Years teachers	Direct teaching (stimulus) followed by praise (response)	Hierarchical view of mathematics led to widespread use of published schemes and 'pre-number' activities	Relate mathematical activities to children's own experiences	Emphasise both the individual and shared meaning which children attach to what they say and do
Role of family and culture	Families not involved	Families not involved	Encourage talk about mathematics used by and within the family and society for real purposes	Involve children in the mathematical practices of the family and community

- There was no room for creative thinking.
- Learning was seen as passive rather than active and dynamic.
- The value of language and social discussion was not recognised.
- There was no appreciation of the role of the child's culture within the home and community and in the education setting.

Constructivism

Piaget's scientific studies of individual children led to a view of the child as a 'lone scientist'. Piaget viewed children's learning as biological development. Although children were considered actively to construct their understanding of the world through interaction with peers and their environment, the overall view was of children working individually and at their own pace.

Piaget's four 'stages of development' and experiments on conservation have been very influential in the teaching of mathematics. Piaget's hierarchical view of learning unintentionally influenced the content and use of mathematics schemes that continue to be extensively used in schools and in some Early Years settings. In the Early Years this led to a focus on sorting, sets, matching, one-to-one correspondence and classification as precursors to work with numbers that has only recently been questioned (Carruthers, 1997c; Thompson, 1997).

Piaget's work also emphasised the idea of 'readiness': children were not believed to be 'ready' to understand particular concepts until the appropriate developmental stage had been reached. The child's culture, the role of language and social interaction were not emphasised in Piaget's work.

Social constructivism

Vygotsky believed that children actively construct their understanding through solving problems in their own way. Children were believed to have a current level of learning and a level that might be reached with the help of more knowledgeable others (an adult, peer or older child): he termed this second level the 'zone of proximal development'. According to this theory, the child's understanding is constructed through talk, social interaction and shared meaning.

The theory of social constructivism implies that teachers encourage children to talk about their mathematical understanding. Social interaction is emphasised since individual children construct their understanding through talk and interaction with others. Sharing of ideas and meanings are negotiated with others. Learning that is socially constructed continually challenges learners' thinking and emphasises the personal meaning individuals make.

Sociocultural perspective

This theory emerged during the 1990s. Compatible with many aspects of Vygotsky's work, Bakhtin (1981; 1986) and Bourdieu (1977; 1991) have extended our understanding of the importance of creating knowledge together and of the central role of talk. The belief is that higher-order functions such as learning grow out of social interactions; therefore, the context of learning is highly significant, whether at home, in the community or in the Early Years setting.

Bakhtin focuses on different aspects of talk including the child's 'voice' and the role of dialogue. Wertsch proposes that these new perspectives 'suggest major new ways' to extend young children's understanding of literacies: he concludes that the implications of Bakhtin's theory 'are enormous' (Wertsch, 1990, p. 119).

When young children begin to engage in literacy practices or what Bourdieu refers to as 'exchanges', Bruner asserts that they 'bring their excellencies and receive distinctions, they become members of an exchange to be recognised as members of a culture' (Bruner, 1996, p. 13). For Bourdieu, literacy is a form of 'cultural capital, in which knowledge is defined as competence that can be converted into 'status, wealth and mobility' (Luke, 1993, p. 7). Bourdieu's description of the participation of learners in these learning contexts is 'a way of thinking, of negotiating and that is what we need from the start' (Bruner, 1996, p. 13).

Early Years practitioners and educators have long believed that children's earliest experiences in educational settings are highly significant for young children. Viewed from a sociocultural perspective, creating positive learning cultures within our settings will best support children's developing understanding. In such positive cultures, children's own knowledge and understandings – 'their excellencies' – are valued and meaning is co-constructed by adults and children; they will become full members of a mathematical literacy club (Carruthers, 1997a). But it is within their homes and communities that children first learn about literacies.

Sociocultural contexts of home and the community

Like writing and reading, mathematics learning is embedded in the sociocultural practices of the child's family, community and culture. These sociocultural contexts are interdependent and are created by children and adults together. The learning is also 'mediated through the values and behaviours of the child's culture' (Barratt-Pugh and Rohl, 2000, p. 7).

Sociocultural practices, tools and technologies

In their studies of the literacy practices children have access to in their homes, Weinberger (1996) and Hill et al. (1998) found 'a great deal of rich and diverse literacy learning in the home' (Barratt-Pugh and Rohl, p. 6). Adults may read television listings in a newspaper; go to the supermarket where they read signs, labels and prices; write a cheque; choose a video (reading the picture and text on the box) in the video shop; read instructions from television, computers, museum displays; read a menu from a Chinese restaurant or a catalogue dropped through the letter box. The evening weather report we check to see if we should go for a picnic the following day and the many road and shop signs we pass when walking or driving in urban areas also surround us with literate symbols, marks and images. Other literacy practices in the community outside the home are often within the child's experiences, such as a poster with details of a school fête or a noticeboard outside the local mosque.

Reading and using mathematical graphics

In these literacy practices, written words, pictures, logos, numbers, advertisements, charts, timetables, prices, lists, symbols, data, instructions or cartoons may feature. The text messages sent by mobile-phone users have created a new 'language' of communication. Furthermore, members of a family may be engaged directly in representing meaning through direct, specific practices such as writing a birthday card, doing homework or typing a report on the computer. And young children may be involved, either on the periphery or directly, in any of these (Lave and Wenger, 1991).

In the following examples, Matt, Sovay and Pauline are all learning something about mathematics within the sociocultural contexts of their families.

Sovay's dinner money envelope

Sovay (aged 2 years and 11 months) likes to imitate her sister. The family rush around in the morning getting ready for the day. Mhairi, Sovay's sister, writes £1.05p on an envelope and puts her name on it with the words 'dinner money'. She reads it to Sovay who is sitting beside her. I then open my purse and count out £1.05p and give Mhairi the money to put inside the envelope.

After Mhairi leaves for school, Sovay gets an envelope and puts marks on it with a pen. Sovay tells me 'Dinner money – £1. 00'. I smile and give Sovay some money to put in her envelope. I ask, 'Is that enough dinner money?' Sovay then takes the money out of the envelope and counts, '1, 50, 52, 53' (Carruthers, 1997c). Sovay is learning about mathematics from a sociocultural perspective.

The wider social perspective
A number of features are evident from this incident, showing that Sovay recognised that:

- you can write down mathematic including numbers and money
- doing this has meaning
- what is inside the envelope relates to what is written outside
- money is important and valued enough to take to school
- money can be counted.

Cultural context of this family
- The mathematics was influenced by the older sibling's need to communicate with the school.
- Sovay knows that money is important.

- Exchanges in the morning centred around who has and who has not money for the envelope.
- The school's culture expected dinner money to be brought daily rather than weekly.
- Sovay is included in mathematical events in this family.

The mathematical learning: beliefs within this family
- Everybody can write mathematics.
- The child's own marks are accepted.
- The mother responds and supports the child's mathematical play.
- The child wants to be part of the family activities of the morning and the child is accepted into this world at her level of response.

Within this family it seems that writing down numbers is accepted by everybody. There is no expectation that the 2-year-old needs to be right, since Sovay's own marks are accepted. I was delighted when Sovay showed interest and communicated what she knew to me. The child leads her chosen action. In this example, Sovay moved from being on the edge of this literacy event, to a central and active role, making personal sense of the dinner money episode.

In her study, Anning found that there were 'various rites and rituals associated with the meaning making across communities of practice in children's home contexts' (Anning, 2000, p. 9). Each family has its own way of doing things: in Sovay's family, one of the daily rites is the morning hunt for change for her sister's dinner money. Different family rituals contribute to the wide range of literacy practices to which young children are exposed before they enter an Early Years setting, and to the child's understanding of mathematical literacy. Anstey and Bull (1996, p. 153) argue that 'literacy is an everyday social practice'. Literacies are not only socially constructed on a daily basis, they are also culturally specific (Crawford, 1995).

Matt's marks

There are pens, pencils and paper for the boys to use – in the sitting room, their bedroom and in a kitchen drawer that they can easily reach. Matt produced these examples (Figure 2.6) in a burst of activity, on the same occasion that he 'read' 'I spell 80354' (see p. 12).

In figure 2.6a Matt made a variety of marks that he did not name. He then showed me other pieces. The scribbles on one he read as 'my number's 1, 2, 3, 4, 6, 7 and 11'. On one 'Post-it' note he had made marks that he termed 'song' and on another he 'read' 'I care and love you both and same day'.

On another piece of paper (see Figure 2.6b), he read 'I love you'. Matt knew a heart symbol and asked me to write one. He said 'I love the number eight' and then 'when someone's being mean to you, you say "don't even think about it!"' Other marks he 'read' as 'You have to put names on the board'; this appeared to relate to a practice at the day-care centre the boys attended at the time.

Figure 2.6a Matt's marks   **Figure 2.6b** Matt

Matt was exploring a variety of 'messages' that marks can convey. During this one session of about half an hour, he explored several different purposes for marks. These included:

- several 'drawings' (Matt's term) in which he explored marks made with circular actions
- a 'song'
- a reference to spelling
- two pieces that he labelled as a string of numbers and a favourite number
- one piece of persuasive, or perhaps we might use the term 'assertive' writing, in the last comment
- several personal messages including his use of the heart symbol
- something he had heard adults say in the day-care centre.

Wider social perspective
- People talk about what marks on paper 'say': some marks say something but they do not all have to.
- Different marks can say different things.
- We can make marks to tell someone something: some marks are like talking, but on paper.

Cultural context of this family
- In this family, people read and make marks for many different purposes.
- Making marks is a valid activity – 'my aunt does it as well as my mum, dad and brother'.
- 'The grown-ups in my family like my marks – they listen when I talk about what I've done and sometimes put them on the wall or the fridge'.

- Making marks on paper is important: 'my mum writes for work and writes letters to people, my dad works at home a lot on the computer and they both type emails to people'.

The personal messages, comments about behaviour, the heart symbol, song, use of the term 'spell', reference to practice in the day-care centre and several references to numbers reflect the importance of the child's sociocultural contexts of the home and the community beyond the home. These examples of Matt's marks from just one episode also show the tremendous knowledge he had developed about different purposes of literacy by 3 years of age. Matt was making use of his observations, drawing on a great deal of knowledge of marks, of meaning and about communicating with others. He was also finding out the sort of responses his marks and meaning might evoke from me, since I had only just arrived in Canada where he lived – and the previous time I'd seen Matt he'd been a small baby.

Pauline's address

In their study of 4-year-olds learning in a home environment, Tizard and Hughes documented many interesting conversations. One such conversation is described in the following passage.

> Pauline's mother was discussing with her what she could say to a policeman if she was lost. Pauline's mother pointed out that you must say where you live. Pauline replied 'down by the grass'. Her mother was upset because she thought that Pauline knew her address. Pauline may not have known the word 'address'.

CHILD: Eh?
MOTHER: Do you know your address?
CHILD: Yeah.
MOTHER: Yeah and what do you say to him?
CHILD: Um? I've ... I said ... (hesitates)
MOTHER: What number house?
CHILD: Um ... number six.
MOTHER: No, you don't live at number six.
CHILD: What?
MOTHER: You say 'My name is Pauline Robinson'.
CHILD: Yeah.
MOTHER: 'And I live at seventeen ...'
CHILD: Yeah.
MOTHER: ' ... Fleet Flats.'
CHILD: Yeah.
MOTHER: You say it.
CHILD: Seventeen.
MOTHER: Sally does. She says it. (Sally is the older daughter.)
CHILD: Seventeen.
MOTHER: No. You tell him your name.

CHILD: Yeah. I say, 'Seventeen Fleet Flats.'
MOTHER: Seventeen Fleet Flats.
CHILD: Yeah.
MOTHER: So when you're lost you tell him that.
CHILD: Yeah.
MOTHER: He'll say, 'now we'll take you home to see your mum.'
CHILD: He don't (laughs).
MOTHER: He will if he knows where you live.
CHILD: He won't. He say, 'Where you live?' I say, 'I live down Fleet Flats.'
MOTHER: Yeah, but you gotta give him the number.
CHILD: Look! Number six.
MOTHER: He'll take you to the wrong house. If you tell him number six. You have to tell him the proper number.
CHILD: What?
MOTHER: You say, 'Seventeen.'

At this point in the conversation, in addition to having forgotten the number of the flat, Pauline appeared to be anxious about the idea of being lost and of being found by a policeman.

CHILD: He (the policeman) don't come today.
MOTHER: Well, you never know. 'Cause you're going down the beach in the summer, aren't you?
Pauline's mother explained to her daughter that she might go to the beach with their neighbour Irene.

MOTHER: And if you lose her?
CHILD: Yeah.
MOTHER: And you see a policeman.
CHILD: Yeah.
MOTHER: And the policeman comes up to you 'cause someone's bound to pick you up on the beach, aren't they?
CHILD: Um. I'm gonna see a policeman on the beach tomorrow.
(Tizard and Hughes, 1984, pp. 69–71)

Wider social perspective
- Pauline knows that her house number is important.
- She needs to know her house number to communicate this to others.
- House numbers have purpose (if you say 'six' the policeman will take you to the wrong house).

Cultural context of this family
- Safety is important: you need to know your address to keep safe.
- Mum thinks this is important enough to repeatedly ask Pauline her address.
- Mum gets anxious about addresses.

Mathematical learning: beliefs within this family
Pauline knows that:

- her response is not always accepted
- her sibling gets it right
- numbers can be confusing.

Within this family culture, there are sometimes rules – especially about safety – and these may make something that would be accepted normally, i.e. getting your address wrong, unacceptable. Each family's culture has different beliefs about this. The child getting lost is most parents' nightmare and this is therefore reflected in Pauline's mother's anxiety. Getting the door number right is important: numbers are important. In addition to being involved in literacy practices, Sovay, Matt and Pauline are also learning about who can be literate, from siblings and parents to aunts and policemen. In this example, Pauline is in no doubt about her older sister's knowledge of her address.

These examples highlight the central role of language in sociocultural contexts: we use language to change our experiences into understanding. In their study, Tizard and Hughes found that conversations in the home were more frequent, longer and more evenly balanced between adult and child when compared to talk in nursery schools (Tizard and Hughes, 1984).

The questions Pauline's mother asked are genuine, are asked out of real concern and for genuine reasons, whereas Smith and Elley propose that most questions asked by teachers are of the 'guessing-what-I-am-thinking' variety (Smith and Elley, 1998, p. 27) or 'testing' (Tizard and Hughes, 1984). The Tizard and Hughes study raised many important questions. From their findings, Tizard and Hughes found that 'working-class' families provided equally rich learning environments in terms of activities and parent–child interaction when compared to 'middle-class' families. There were different values and beliefs from home to home within both class structures (Tizard and Hughes, 1984). Bruner, writing of the notion of cultural deprivation proposes that this concept requires rethinking: 'cultural deprivation blames the victim, even if only indirectly'; this implies that the culture is at fault (Bruner, 1996, p. 14). Bruner also argues that from home to home, family values and cultures are different, not better or worse than another.

Tizard and Hughes highlight the importance of learning in the home and compared this to learning in nursery schools. Conversations in the home were based on history, of knowing the family routines and values: conversations in the nursery are based on the here and now. They suggest that in order for children to thrive in educational settings, staff in the educational setting needs to understand the home cultures and values. Children will feel more accepted and the teacher will understand the children's thinking more (Tizard and Hughes, 1984, p. 255). The sociocultural theory of learning is based on this premise.

Sociocultural contexts in Early Years settings

When children move into an Early Years educational setting, they enter a different culture where values, beliefs and literacy practices may differ from those in their homes. Different beliefs about literacy practices across the contexts of home and early education settings and the ways in which children experience them, shape children's understanding of literacies.

In educational contexts, children may experience literacies and the abstract written language of mathematics in very different ways. In Bruner's view, education is a constant quest for meaning. From a sociocultural perspective, teachers can create 'communities of practice' in which learners and adults 'co-construct' understanding in ways that make sense to the children. Bruner believes that the aims of educational settings should be to create an 'enabling culture in which the child is involved in re-inventing, refurbishing and refreshing' the culture. He emphasises the need for pre-schools and schools to create communities of learners: 'on the basis of what we have learned in recent years about human learning, that it is best when it is participatory, proactive, communal, collaborative and given over to constructing meanings rather than receiving them ... learning in its full complexity involves the creation and negotiation of meaning in a larger culture' (Bruner, 1996, p. 15).

The scenario at the beginning of Chapter 8 illustrates a community of learners in which children are building on their rich, informal knowledge from home. Through their interactions with peers and adults they are co-constructing their understanding of marks and symbols.

In enabling cultures, teachers also learn from parents and carers about the child's knowledge and experience of mark-making and representation that their children bring. Early Years settings can then build on what the child already understands and can do. Staff also need to communicate with families about the culture of the setting and their beliefs and practices in supporting emergent learners. However, due to different values and beliefs about the nature of learning, curriculum demands and the very many pressures on teachers in Early Years settings, there may be a conflict between the sociocultural practices of home and the educational setting. Children may find that there is an inconsistency between beliefs and practices at home and in their educational setting. Barratt-Pugh and Rohl argue that 'those practices that are valued by the family and the community may not be valued in formal learning contexts, and therefore hold little cultural capital' (Barratt-Pugh and Rohl, 2000, p. 4).

In terms of representing mathematics, the focus may be on completing a task or page. Cullen and St George point out that 'when teachers over-emphasise teacher directed tasks such as worksheets, children view learning as dependent on the teacher' (Cullen and St George, 1996, p. 4).

In her study of the influence of different cultures and beliefs in home, pre-school and school settings on the children's strategies for mark-making, Anning observed that finding time to: 'tune into children's meaning making and listening to their personal "voices" was a challenge for adults. In educational contexts, children's personal representations might even be discouraged if they were framed as a distraction from the school rites and rituals dominated by the imperative of turning children into pupils' (Anning, 2000, p. 12).

In her study Anning observed that staff in a family day-care centre had changed 'from a relaxed attitude to children's meaning making' after they had been 'colonised by educational beliefs and practices' (Anning, 2000, p. 12). This had led to an adult-led agenda and a curriculum which shaped predetermined outcomes for activities. Anning refers to this as the 'checklist phenomena' where staff concerns often focus on teaching children to write their own names, 'to know his colours' and 'know his numbers and shapes' (Anning, 2000, p. 13). In such contexts, children are limited to learning what the adult wants. When the teacher imposes her kind of symbols – including standard symbols – on the child, the child's enthusiasm may be dampened and her impulses to explore creatively or to put thoughts on paper suppressed.

Lave and Wenger point out that children learn to do what they think is expected of them by members of a 'community of practice' (Lave and Wenger, 1991). Unfortunately when adults have the agenda for what children learn and how they learn, it follows that children will stay within the boundaries that teachers have set. The children may learn to write their names, but they are also learning that the teacher in fact expects correct spelling, legibility and neatness; content and meaning are valued less. From this the child also learns that personal marks and emergent literacies do not belong in this new culture.

In such a learning culture, because children have very limited opportunities to make meaning, they soon learn that mathematics – especially mathematics represented on paper – does not always make personal sense. In the mathematical culture of the school they may learn that it does not always matter if it makes sense. Whereas learning mathematics informally at home was natural, learning mathematics in the educational context has been transformed into a 'subject' that may not always make sense. Mathematics is now difficult.

Loris Malaguzzi's poem, paraphrased below, captures these conflicts well:

'The child has a hundred languages, (and a hundred, hundred, hundred more) ...
But they steal ninety nine, the school and the culture ...
They tell the child to discover the world already there ...
The child says:
No way. The hundred is there. (Malaguzzi, 1996, p. 3)

When children make marks and represent their mathematical thinking in a variety of ways that they have chosen, they are using some of these 'hundred languages'.

Teachers' beliefs

The four learning theories we have explored in this chapter have also influenced teachers' beliefs about if, and how, children can represent mathematics. The educational theories summarised in Table 2.2 indicate the extent to which educational theories have influenced teachers' beliefs; contemporary theory may not yet have influenced practice in all Early Years settings. Anning emphasises how children struggle to make sense of the 'continuities and discontinuities' of home, pre-school and school settings. She asserts that 'for many, the discontinuities are on children learning to be readers, writers and mathematicians' (Anning, 2000, p. 22). It appears that of all the curriculum areas, mathematics – especially the ways in which young children represent mathematics – is where the greatest discontinuity exists.

Table 2.2 Beliefs about young children's ability to represent mathematics

Behaviourism	• Children cannot represent mathematics unless they are shown what to do and how to do it
	• There is a standard format for every aspect of written mathematics that children can only learn by direct teaching.
	• Mathematics is either 'right' or 'wrong': provide a carefully sequenced structure in small steps to record arithmetic
	• Teach skills in isolation
	• Repetition and practice of written mathematics is vital
	• Praise right answers and neat work: this reinforces 'good' work
	• Children should work independently.
Constructivism	• Children can only understand certain aspects of mathematics at each stage of development.
	• It follows that young children need a lot of groundwork (pre-number work), before they are ready to work with numbers.
	• Although 'active' learning is encouraged, in terms of representations, the outcome has been an emphasis on actively thinking about adult–prepared materials.
Social constructivism	• The value of the child's own marks should be recognised because the child has constructed them herself
	• Adults ask the child to explain her marks and through discussion helps the child achieve what she could not do on her own
	• A variety of marks are valued: these might include informal 'scribbles', pictures, child's own marks, tallies and approximations of standard symbols and numerals
	• Emphasis needs to be on the meaning made by the child
	• Teachers recognise, understand, support and extend children's emerging understanding
	• Teachers recognise that there is a development of children's emergent mathematics in a way that is similar to emergent writing

> - The setting also values and supports all aspects of emergent learning including writing, mathematics, science and the child's art and model making.

Sociocultural	*In addition to the points made under 'social constructivism' above:* • Adults need to build on from the sociocultural practices of the child's home and community of representing, 'reading' and using mathematics • The emphasis needs to be on adults and children co-constructing their understanding of representations and symbols of mathematics • Encourage children to move between their informal 'home' mathematical representation and the subsequent formal and informal forms of written mathematics in early childhood settings • Early childhood settings create cultures of practice for learning mathematics • The culture of the early childhood setting supports the use of critical mathematical literacy.

The model in Table 2.2 demonstrates the gulf that may exist between the home and Early Years settings in terms of beliefs, values and practices about early literacies, including mathematics.

The challenge for Early Years educators is to value and build on every one of the child's 'hundred languages' in ways which make sense to the child and connect with their early experiences within their homes and cultures. The challenge is to help children 'translate' between informal ways of representing mathematics in the home and 'formal' ways in educational contexts (Hughes, 1986). If we are unable to achieve this there will be a discontinuity between their early learning at home and that of the Early Years setting: the implications for the children's beliefs about themselves as learners and about the nature of learning mathematics are enormous.

Summary

We have shown how young children struggle to make their own meanings in many different ways. We argue that emergent mathematics generates success 'through social interactions and the contexts in which they take place, as children struggle to master skills and make meaning' (Worthington, 1996a, p. 16).

Teachers can support children's mathematical literacy by:

- recognising and supporting the sociocultural context of the children's home learning

- creating a positive learning environment in which children's own contributions are valued
- listening to what children say about what their marks mean
- looking at what children do know about mathematics through their own marks
- building on children's own early marks and representations
- recognising that there are many ways in which children represent their mathematical thinking on paper.

Without the rich experiences of diverse literacy practices within the children's families, communities and cultures and the very specific cultures created by their teachers, the many examples of mathematical literacy in this book would not exist.

In this chapter we have used several examples to introduce some of the possibilities. In the next chapter we explore children's mathematical marks in a different way, through their mathematical schemas.

3

Mathematical Schemas

The cat from France likes to sing and dance but my *cat likes to hide in boxes (Sutton, 1984, pp: 4 and 6).*

We have found that our knowledge of young children's schemas has informed our teaching immensely. It has helped us understand young children's actions and thoughts and therefore respond to their educational needs. Our constant discussions about children's schemas have given us great insight into children's development.

What is a schema?

Chris Athey (1990) led a research project that identified developments in young children's thinking which 'entailed developing a new approach to the description and interpretation of cognitive behaviour' (Athey, 1990, p. 49). Over 5,000 observations were collected from 20 children, aged 2–5, over two years and then analysed. Athey focused on the particular patterns of behaviour that 2–5-year-old children have, which she termed schemas. She defined schemas as 'a pattern of repeatable behaviour into which experiences are assimilated and that are gradually co-ordinated. Co-ordinations lead to higher levels and more powerful schemas' (Athey, 1990 p. 37).

Skemp explains the functions of schemas by saying that they integrate existing knowledge, act as a tool for future learning and that they make understanding possible. Skemp recognises the importance of schematic development in understanding mathematics. Like most mathematicians, Skemp's analysis of schemas is from a mathematical viewpoint: these are the logico-mathematical concepts that children need to learn first before they can understand higher concepts. As he reflects on teaching young children, Skemp acknowledges that they already know some number concepts before they start in an educational setting. He asks if it matters that they do not yet have an understanding of sorting, sets and matching and one-to-one correspondence, as long as they 'tag on' these concepts at some time. Skemp seems to wrestle with young children's schemas because his ideas somehow do not totally fit into his current knowledge of young children's development. He has followed the Piagetian theory and the research model of clinical tasks and has not balanced this by following the young child in real-life situations, at home, at play or in autonomous situations where they are following their own thinking (Skemp, 1971).

Figure 3.1   Imogen constantly lines things up

Piaget particularly looked at children's very early schematic behaviour such as the baby dropping an object on the floor and the parent retrieving it, only to find five seconds later that the baby has dropped the object again. This, Piaget called 'object permanence' (Piaget, 1958): the child may be thinking 'is the object still there if I cannot see it?' This links with babies' fascination with the 'peek-a-boo' game. In his observations Piaget saw that early schemas of 2- and 3-year-olds included children grouping and sorting. This was unfortunately translated into the 'pre-number' theory of the 1960s and 1970s. It was believed that children needed to sort and do sets before they were ready for number. Five-year-olds, who had long passed this concept when they were 3, were made to sort objects such as green and blue frogs. The published mathematical schemes of this time had workbook pages, so that children could colour in sets of green frogs and blue frogs or suchlike: then the children had to partition the sets. Very little mathematics went on, the main time was taking up colouring in.

Athey took Piagetian research further and, more importantly, observed children's actions from a positive stand, looking for what children know, not what they do not know. For example, from a Piagetian perspective the acquisition of one-to-one correspondence is seen as the watershed of the child's knowledge about number. From this perspective the child had little knowledge of number before he understood this concept. Athey's research, right from the start, threw out the deficit model and therefore brought out many enlightening details about children's knowledge. It is vital to note this because it gives us as teachers an important observational strategy. The studying of schemas is a useful observational tool. As Athey has documented, it is a wonderful way to share children's experiences with parents and for parents to share their experiences of their children with teachers. Done in an open, honest, way it forms a true partnership (see for example the letter from Chloë's mother, Figure 3.2).

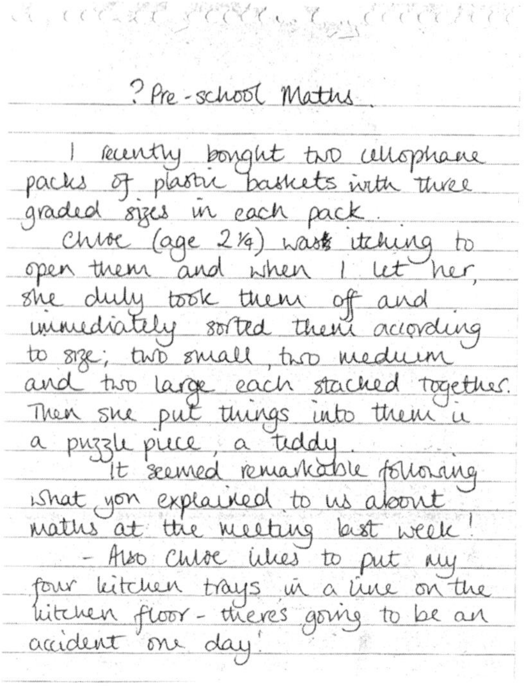

? Pre-school Maths

I recently bought two cellophane packs of plastic baskets with three graded sizes in each pack.
Chloë (age 2¼) was itching to open them and when I let her, she duly took them off and immediately sorted them according to size; two small, two medium and two large each stacked together. Then she put things into them a puzzle piece, a teddy.
It seemed remarkable following what you explained to us about maths at the meeting last week!
– Also Chloë likes to put my four kitchen trays in a line on the kitchen floor – there's going to be an accident one day!

Figure 3.2 Note from Chloë's mother

Bruce argues that schemas are 'biologically pre-determined and socio-culturally influenced ' (Bruce, 1997, p. 73). In our experience as teachers, there is also a strong connection to children's feelings, connecting with the work of Goleman (1996).

The easiest way to explain schemas is to give an example. Nearly everyone who has studied schemas has a story of how they first understood this concept and when they really started to understand. In our experience of leading professional development in this area, teachers of young children and parents can easily identify very quickly what a schema is. They often talk about unexplained behaviours of young children, something they, the adults, did not understand and then realised it might be a schema.

My schema story is about my youngest child, Sovay. When Sovay was 2 years old she used to put objects (any she could find) into plastic carrier bags and hang the bags on the doors in our house. At any one time there could be up to 13 carrier bags hanging on our doors! At first I thought she was playing at shopping, but then I read Chris Athey's work on schemas. This highlighted for me that Sovay was in a containing schema, she liked putting things inside. She did not seem to be interested in the objects but her concern lay with putting things inside containers. If anything went missing we knew where to look.

Most frequently observed schemas

Athey identified many kinds of schemas in which young children were engaged. In a study by Arnold (1997) the most frequently observed schemas were:

- *Envelopment* – enveloping, covering or surrounding oneself, an object or a space. You might see children interested in dens, things in boxes, envelopes, dressing up, wrapping 'presents'. Often children will paint or draw then fold the painting or drawing to give it to you.
- *Trajectory* – this can be an unsociable schema where children might throw things as their interest lies with straight lines, arcs or curves. Children in this schema might kick balls, throw things from one point to another, or be interested in playing with toys that take them from one place to the other, for example tricycles, bikes and scooters.
- *Enclosure* – enclosing oneself, an object or space. Children in their play can be seen putting a 'fence' around objects, building walls around them in block play.
- *Transporting* – carrying objects or being carried from one place to the other. Have you ever observed children filling up a pram with objects not necessarily dolls, then transport the objects to another place in the nursery and unload and go and fetch other objects and unload again to make several other similar journeys? Children also do this outside with trailers.
- *Connecting* – an interest in connecting themselves to objects and objects to each other, for example, children like to make and join things. They are very interested to use sticky tape and paper clips. They like construction play.
- *Rotation* – turning, twisting or rolling oneself or objects in the environment around. Children playing circle games, running in circles, interested in windmills, wheels and roundabouts.
- *Going through a boundary* – causing oneself or material or an object to go through a boundary and emerge at the other side. Children in this schema are usually interested in going through tunnels and under fences. They like to sew, thread beads and perhaps you might see them go in and out of doorways.
- *Oblique trajectory* – moving in, using or drawing oblique lines. Children might put the water tap full on to see the angle of the water flow. They make dens using a table with a sheet that goes at an oblique angle from the table.
- *Containment* – putting materials inside an object which is capable of containing them. Children put objects in boxes, bags, suitcases and fill up containers in the sand and water area.
- *Transformation* – transforming oneself by dressing differently or being interested in changes in state. Children try on hats in front of the mirror in the role-play area. Often children are interested in cooking and making things.

This list of frequently observed schemas, recorded by Arnold, may be compared to those identified in our study within a school setting on page 43.

Schemas and mathematics

If we look at the schemas identified by Athey in the Froebel study we can see that almost all are linked to mathematics (Athey, 1990). Perhaps this is not a surprising finding because, as most mathematicians would argue, we live in a mathematical world. Children explore this world and therefore they build on their natural curiosity about mathematics.

In her study of 3–5-year-olds in a nursery setting, Nutbrown describes the many mathematical ideas being investigated by these young children through their schemas (Nutbrown, 1994). When children are exploring one particular schema, they can be finding out about different aspects of mathematics through this exploration, for example:

> The nursery staff have observed John, 4:2, over a period of five weeks. They have noted he is in an enclosing and containing schema. John often chooses to go in the play telephone box in the nursery. He goes in the telephone box with two cars and moves them around the box, on the floor, up the wall and around the wall. He often plays in the sand, filling up the containers with small-world toys then sand. He chooses containers with lids and shuts and opens the lids, taking toys out, rearranging them and putting them back in.

John is finding out about capacity, area, perimeter, shape, space and volume through his schemas. When he is inside that cuboid (telephone box) he explores the space, the shape, the corners, the vertices, the angles. He also explores these concepts in different ways through smaller containers. He may be asking himself: 'is this the same? Is this different? What else can I do to explore this kind of inside. I am curious, I want to know.'

Children's schemas help them grasp ideas intuitively. They notice certain aspects of their environment that they want to use. Athey (1990) wrote that children will use whatever they can in the environment to try out their present concern. Children in a *transporting* schema will use any object at hand to move the object from one place to the other. Adults may often not see the logic of this because it is not the adult's logic.

Many early schemas provide a thought 'footstool' for many more complicated mathematical ideas. Very early schemas can combine together, for example:

- *horizontal* schema – carefully lining objects up horizontally
- *connecting* schema – lining objects up, one touching the other
- *number* schema – putting numbers to objects but not necessarily in the standard way. Children use numbers in their everyday talk.

Eventually all these schemas can work together to produce counting (Carruthers, 1997c).

Key points about mathematical schemas

- The majority of schemas identified are mathematical.
- Through observations of children's schemas we can see the early development of mathematical concepts.
- We can support this mathematical development.
- Mathematics can be seen in its broadest sense through children's schemas.
- It may also help the practitioner understand the mathematics through the children's schemas.
- Schemas highlight the mathematics in the world.

In later childhood, mathematical schemas develop into mathematical concepts though, as Bruce argues, 'we are only at the beginning of understanding this' (Bruce, 1997, p. 78). It is possible to see the links between the examples of children's schemas and specific mathematical concepts when we consider the examples of Sovay, Naomi, Zoë and Aaron in this chapter.

Schemas and mark-making

We have both found our study of children's schemas fascinating. It has helped us understand one way children explore their worlds. This schema interest is a window into children's minds: it is extremely mathematical. We have provided a background on mathematical schemas and are now going to focus on children's mathematical schematic mark-making on paper.

> Sovay, 4:3, is interested in *containing* and *enclosure*. We referred to Sovay's interest in containing/enclosure when she was 2 years old. Her drawings are to do with her interest in inside. In this period of her life she drew a cluster of graphics which seemed to move from action of doing at 2 years to the actual representation of ideas at 4 years. For example, one of her drawings was an 'apple with the rotten bit' and she pointed out the rotten bit.
>
> In another of her drawings she drew a truck and said 'this is the oil in the engine' and again she pointed this out. Her attention to where the oil was inside the engine, and the engine inside the truck, is her revisiting her earlier schema of containing: now it had gone beyond the action right now, to symbolic representation of some of her *containing* ideas. Figure 3.3 is an example of Sovay's engagement with her *containing* schema. At four years seven months she drew a house for me. Her focus was on the inside of the house. She told me what each room was in the house and I wrote what she said.

The drawings collected in the Froebel study were analysed by looking at form and what the child said about the graphics. This is important because many studies of young children's drawings have not placed an emphasis on meaning.

Some studies, for example Kellog's, looked at developmental sequences at the expense of what the child said about her drawing (Kellog, 1969). Other studies such as Eng's, looked at changes in content (Eng, 1999). In the examples we give, we are looking at children's schemas on paper: these are often when children express their schema as an action. For example, children in a circular schema might be interested in the actual action of making a circle on paper. Children may also express their schema on paper as a representation of a pattern of thought.

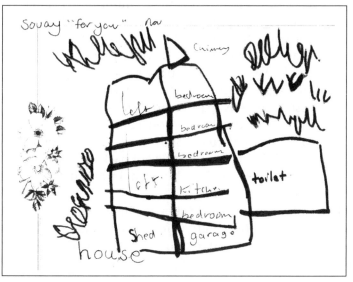

Figure 3.3 Sovay's house plan.

Children often transfer their schematic experience on to paper.

Supporting schemas

To support children's schemas it is important to first observe children closely (see Chapter 10). Early Years teachers need to acquire skills in observing young children to detect their present cognitive concern. It is also important to be aware of a range of schemas and have knowledge of the current theory which relates to this area of child development. Having identified a child's schema, there are many ways teachers can expand that child's interest. Often a group of children will have the same schema: if it is a *containing* schema then the teacher might read books that have an 'inside theme' such as *My Cat Likes to Hide in Boxes* (Sutton, 1984) and provide a range of containers in different areas for children to fill. There are many possible ways to support schemas, for example, see pp. 45–47.

Both the psychological and the physical atmospheres that are created within a setting are of the utmost importance if teachers wish to nourish schemas. The psychological atmosphere sets the scene. Teachers must be willing to be flexible, encouraging and caring, and allow the children to be themselves. 'Transporters' can cause concern to a teacher who likes everything to be in its place. For

schemas to flourish then the Early Years setting has to be democratic where children and teachers can negotiate. Play that is valued by the teacher is essential in
a schema environment.

The physical environment needs to be well stocked and easily accessible.
Resources do not need to be expensive and objects such as cardboard boxes
provide many interesting experiences for children in a containing schema. Good
Early Years settings provide open-ended resources with creative potential, rather
than those that are plastic. Plastic toys are not multi-dimensional and are not as
mathematical as real things. A plastic apple, for example, has no significant
weight, you cannot cut it and you cannot eat it. Each plastic apple looks the
same, so children cannot even compare it with others.

Many of the usual play areas in a nursery will foster children's schemas,
including painting, clay, mathematics, science, music, stories, books and
cooking. The outside area is particularly important to extend children's
schemas. Many of the mathematical concepts bound up in visits nourish
schematic development. Athey found that the details picked up from the visits
were explored by the children when they went back to their nursery setting. On
page 47 we focus on the way in which an informal local visit supported
children's current interest in spirals.

To support the mark-making of children's schematical thinking, teachers first
have to value the marks the children make. Secondly, children need opportunities to make marks both inside and outside. Materials need to be readily
accessible (discussed in Chapter 8).

Observing schemas in a school setting

Studies of schemas in England have focused on children in pre-school and
nursery settings (Athey, 1990; Bruce, 1997; Nutbrown, 1994). There are now
indications that teachers' interest in schemas extends further afield (see, for
example, Meade, 1995). However, the schema examples in this chapter show
that the school environment can also support schemas and high levels of
cognitive challenge.

Athey (1990) argues that rich experiences enhance and extend children's
schemas, contributing to the active construction of knowledge and development of children's cognitive capacities. But when young children sit at tables
following teacher-directed tasks, or on the carpet listening passively for long
periods, they will not be able to explore their schemas. This has considerable
implications for their cognitive development in the long term, including their
mathematical understanding.

Starting with the home

Parents are vital partners in sharing knowledge of their children's behaviour.
Families' knowledge of their children can contribute to a fuller understanding of

the young child's history and sociocultural background in all areas of their development. Through their observations of children – especially of children playing – staff in Early Years settings continually increase their knowledge of the children's personal interests, skills and concerns. When staff and families share information, this can contribute to appropriate support and extension of children's observed schemas and mark-making (Athey, 1990).

A group of parents of children in my class of 4–6-year-olds had become very interested in sharing ideas of ways of supporting their children's development at home, first of reading, then writing. The parents' group suggested they focus next on mathematics. I was excited about the observations of children's schemas I was making daily, and the parents were interested to know more. A meeting open to all families triggered many responses from parents who recognised similar schema behaviours in their own children at home. Subsequently several parents responded to an invitation to keep a diary of their own children's patterns of behaviour for several days.

Chloë's older sister, Lydia, was already in the first class in school. A week after the meeting about schemas, Chloë's mother sent the note at the opening of this chapter (see Figure 3.1).

Schemas within child-initiated play

One aspect that is significant for the development of schemas is that whilst time and opportunities for children to explore in their own ways are crucial for schema exploration, certain experiences and materials appear to offer especially rich sources of exploration.

Painting and drawing, modelling with clay and play-dough design/technology, construction materials and block play offered particularly rich opportunities for schema exploration for the children in this study. When analysed, observations of play with these resources also had the highest percentage of cognitively challenging minutes recorded, with art the highest (Worthington, 1996b). Sylva et al also found art to be the most challenging experience for children whilst Gura's study of block play illustrates its potential for learning (Gura, 1992; Sylva, Roy and Painter, 1986). Like the example of Naomi below, many of the observations with these resources were of mathematical schemas. It is also interesting to note that the resources listed above allow children to represent their thinking: this may be significant for later representation of abstract ideas and symbols, especially in mathematics.

Intense involvement and challenging learning

Naomi, 4:10, was with a group of children. They had had free access to clay since entering school, during their child-initiated play. Today the nursery nurse was leading a group who were exploring clay with their hands but without other tools.

Naomi is rolling a long sausage of clay: several other children have used similar clay 'sausages' to make parts of a person or animal. She joins the ends of her sausage to form a circle and then rolls some small balls of clay that she places inside the circle. She stands up for a moment, looks at what she has done and then places an additional ball on the outer edge of the circle and sits down. Taking some more clay she twists and moulds it in her hands and breaks the piece in half, then combines the two pieces. She appears to be oblivious to the busy noise and movement in the room around her while she rolls another cylinder. At first the clay in her hands is short and thick but with careful attention it becomes thinner and longer: it is about 46 centimetres long and of even thickness. Naomi looks up briefly to see what the other children are doing, then rolls her cylinder into a ball. Again she transforms the ball of clay into a long cylinder.

A boy nearby shouts loudly to another child but Naomi appears untroubled and continues to roll the clay with regular movements. Next she places her long cylinder above those she made earlier, so that they are arranged in order of length. The shortest is nearest to her on the table, ascending to the longest cylinder furthest away. Naomi lifts the cylinders one at a time and joins each to the end of the previous one. The nursery nurse asks if Naomi is going to join them all: Naomi smiles but does not answer and looks down at her long 'rope' of clay on the table.

Now she stands up for a moment and begins to roll more clay with increasing vigour. She has a sufficient length of clay to stretch along one side of the square table where the children are seated. Naomi begins to add more clay cylinders around the perimeter of the table. The other children silently co-operate by taking care not to remove her clay: they move out of the way as she walks round or reaches across the table.

Naomi has used all the clay she had but a gap remains along of one side of the table. She walks away from the table, looking around at various objects in the room. After a few minutes Naomi returns to the table with some wax crayons, bottles of paint and paint brushes — all are cylindrical. Thomas reaches to take some things from her, occasionally instructing 'move this one up' and 'one more'. Together the two children fill the gaps to complete the perimeter enclosing the table.

This observation was 25 minutes long. During this session Naomi explored *going round a boundary* or perimeter and other mathematical concepts. These included length, comparison, lining up end-to-end (also related to measuring length), ascending order and ordinality, and thick/thin and *transformation* (from cylinder to sphere and back again).

Observations of schemas in this study with children 4 to 6 years of age, appeared to share a number of features highlighting the fact that:

- the children's involvement at the time was often very intense
- children exploring a schema often concentrated for extended periods of time.

These qualities were certainly clear in the observation of Naomi exploring *going round a boundary* with clay. Such high levels of involvement resonate with the 'child-involvement scale' of the Effective Early Learning Project (Pascal and Bertram, 1997).

Exploring spiral schemas in one classroom

We had been very excited by our early observations, but shorter observations of schemas are more manageable in a busy classroom. These informal observations were spontaneous and usually only took two or three minutes. During a period of nine months we found that the most popular schemas for these 4–6-year-olds in a school classroom were *spirals* and *rotation, grids, shapes, connection and trajectories* (often explored through maps). This list can be contrasted with Arnold's list of most frequently observed schemas in one nursery (see p. 36).

> For over two terms everyone in the class knew that Zoë, 4:7, had a passion for *spirals*. She drew them, cut out spirals and talked about them endlessly. Outside she often walked in a spiral formation in the playground saying 'I'm winding myself up', and then, reversing her direction, announced 'I'm unwinding myself'. At home she loved playing with a 'spirograph' set on which she made circular patterns with the help of rotating wheels. One day her mother brought in some Greek cakes called 'baklavas' for the children to share: as she handed the plate round, Zoë proudly told her friends that 'they're spirals'.

Zoë's schema was dominant for such a long time that some of the other children were drawn into her interest and explored them in their own ways. When the other child's schema interests were mapped (see, for example, Figure 3.7), it was clear that only the children who were already interested in aspects of rotation, circles, arcs, trajectories and semicircles chose to explore spirals. These children were at a point where exploring spirals fitted with their current schemas and added to their understanding. At the same time other children's new perspectives on spirals and rotation added to Zoë's understanding by exploring an ever-widening range of behaviours, resources and opportunities.

Children's representations and marks of their schemas

The children's current schemas appeared to captivate them and often surprised us by their endurance. In the middle of a class discussion one day, David put his finger in his ear and said 'Oh! Our ears are spirals!'

Several children used construction apparatus to explore spirals. Daniel, 5:1, drew a circular scribble saying 'It's like my stirring wheel' (that he'd made the previous day with construction materials). Several weeks later when he was drawing, he found some blunt pencils and fetching a pencil sharpener said 'I'll get my little stirring thing'.

A group of children in the same class decided to make a 'spiral road' with the big wooden blocks. This resembled a circular maze and drew lots of children to it, to make their own journeys to the centre and out again. James, 5:4, and Mitchell, 5:2, cut out paper spirals and stood on the blocks waving them, repeating 'Spirals and spirals and spirals'.

Figure 3.4 James and Mitchell construct spirals

The circular paper spirals led to an interest in making different shaped spirals – all ideas that came from the children in their play. At first they drew these shapes and later progressed to cutting them out. The act of cutting out changed their two-dimensional representations to three-dimensional objects that they could manipulate. Analysis of cutting out as a process of animation 'offers a different opportunity to make meaning' (Pahl, 1999b, p. 115) and one in which 'represented objects come off the page and are brought into the world of physical objects'(Kress, 1997, p. 27).

Several children decided to make square, oblong, triangular, oval, diamond and pentagon 'spirals' over a period of several weeks. Their interest in different shapes then led to a comparison of the different widths apart of their cuts as they created spirals. They were developing their own theories: spacing the cuts further apart led to wider strips but shorter lengths when the paper spirals were extended.

Aaron, 5:0. Spirals were one of Aaron's dominant schemas. One day he decided to make a 'spiral map' (see Figure 3.5). Starting with a small square of paper, he added successive strips joining them with paper clips and brass fasteners to create his map. Finally he drew a 'spiral road' on it, with arrows that included some with right-angled turns. In traditional American patchwork this arrangement is known as 'log cabin' but at that time Aaron's mother thought it unlikely that he had ever seen this pattern.

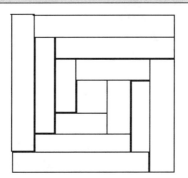

Figure 3.5 Aaron's spiral map

Spiral marks and representations

Spirals and spiral-like marks appeared on paper, in painting and drawings. They embellished drawings as hair, fingers, sun and flowers; one shape within another; as patterns and as explorations of shapes (Figure 3.5). This last example is of interest since these older children were also trying to relate other aspects of their play to their dominant schema, though it was not clear to adults what a 'spiral play' or 'spiral aliens' (Figure 3.6) were.

At one stage in his writing, Mitchell used tiny spirals to represent meaning (see Chapter 4, p. 56).

Adults supporting and extending children's spiral schemas

Adults need to support children's play, although this is not to imply that with 25 children there will be 25 individual schemas. As these examples of children exploring spiral schemas show, their schemas often cluster together.

For Zoë and her friends we provided further opportunities and resources for the children to explore both rotation and spirals including the following:

Figure 3.6 Spiral aliens

- We put plain yoghurt in the fridge with some fruits and jam for children who wanted to stir. On another occasion we provided ready-made pastry and dried fruit for rolling up, and juices to mix and stir for drinks.
- We brought in two giant African snails in a glass tank and put out some magnifying glasses.
- A basket of ropes and wools that we took outside for play subsequently led to some complicated spiral mazes outside. Following this, when the grass was mown on the school playing-field, some of the children decided to create grass mazes.

Exploring spirals together

- With the whole class, we played a circle game that involved winding and unwinding actions.
- A group of children made coil pots with clay.
- At the beginning of Advent we created an 'Advent Spiral' on the floor of the hall, the pathways marked out with moss. Children took it in turns to walk in the dark hall from the outside to the centre, to light their own candle from the central candle that was already lit – and then to retrace their journey.

Enriching schemas through visits

When planning to support and extend children's schemas, we often included informal, local visits. Chris Athey's study supports the 'critical importance of first-hand experience in providing the content of representation'. She argues that these first-hand experiences could be called the 'stuff' or 'content' of mind (Athey, 1990, p. 58).

For the spiral explorers we walked across a pedestrian bridge that crossed a major road near the school. At either end the bridge descended in a curve which the local children referred to as the 'curly-whirly bridge'. Many children had been exploring *rotation, linear movement, trajectories, maps, zigzags, spirals* and *arrows,* and linked these to *spirals.* Because schemas are rarely explored in isolation, there were links between different schemas as Figure 3.7 shows.

Mapping patterns of schema exploration

We had been looking for the 'pattern' of repeatable behaviour to which Athey refers (1990). When we looked at several weeks of observations of each child and traced their development, a visible pattern began to emerge that was quite unexpected. When represented on paper the pattern looked like the highs and lows of a patient's temperature chart or the stock exchange (see Figure 3.7).

Tracing Aaron's schema development

(See also pp. 48–51 'Observations of Aaron's dominant schemas'.)

Beginning with the first observation of Aaron, I noted his interest in *'millions'* and large quantities at the top of the chart (see Figure 3.7). I wrote subsequent schemas he explored across the top of the chart in the order in which they were observed. I gave each written observation a number (starting with 1 for the first observation) and mapped these onto the chart. Where a number is repeated, this shows that I observed more than one schema on one day: Figure 3.7 shows that three observations were made on the first day (1,1).

Mapping the children's explorations of different schemas provided us with a great deal of information and all the children's 'maps' shared certain features. The most significant of these are that:

- when represented, each child's 'journey' traces a similar zigzagging pathway that moves gradually forwards
- all children revisited some earlier schema interests, allowing them to add new understandings.

Understanding Aaron's pattern of schema explorations

Aaron appeared to move through seventeen schema interests during nine months (Figure 3.8).

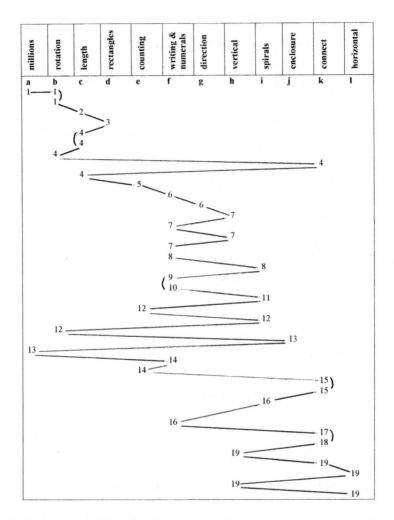

Figure 3.7 The pattern of Aaron's schema journey (part)

Aaron's dominant schemas during this period were what he referred to as 'smokers' which we understood to be an interest in *vertical* chimneys. This developed later to include *horizontal* cylinders (exhaust pipes). Aaron was clearly interested in the movement of smoke and other objects *up, down* and *through* the cylinders (chimneys, tubes, tunnels).

Observations of Aaron's dominant schemas

(See Figure 3.7)

We have selected observations of Aaron's dominant schemas from a period of nine months (see below). *The numbers in column one refer to the observation (day): '1' was of notes made on the first day of observing.*

Millions and large quantities
Rotation and rolling up/unrolling
Length, long/short, height, comparing, measuring and estimating length
Rectangles
Counting one-to-one
Writing and numerals
Direction
Vertical, up, down and through
Spirals
Enclosure
Connection
Horizontal, along and through
Zigzags
Grids
On top
Trajectories
Right angles

Figure 3.8 Key to the pattern of Aaron's schema journey

Rotation, rolling up and unrolling

Day	Observation notes:
1	• Made a long 'car' and rolled it up and unrolled it.
1	• Made 'helicopters' and a 'roundabout' and spun them above his head.
4	• Made a motorbike with a wheel at either end. Said he wanted 'to make them go round together' and he suggested using a 'big rubber band' (we had none large enough). He tried a long strip of paper (it broke) and then string which he estimated correctly to within 10 cm. He was thrilled when his idea worked.
12	• Intrigued when watching liquid swirl in a cup, explaining 'it's the stirring'.
24	• Explaining part of a tall construction, said 'this bends for the smoke to go round' (i.e. it both curved and rotated).
24	• At the base of his model was a cross with wheels which could rotate. He explained 'it's the propeller'.
33	• Made a spaceship with a steering wheel, lock, tools, microphone and dumb-bell, all of which he demonstrated could rotate.
34	• Brought in off-cuts of a roller blind which he repeatedly rolled and unrolled.
35	• Again unrolled and rolled the off-cuts of the blind.

35	• Made a road with a ramp either end for the off-cut of blind to unroll on.
35	• Involved Katie, spending ages rolling and unrolling – pleased to demonstrate to anyone who would watch.
35	• Brought in a door catch he'd found outside and showed me how it worked (it rotated).
35	• Excited to watch the builder's cement mixer rotating.
35	• Unrolled the entire length of his off-cut of a blind and compared its length with a track he'd made.

Spirals

8	• Observed snails and commented that they 'might crawl in a spiral'.
11	• Brought in a small metal spring and told us 'It's a curly, spiral thing'.
12	• Said 'I'm doing a spiral drink' (making a drink) and explained that it was 'the stirring'.
16	• Drew a spiral.
22	• Brought a banded-snail to school and said 'I like spirals'.
24	• Showed how the imaginary 'smoke' moved in spirals through a curved tube on his construction.
35	• Joined two pieces of off-cuts of a roller blind, saying, 'Let's make a longer spiral'.
36	• Made a square 'spiral map' (see p. 45).
36	• Completed his 'map' by drawing a spiral 'road' on it.

Vertical up, down and through

7	• Decided to use a sand-timer, explaining that it would be his turn when the sand ran through (interested in movement of the sand).
7	• Whilst investigating soil asked 'Can snails climb up?'
19	• Made a shadow puppet and added a 'smoker' (chimney), fixed to its head.
19	• Made two houses with small bricks, with 'smokers' on top.
24	• Used 'Tic-Tac' to make a tall, vertical construction.
28	• Aaron was very excited to find a computer program to build a house, with chimneys.
31	• Recorded a traffic survey with ticks.

Horizontal, through and along

19	• Saved a piece of card and commented on the hole in it: held it to his eye to look through.
19	• Pointed to an aeroplane crossing the sky, 'It's got two smokers!' – he pointed out the plane's vapour trails.

24	• Turned his tall, vertical construction on its side so that it was horizontal and said it was a plane.
24	• Fixed two tubes at one end of his 'plane' that he called 'smokers' – this was the plane's exhaust.
25, 26, 27	• Made a complicated system of tunnels in the sand (on three consecutive days).
27	• Aaron was fascinated by the idea that water would go through the (horizontal) pipes beneath the floor, shown by the builders who were working in school.
29	• Made Lego 'flowers' with bricks arranged in a horizontal arrangement, one on top of the other.
35	• Made a road with a ramp at either end on which to unroll his off-cut of roller-blind.
35	• Added horizontal tunnels for his roller blind off-cuts to go through.
35	• Unrolled piece of roller blind to measure its length.

Rotation and *spiral* schemas also complemented each other. The observations above show the way in which Aaron added to his understanding over an extended period of time and it is important to remember that all these observations were of child-initiated and often spontaneous play, and not direct teaching. This underlines the significance of opportunities for children to play in ways that support their deep cognitive concerns. Aaron could not have explored these schemas in a setting in which child-initiated play was not valued or where staff gave no time and opportunities for this.

During the nine months in which these observations were made, Aaron also explored various schemas when choosing to write letters and numerals: these were clearly linked with *vertical, horizontal* and *connection* schemas, and this is explored further in Chapter 4.

Looking at Figure 3.7, Aaron's 'journey' of schema explorations can be seen to move forwards, as he visited new and often related schemas, then revisited previous schemas. Although Aaron appears to be constantly changing his focus, it is clear that there were relationships between his behaviours. Athey proposes that rather than describe children's changing interests and play behaviours as 'flitting', through knowledge of schemas we can often see that the child is 'fitting different but appropriate content' into their latest 'form' (Athey: 1990, p. 107).

Making meaning through mark-making

As the children's schemas developed from action to thought they recorded and represented their schemas with resources and materials to hand. As we have shown, the children represented their cognitive constants using objects such as their actions with their bodies, toys, cut-outs from paper, sand, grass, clay, block

play, objects made with different materials (technology), constructional apparatus, pencil sharpeners, yoghurt and cakes. They also recorded and represented
their schemas through making marks on paper with pens, crayons, paint and
pencils. In his significant study of young children's art, Matthews uses an alternative term to 'schema'. Describing aspects of the infant's and young child's
worlds to which they are drawn, Matthews argues that their 'attractor systems
operate like searchlights, which illuminate for the child aspects of the world in
a systematic way' (Matthews, 1999, p. 80). Reading the observation notes of
Aaron on pp. 48–51 the extent to which certain forms and actions acted as
attractor systems for him, is clear.

Schemas highlight the mathematics in the world

When we observe children exploring a schema it enriches our experience of how
children think and learn. Mathematics can be seen in the broadest sense
through the children's schemas. Compare a less stimulating mathematical curriculum where the teacher has a script to 'teach' shapes. The teacher in this situation shows a triangle (usually equilateral) and says 'this is a triangle', she
repeats this for the four basic shapes. Very often the geometry of the given curriculum never goes beyond the naming of the shapes. If we give children experience and opportunities to explore their schematic concerns then we will see
that children will be engaging with the properties of shape that define this
mathematical area. They will have gone beyond the narrow curriculum and be
investigating perimeter, angle, circumference, height, position and area. This is
a much more useful and cognitively challenging curriculum, on an intellectual
level, that befits young children's capabilities.

Key points about schemas

- Schemas can be described as a child's repeated pattern of behaviour.
- Schemas cannot be taught, they come from the child's own self-interest.
- When children are involved in a schema the level of involvement can be very
  intense.
- Some of this schematic thinking is represented in their drawings.
- These schemas, whether graphic or actions, form 'footstools' for more
  complex structures and mathematical ideas.
- The schematic marks, like other mathematical mark-making, help bridge the
  gap between informal and formal mathematics.
- Supporting children's schemas feeds their natural curiosity which, in turn,
  extends their thinking.

In the following chapter we focus on children's early writing, showing some
links with their schemas. We look at the relationship between early writing
development and early mathematical graphics.

4

Early Writing, Early Mathematics

Figure 4.1 Alex's letter

Alex, 4:7, read his letter (Figure 4.1) to me: 'Hello! I want you to write to me –
I'd like that. School's exciting: you can do typing and we've got paper clips. I
made an aeroplane today and a puppet – two puppets! I made a sandwich with
pocket-money bread.

Love from Alex'.

The significance of emergent writing

Two voices

Elizabeth: one of the major turning points in my teaching career came, in the
early 1980s, when I took an early writing course at the Centre for Language in
Primary Education in London. This introduced me to a developmental writing
approach to teaching. Later, in 1987, at the University of Louisville in Kentucky,

I took another more intensive course on early literacy development tutored by Jean-Anne Clyde. This helped me in my enquiry about children's literacy and directly supported me in my teaching of reading and writing. This developmental theory or emergent approach was developing slowly in pockets of England, McKenzie (1986); New Zealand, Holdaway (1979) and Clay (1975); and in the USA, Goodman (1968). The significant change in my teaching was that I started to observe what children were actually doing in writing when given the freedom to explore their own thinking.

Maulfry: at about the same time, I also came across emergent writing, but via a different route. A local teacher had visited several Early Years settings in the USA and had seen children using the 'writing station' (or writing area). She talked about the way children made their own marks and that these were accepted by the teacher. I was intrigued by this idea and took it back to my classroom.

Gradually I encouraged children to use their own marks and, with the children's help, I developed a writing area. Their growing confidence and deep levels of understanding were soon evident. At the time I called this 'thinking writing' since I emphasised the need to 'really think' about all aspects of their writing – and especially their intended meaning, the content. At first I had no idea that other teachers were supporting children's early writing in England in this way. For two years I kept every piece of the children's writing – including writing they chose to do in their play – in order to assess and be able to justify what the children did. Gradually I was able to trace a developing pathway that included content, understanding of phonics, spelling, punctuation and handwriting. As I did this I came across texts that highlighted this development within the context of 'whole language'. This was a major turning point in my teaching and, like Elizabeth, it was the observations of children that helped reveal the children's thinking.

The literacy movement also heavily influenced many other teachers. This was a theory based in classrooms and homes rather than specially set-up clinical tasks. This grounded theory is based on the social environment, about the lived experiences of participants (Glaser and Strauss, 1967). It is effective because, although it is complex, it is based in real situations and therefore manageable to do in classrooms, because that was where the research was based. It was argued that: 'the classroom practice of tens of thousands of Key Stage 1 teachers has been changed by the findings of emergent literacy. Teachers are better equipped conceptually to exploit children's knowledge of reading and writing as a bridge to what is conventionally required' (Hannon, 1995, p.16).

Both of us therefore constructed strong classroom practice in literacy teaching. An objective view of your classroom is always useful: a visitor once walked into my classroom and remarked 'the children are really developing their literacy but where is the mathematics?' Criticism is always hard to handle but once you have recovered from the initial shock, then you sort out whether you accept it or not. I decided this criticism of my mathematics teaching was a fair comment, but what was more difficult to understand was the visitor's suggestion of applying the same learning principles to mathematics that I did with literacy. Since 1990 both of us were able to develop this idea with others who were also struggling with this concept, but wanted to find out more: thus the Exeter Emergent Mathematics Teachers' group was born (see Chapter 1).

In this chapter we review children's literacy development and make links to mathematical development since it is from this basis and this view of children's learning that we began our journey into a better way of teaching mathematics.

Young children explore symbols

Newman (1984, p. 12) proposes that 'from an early age, young children expect written language to make sense' and show 'their amazing ability to coordinate the meaning they want to express with the form appropriate for expressing it'. Children's ability to link early marks with meaning and their ability to communicate through these marks is an important stage in becoming writers (and mathematicians). These early marks will not look like standard letters or numerals. As Newman argues: 'the notion that their scribbles are merely random marks on paper must, I think, be replaced by an understanding of how these early writing attempts are intentional efforts by children to create and share meaning' (Newman, 1984, p. 12).

Alex and the 'pocket money bread'

Alex, 4:7, was interested in things high above him. One day he repeatedly told us a dramatic story about his father falling off a ladder: we found out later that it was an invented story. When the window cleaner came to school Alex watched him working for a long time. In the same week Alex wrote a letter to his mum using many capital 'H's'. Towards the end of his letter he joined a string of 'H's', like a fence or a ladder on its side. He was interested in making things: a 'machine to make bubbles', 'a space rocket', several planes and a kite – all things that move above the earth. Next he told stories about huge eagles – birds unknown in southern England – which he had watched fly away with various items. A pattern seemed to be emerging: Alex was interested in *vertical movement*, *trajectories* and *grids*, and these movements and forms were mirrored at the time in his writing. He was also exploring *containing* and *enveloping* at this time.

To encourage the children to write letters I had arranged that they could write to children of the same age in another school in the city. Alex's schema concerns were revealed in the development of his writing (see Figure 4.1).

Alex used both the first letter of his name and his full name. The strong shape of the capital 'H' is similar to the 'A' of his name: both letters need either strong *vertical* or *oblique* lines. Lower down on the page he joined three capital 'A's and then a series of capital 'H's which link with his schemas at that time (*height, grids* and *trajectories* and *vertical* and *horizontal lines*) and is like the 'fence' he'd used in the letter he'd written to his mother. The letter also included a face and several approximations of letters, and the word 'Hello' (see Figure 4.1).

Alex was in his first term at school. His 'voice' shines through his text. Although he had not then met his pen pal, he was able to communicate some features of his own school that were significant to him. To support his *containing* and *enveloping* schema that week I had put 'pitta' bread and some salad to fill it in the fridge, for those children who were interested. Alex's reference to 'pocket money' bread is his personal way of naming the bread – the action of filling the bread reminded him of putting his pocket money *into* a purse. At home he enjoyed making 'houses' out of boxes which he then *filled* with snails from the garden. The content of his letter therefore reflects part of his schema interest (*containing* and *enveloping*) at that time, whilst the form of the letters he used to represent meaning was also influenced by schemas (*height* and *grids*) in the grid-like letters and use of vertical and oblique lines he wrote.

We believe that the content that children explore through their early marks and the meanings they make are of the utmost importance. At the same time the function and form of children's early mark-making can be seen to develop in tandem with the content if their schema interests are viewed as relating to their early writing. We can see how both Alex's schemas and his emerging skills support the development of his writing.

Ferreiro and Teberosky have argued that from 3 years of age children test out their hypotheses about both print and the process of writing in systematic ways (Ferreiro and Teberosky, 1982). In her challenging study of schemas, Athey identified a clear relationship between children's schemas and their early mark-making and writing that the example of Alex's letter demonstrates. Alex's understanding of the social and cultural purposes of writing is also continually developing through observation and co-construction within his home and early childhood setting.

Marks and approximations

At an early stage Mitchell, 4:9, used tiny spirals to represent letters, also experimenting with continuous wavy lines and his own approximations of numerals and letters. To these he gradually added standard letters, increasing his repertoire. He used the first letter of his name to stand for many words and then, having made the link with the sound of this initial letter, widened the range of initial letters of words, often matching the sound. Mitchell began to put dots between letters, explaining 'so the letters don't get bumped' and at this time also used spaces for the same reason. During this period of observations Mitchell was fascinated by counting everything he could and often labelled things he counted with numbers on small pieces of paper. He was interested in series of numbers and experimented, for example, 20, 60, 90 and 1, 6, 1, 2, 3, 4, 8, 8, 30, 8 before counting for the first time in a standard sequence of 1–7.

Nicola, 5:0, used the letters of her own name and zigzag lines on different areas of the page. She then wrote the names 'Mummy' and 'Nicola' to stand for what she wanted to say, gradually increasing her range of letters to include others. The strong visual shapes of capital letters and their relationship to zigzags had impressed Nicola, and she concentrated on using these. At this stage she also used some small circles and squares to stand for letters. Occasionally Nicola used numerals to represent 'writing', repeating 1, 2 and 3 across the page.

Young children do not see the division between different marks of 'writing' and 'mathematics' and 'drawing', and often combine them on one page. This can be seen in the example of the birthday card that Mhairi, 4:7, made for her daddy (Figure 4.2). Using a Christmas card that she had received, Mhairi added her special message for her Dad's birthday. The smiling faces and the letter 't' for her dad's name Tom, are appropriate symbols that she has met elsewhere and she has used balloons since she knows these are important items for birthdays in her family. Finally she added 'from Mhairi'.

Figure 4.2 Mhairi's card

There is some wonderful software available for children to use but we have rarely seen children in Early Years settings using a computer for their *own* early writing or mathematics. I was teaching in a local class with 4- and 5-year-olds for a few days and set up a noticeboard for their use. Robert, 4:8, was new at school and used this as an opportunity to develop friendships (Figure 4.3). Several children subsequently invited him to play, adding their names on 'Post-it' notes.

wilyoplawivmeRITYON
AMROBERT

Will you play with me?

Write your name.
Robert.

Figure 4.3 Robert's notice

Early writing and links with schemas

In the previous chapter we saw how Aaron's attractor system or schemas helped him focus on certain aspects within his environment and actions. Threaded through the observations of his schemas are notes of his developing interest in writing and mark-making.

While sharing a book, Aaron asked 'how does writing go?' The following day when writing, Aaron used some numerals he knew (rather than his own marks, letter-like symbols or letters). Soon he was observed to use a capital 'A' and subsequently 'A' and 'H' to represent his own meaning when writing. Some of his schema explorations during this period focused on comparison of *lengths, vertical* and *horizontal lines, movement up and down* and *connection*. He was also interested in triangles and diamonds which share some features with the written letter 'A'. A later interest was *zigzags*, which when represented with a pen on paper mimicked both the movement of an adult's hand as it writes and the 'joined-up' writing itself. Aaron's interest of *zigzags* also developed the use of *oblique lines, movement up and down* and *connection*. This interest coincided with his increased use of 'M', 'N', 'V' and 'W' in his writing of the time.

While Aaron was busy comparing the length of constructions he had made, building tall chimneys and pointing out exhaust pipes on cars, he was adding to his understanding of 'how writing goes' at a deep level, for example, of how 'A' and 'H' are written. It is significant that many of the first letters he focused on share the same 'up and down' movement and orientation as his 'smokers', in addition of course to one being the first letter of his name. Whilst he was developing theories about writing, the observation notes show how Aaron was also developing his understanding of the relationship between reading, writing (letter symbols), writing numerals, number patterns and counting. At the same time Aaron was also assigning his own meaning to the marks he made and listening to the meanings that other children and the teacher gave to constructions, text, numbers, symbols and pictures they 'read'.

Understanding development

Knowledge about schemas and an appreciation of their significance in children's development can therefore help teachers to understand individual children's writing development and mark-making. But such knowledge can only be gained through observation of children who have opportunities to initiate their own play and learning, and an appreciation of children's early (emergent) writing development. Athey argues that when teachers closely observe children, this leads to: 'attempts to evaluate (children's) valid contributions to the negotiation of meaning, the teacher is able to accumulate deep understanding of stage levels of cognition in children as well as other aspects of development' (Athey, 1990, p. 31). In our own settings, we found we were able to appreciate and gradually understand the rich abundance of children's visible schemas and marks from our informal observations. In Chapter 6 we explore the early development of young children's mathematical marks.

Research into early literacy has established that there is a great deal of development before formal instruction (McNaughton, 1995). Whereas formerly children were seen as passive learners needing 'pre-reading, writing and number' activities, their active involvement has been recognised. The research into early writing development during the past 30 years builds on a long tradition of study of what children themselves actually do, that reaches back to Vygotsky and Luria: 'writing must be something the child needs … writing must be "relevant to life" – in the same way that we require a relevant arithmetic', 'and should become necessary for her in her play' (Vygotsky, 1983, pp. 290–1). In researching the early development of writing in 1929, Luria observed that:

> before a child has understood the sense and mechanism of writing, he has already made many attempts to elaborate primitive methods; and these, for him, are the pre-history of his writing. But even these methods are not developed all at once: they pass through a number of trials and inventions, constituting a series of stages with which it is very useful for an educator working with children of school age children and pre-school children to be acquainted. (Luria, 1983, p. 276)

As we shall show in Chapters 6 and 7, children's 'trials and inventions' are at the heart of their understanding of abstract symbolism in mathematics.

Marie Clay's research in New Zealand highlighted the way in which new skills continually emerged during development. This definition led to the term 'emergent writing' which has also sometimes been called 'developmental' or 'process' writing. Since the publication of Clay's study of young children's writing in 1975, there has been a considerable number of texts published on early or emergent writing, for example, Cambourne, 1988; Hall, 1987; McNaughton, 1995.

Early writing and early mathematical marks

In my own research, in a study of my own child's development of number, I found parallels with the way the child in the study developed number language and Clay's analysis of writing development. (Carruthers, 1997a; 1997b; 1997c)

Below is a concept map to show the possible link between the development of early writing and Sovay's number development (Carruthers, 1997a; 1997b; 1997c).

Clay's analysis of early writing	*Sovay's acquisition of number*
The sign concept – letters and their own letter-like shapes represent a message they can read	You can talk number words for counting in different ways and you need numbers in different situations
The message concept – you can write down a message you want to convey	Numbers can be written down for purposes, e.g. Sovay wrote marks on her sister's dinner money envelope to convey how much money was there
Recurring principle – where children use any letters and words they know over and over again	Sovay – 1, 2, 1, 2, 1, 2, 1, 2; counting pebbles. '6' became all numbers
A generating principle – in which they combine the letters they know in different ways to produce strings of print	Playing with her sister using pencil and paper saying '26, 29, 24, 3, 6, 9, 17, 16, 2, 3, 1, 7'. Making her own symbols on the paper
A directional principle – children become aware that writing is formed in horizontal lines from left to right	Sovay's data from this period (before she was 44 months of age), came from her talk. In 90 per cent of her recorded talking and counting numbers she began with the lowest numbers and graduated to the highest e.g. '1, 59, 51, 52, 53'

The child in the study above demonstrated her understanding of numerals through her number talk (Carruthers, 1997a; 1997b; 1997c). Although we found that young children in general do not seem to be so prolific at putting marks on paper as older children (there are exceptions and periods they go through where this is their chosen way to represent) they do put their mathematical marks down on paper. In Chapter 6 we have traced a pattern of early number development; young children make marks, some of which have mathematical meaning to them. It is notable to point out that many of their marks are ways of expressing their thoughts and as such they may not fit neatly into the art, writing, scientific or mathematical category. The children represent what they want to in a way that crosses 'subject' boundaries.

We have argued previously that early (emergent) literacy shares certain attributes with early mathematical marks and representations:

- Children exhibit behaviours that demonstrate they acquire conventional knowledge of reading and writing in a gradual way.
- Children's approximations are accepted.
- The developmental process is viewed as a continuum from birth throughout life.
- Teaching is based on the observations of children's learning and behaviours: teaching and learning are therefore intertwined.
- Children are seen as powerful learners, constantly making sense of their world.
- Learning is most effective when it is experienced as a whole picture which is not being broken into meaningless parts.
- Learning is best when it is presented in meaningful contexts.
- Children have real choices in their learning.
- The role of the teacher is not as sole giver of knowledge, but she understands that environmental and social factors and the child's own knowledge are important contributory factors to the learning process. She sensitively takes these aspects into consideration (Worthington and Carruthers, 1998).

We would also add that:

- the child's continual search for *meaning* in all contexts is one of the most significant features in the development of early mathematical marks, symbols and written methods
- the development from informal 'home' mathematics, to subsequent abstract symbolism of 'school' mathematics is negotiated and co-constructed by the members of the learning community, whether in the home or the Early Years setting.

In this section we map out some existing research that links the development of mathematics and language.

As can be seen in the concept map on p. 62, there are parallels with research and writings of literacy and mathematics development. It is interesting to note that what was discovered about knowledge of young children's development is considerably behind in some areas compared with literacy. However, if one could claim there is a similar pattern of development between literacy learning and mathematical learning, then there could be a strong argument to suggest that we teach both subjects in similar ways.

Literacy	*Mathematics*
Chomsky's (1965) Language Acquisition Device (LAD) innate structures somehow guide the child to consider the 'right' possibilities among an abundance of logical alternatives	Gelman and Gallistel (1978) suggest that similar innate structures as in LAD guide children learning to count. They claim infants are born with a non-verbal mechanism called an 'accumulator'
The social learning aspect was a significant factor in children's language and literacy learning. Harste, Woodward and Burke (1984): 'Language whether oral or written is a social event of some complexity. Language did not develop because of the existence of one language user but two.'	'Mathematics knowledge is a social category of knowledge' (Nunes and Bryant, 1996).
'Meaning is the key to reading' (Smith, 1978)	Hughes (1986) proposes that children need meaningful and relevant mathematical tasks
Children are powerful learners and they know a considerable amount about literacy before they come to school (Clay, 1975; Hall, 1987)	Aubrey (1994b) found that pre-schoolers had a considerable amount of informal mathematical knowledge before they enter school
Pre-reading and readiness are questioned. Coltheart (1979) demonstrated that reading readiness has no basis. The way to learn to read is by reading	Durham Project (cited by Pettitt and Davis, 1994) questions pre-number concepts. From the evidence of their research children learn about number by counting objects in a variety of ways and not by traditional pre-number activities, e.g. sorting and matching
Markman (1990) suggests that children narrow down alternatives by making certain assumptions about word meanings which constrain their guesses	Gelman (1991) proposes that the counting principles (Gelman and Gallistel, 1978) function as constraints for number
Barratt-Pugh (2000) proposes that literacy learning is embedded in the sociocultural practices that children are involved in	Worthington and Carruthers (Chapter 2 in this volume) argue that mathematical learning is embedded in the sociocultural practices of the child's family, community and culture

(*Source*: adapted from Carruthers, 1997c.)

Early (emergent) literacy is often misunderstood

Whatever teaching approach is used in education, there are dangers of poor teaching or the concept being misunderstood. For example, Munn (1997) explains emergent literacy in terms of 'emergent literacy scheme' and 'pre-literate children'. These terms are questioned in texts on emergent literacy (see, for example, Hall, 1987). Munn also talks about communication as the overriding factor in emergent literacy. In her analysis of her research findings, she concludes that 'there can be little similarity between the development of children's understanding of numerals and their understanding of writing' (Munn, 1997, p. 95). Her research findings stated that children cannot communicate their own pictographic and tally marks in numeracy because they cannot read them back. However, there is also a stage in emergent writing when children cannot communicate their marks to others but they do know that they have meaning, as when a child says 'I am doing writing' (for example, see Hughes, 1986, p. 57). In Mills's experience of children's literacy she describes an incident where, several days later a child read her same piece of writing and had completely changed the meaning. Mills's salient questions help us think through the dilemmas:

- Can you pinpoint the exact moment a child attributes a sound value to a letter or transfers from syllabic to alphabetic recording?
- Is it really necessary for every child to read back their early attempts at their own invented numerical recordings several days after writing them? (Mills, 2002, p. 9)

In our experience there is no definite line where a child moves from one kind of understanding to another. The overriding point is that they do have an understanding on which they build and develop. An emergent approach to mathematics has no easy clear-cut pedagogy and can be fraught with difficulties. However, in reply to Munn's doubts about such an approach Mills asks: 'Is the ambiguity over the point of understanding enough to discount an emergent approach to numeracy?' (Mills, 2002, p. 59).

In our study we have found that children use a variety of non-conventional marks in different ways to communicate their mathematics. It is, we believe, because they have chosen to do it and it makes sense to them. Our findings are different to those of Munn because, instead of the clinical interview model of research, we used situations that were based on everyday conditions in real classrooms and in the home. Bruce (1991) describes this as 'real data'.

Teachers' perceptions of early writing

In our telephone interviews with teachers, one of the questions we asked was whether teachers supported emergent writing. We believe that if teachers already have developed their understanding and practice to support children's own early writing, they will more readily understand how to support children's mathematical graphics.

It is important to point out here that these teachers had already expressed their interest in children's own written marks and in mathematical graphics. We invited teachers to tell us a little 'about what this means for the children' in their setting or class. Teachers' responses show a wide range of understandings. Of those we interviewed, almost 70 per cent appeared confused by the term 'emergent writing' and what this meant in terms of practice. Explanations of their practice included:

- Children copy over or trace. We use 'Jolly Phonics'.
- They need help with spelling and copying writing.
- Near the beginning of the reception class they do need to write over the teacher's writing.
- Their first job is writing over the teacher's writing. I support this with dot-to-dot and tracing. I think fine-motor control is really important.

The remaining 31 per cent of teachers responded with comments that suggest they do have an understanding of emergent writing and are putting this into practice:

- Right from the beginning letting them teach us what they can do – emergent writing is the stage when the marks connect with meaning.
- Their own marks are very important – I respond to the content of what they have written and give lots of positive praise.
- Emergent writing is about the children making marks – they start with a scribble or a bit more and they read and tell you about what they've written.
- We have a language-rich environment: children have their favourite letters. I write a question on what they've written, responding to the content.
- Any marks they make on paper tell me something.
- (Emergent writing means) children's pretend writing – any of their marks on paper. Their scribbles and what they tell you about them, tell you a lot.

These findings illustrate the varied perceptions of what teachers understand about emergent literacy. This confusion seems to be widespread, for example, whilst New Zealand has embraced an emergent or 'process' approach to writing (McNaughton, 1995), elsewhere the extensive research and literature published in this field has not led to high-quality practice that reflects understanding of this. Perhaps because young children's writing does not 'look like' the standard writing and spelling of older children, it has so often been misunderstood. This is also the case with early mathematical graphics. One misunderstanding is that there is no teaching involved but, as Smith and Elley point out, 'it is not enough to provide the motivation for the children to write and then to leave them to get on with it. We do not advocate a laissez-faire attitude to writing instruction' (Smith and Elley, 1997, p. 142). We are in accord with this view in terms of supporting children's mathematical graphics. We argue that teaching in this way involves: 'constantly assessing and providing suitably challenging activities, demonstrating standard forms and "asking questions which may help the student to clarify, to predict, to develop further, to look for alternatives"' (Stoessinger and Wilkinson, 1991, cited in Gifford, 1997, p. 78).

Conclusion

There are important links between children's early literacy and their early mathematical graphics: teachers who understand the theory and practice of emergent writing can benefit because they, like us, can find an easier way into helping children move from their informal mathematics to more standard forms. In this way they have already gone part way because of their understanding of early writing. It is a useful connection to make for this reason.

In early childhood mathematics we are currently in the position that emergent writing was 25 years ago. We have argued that supporting the development of children's early mathematical graphics is: 'provocative maths, that is to say it inspires, motivates and challenges children's minds. It requires them to gradually make existing perceptions explicit, to try out alternative ways of thinking, looking and representing' (Worthington and Carruthers, 1998, p. 15).

In Chapter 5 we consider the difficulties that children experience when they first encounter the formal language of mathematics and its abstract symbolism. We show the difficulties that teachers often experience in trying to help children make sense of mathematics. We propose that encouraging and supporting the development of children's own mathematical marks and written methods helps children 'bridge the gap' between their informal 'home' mathematics and subsequent abstract mathematics. We introduce the concept of 'bi-numeracy'.

5

Bridging the Gap between Home and School Mathematics

Edward is 5 years old and is at school. This morning he tries to do a complete page of addition sums in his mathematics lesson: then it is assembly time. He sits for 30 minutes learning about how God made the world and everything in it. Edward, like all children, tries to make sense of his experiences. As he walks out of the school with his mother, he turns to her and says: 'Why does God make us do sums?' (Adapted from David, 1999).

Disconnections

Daniel's (4:6) experience of 'doing' sums

12 Jan.

$9 + 3 = 11$
$6 + 8 = 41$
$7 + 4 = 11$
$8 + 9 = 17$

1 Feb.

t	u		t	u
2	5		3	5
6	0		4	2
8	5		7	7

2 Feb.

h	t	u
3	2	1
2	5	4
5	7	5

8 Feb.

th	h	t	u
1	3	2	4
0	5	1	3
1	8	3	7

Daniel

I was teaching a class in their first term of school. All of the children were 4 but would be 5 years old in that term. Daniel's mother gave me his arithmetic book from the pre-school he had been attending. Above are typed copies of the calculations that Daniel did in his book. The teacher had written out the calculation in this vertical format and Daniel had put in the answers. His mother said he used some sort of apparatus to work out these sums.

From these examples I do not really know what Daniel knows about numbers. I know he seems to know how to write numerals well, as his written numbers were easy to read. He seems to have made remarkable progression in the space of two months: he counted in ones through tens and hundreds and then into the thousands!

If we take a closer look at the above examples, we see that Daniel has no complex calculating to do. He does not need to make any adjustments because the calculations could be done as single number addition within ten. What I really believe Daniel knows from these particular examples is how to mechanically add, with the use of some counting bricks, two numbers. He has performed a trick. Hughes's study (1986) highlighted the fact that school-age children as old as 9 who used conventional signs every day in school, were reluctant to represent addition and subtraction with the standard signs when given a situation other than a page of sums. Their ability, it seems, to understand these symbols and transfer and use them in different contexts was lacking. Given this evidence, think how much more difficult it must have been for Daniel, aged 4, to make sense of these sums he was asked to do. He may have desperately struggled to put it into some context of what he knows about the real world. Children are powerful meaning-makers (Wells, 1986). After some confusion Daniel may have fitted the sums idea only into the context of that nursery. He may have thought, 'these are the tricks we perform at nursery'. This is not Daniel's mathematics: this is the adult's mathematics put on the child. If we give children, at an early age, the message that mathematics is not connected to the real world or to any sort of context or to their growing knowledge, then children's understanding of conventional symbols and mathematical algorithms will not go beyond the context in which they are taught.

There is much confusion about how to teach mathematics in nursery settings. Munn, Gifford and Barber (1997) cite research that shows that in nurseries there is a very poor diet of mathematical content. Teachers often provide activities in which they say the children are learning mathematics but the children seem more interested in the social aspects of the play or the materials that are provided. Nursery teachers seem less confident in their knowledge of mathematics learning than of literacy learning. Many teachers often show less interest in developing numeracy than literacy (Gifford, 1997; Munn and Schaffer, 1993). Studies of nursery staff indicate that although many claim that children do maths for 80 per cent of the day the reality is that children are using numeracy skills for less than 2 per cent (Munn, 1994). The difficulties lie with the knowledge of the teacher and this is carried into school situations.

Scott's use of symbols

Scott, 6:6, was new to the school. During this lesson it became clear that Scott had not developed his own understanding of abstract symbols; to Scott the choice of which symbols to use appeared almost arbitrary (see Figure 5.1).

This was a lesson in which children were adding small amounts of grapes that I had brought in. The children were working out their calculations on paper, using their own chosen forms and approaches. Children used a range of responses – writing, numerals, their own marks and pictures.

We can look at what Scott did in a positive way. He can represent small amounts of things he counted: for example, he drew three circles followed by the numeral 3, four circles followed by '4' and seven circles followed by '7'. His problem began when he tried to use some abstract mathematical signs, for example: '0 4 = 3', '4 5 = 6', '4 3 4', '0 = 0 4' and '5 = 5'. Scott has understood that written calculations require numerals and signs. However he was clearly confused when representing these calculations. When I sat with Scott and gently asked him to show me what he had done, he read his final 'calculation' aloud, 'I = 0' (he knew what the '=' sign was called): he was unable to say what he meant by this.

Scott then took a grape from the plate and reached out for two more grapes: I asked if he could think of another way he might show how many he had altogether. His response was to draw round the first grape, followed by the '+' symbol and then draw round the additional two grapes. Beneath this he wrote '3'. He was beginning to make some connections with his marks and the use of an abstract symbol.

Scott's family had moved into the area and he had had to change schools. Approaches in his previous class had clearly differed from that of his new class. Because he was experiencing difficulty in his new school he had been put in a class with children a year younger than he was. Scott was apparently bewildered by the abstract symbolism of both writing English and of mathematics. It seemed possible that Scott had been introduced to formal calculations before he had had an opportunity to make sense of his own marks. Perhaps before he reached 6 years old, he had been expected to write and to represent mathematics as an older child would, even though he had not understood what he was doing. Like Daniel, Scott was also confused by imperfectly memorised 'tricks' which he was then unable to apply in other contexts. As John-Steiner emphasises, representation is one of the important 'uses of language ... [and] may not develop well when children find themselves under severe pressure to acquire a second language' (John-Steiner, 1985, p. 351).

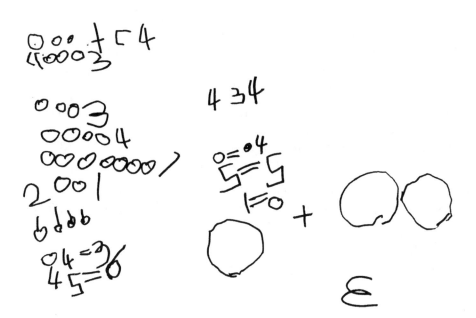

Figure 5.1 Scott's addition

Understanding symbols

Semiotics

Any serious discussion concerning the development of symbols concerns semiotic activity, which, concerning children's representations, Oers defines as: 'the activity of relating a sign and its meaning, including use of signs, the activity of investigating the relationship (changes of) signs and (changes of) meaning, as well as improving the existing relationship between sign (or sign system) and meaning (and meaning system)' (Oers, 1997, p. 239). This is what White termed the *symbolic initiative* (White, 1949). Gardner views our complex use of symbols as 'our final building block'. He argues that 'the disciplines of our world, reconstructed on the basis of symbols; and our capacity to master them, and to invent new systems, also presupposes the symbolic fluency that is launched in the years after infancy' (Gardner, 1997, p. 21).

From a Vygotskian perspective, symbols or graphic representations bridge the gap between 'enactive, perception-bound thinking and abstract, symbolical thinking' (Oers, 1997, p. 237).

Understanding abstract mathematical symbols begins long before children enter school, with a 'pre-history' that Vygotsky believed originates in both gesture and alternative meanings that children assign to objects within their play. An example of this is Melanie's ladybird (Figure 6.1) in Chapter 6. DeLoache observed that children as young as 18 months old can pretend that 'a block of wood is a car, or that a banana is a telephone': in doing this they demonstrate that they are able to represent something in two different ways (DeLoache, 1991, p. 749). This flexibility of meaning and object allows children later to understand that marks – or written symbols on a page – stand for something other than what it is. For example, in our culture a cross drawn on a card or paper may first become associated with a kiss (on a birthday card or letter) but:

• within our written system it is the letter 'x' which occurs in words like box and has a particular sound attached to it
• it can be found on a treasure map to mark where treasure is buried
• it is a warning symbol on a bottle of bleach.

To confuse matters further, when a '+' (the same form but rotated) is used, it carries other meanings. At school teachers may use the similar sign 'x':

• to denote a wrong answer
• as a multiplication sign in mathematics
• signify an 'as yet' unknown number in algebra.

Outside education settings '+' is used as:

• it is on remote controls for video players
• a symbol for a church on a map
• the symbol for an ambulance or hospital.

To bring the interpretation of this symbol up to date, when used in text messaging: '+' is used as an abbreviated form of 'and'.

It is no wonder that young children find it difficult to navigate the various written symbol systems. Moreover, whilst spoken language can be ambiguous – dependent on whether it is used in a natural context or a specifically mathematical one – it appears that written (or graphical) symbols may be even more so. Twenty-first century culture draws heavily on the visual impact of advertising, logos, photographs, film, cartoons, packaging and other visual images, and there is every indication that, because this is a significant feature of young children's culture. There is no doubt that such graphics heavily influence young children. In one nursery that I visited, children of 2½–3 years were 'reading' the names on various plastic bags from supermarkets with ease by recognising the store's logo, in the context of their supermarket role-play. As some parents will testify, their young children may also be influenced by the brand names or logos on clothes, shoes and even wrapping on food, where children's television characters 'sell' items such as bananas and cheese.

Children's difficulties with mathematical symbols

Our central argument is that children come to make their own sense of abstract symbols through using their own marks and constructing their own meaning. However, Deloache, Uttal and Pierroutsakes (1998, p. 325) point out that 'no symbol system is fully transparent'. Letters of the alphabet and numerals for example, 'have no inherent content or meaning, but convey information when combined in systematic ways'. Therefore, young children not only have to make sense of individual symbols but need to understand their role within a system, whether, for example, letters within a written word, musical notation, or a mathematical sign or numeral within a written calculation.

The many studies of young children's early writing development suggest some ways in which teachers support the growth of understanding (see Chapter 4). Ginsburg lists three principles of written symbolism in mathematics:

- Children's understanding of written symbolism generally lags behind their informal arithmetic.
- Children interpret written symbolism in terms of what they already know.
- Good teaching attempts to foster connections between the child's informal knowledge and the abstract and arbitrary system of symbolism (Ginsburg, 1977, pp. 119–20).

Determining ways to foster these connections has been a challenge for teachers but, as Hughes (1986) and others have observed, a failure to do this is likely to be where many of children's difficulties with mathematics lie. Supporting children's early writing development is problematic for some teachers and it appears that introducing abstract symbolism of mathematics is more so. As Hiebert (1984, p. 501) observes, 'even though teachers illustrate the symbols and operations with pictures and objects, many children still have trouble establishing important links. Vygotsky emphasised that – as the examples of Matt's explorations with different marks demonstrate (Figures 2.1 and 2.6) – there is a 'critical moment in going from simple mark-making on paper to the use of pencil-marks as signs that depict or mean something' (Vygotsky, 1978, p. 286). For parents and teachers of young children, witnessing such 'critical moments' is an enormous thrill and a privilege.

Gardener argues that 'given a sufficiently rich environment, many a five year-old is already sensitive to different genres within a symbol system'. Therefore, rather than viewing young children's early writing and their mathematical graphics from a deficit perspective, appreciation of their understanding can be seen as a stunning achievement. It is, Gardner observes: 'hardly an exaggeration then, to say that the five or six year-old is a fully symbolic creature – an individual who has the "first draft mastery" of the major symbolic systems in her culture. The child can "read" and "write" in these systems' (Gardner, 1997 p. 22).

The way we set down mathematical symbols can cause confusion for young children, for example the numerals 6 and 9 may appear the same to children since one is the inverse of the other in appearance. Place value causes problems, for example '2' is different from the two in '25'; they mean different things. The subtraction sign and the equals sign are similar as are the multiplication and the addition signs. Some letters and numbers such as '6' and 'b' also look similar. To further complicate matters, children are also learning about two symbol systems at the same time, writing and mathematics (DeLoache, 1991). It could also be argued that the writing system makes more sense to children. When given the choice some children prefer to use writing instead of mathematical symbols (Pengelly, 1986).

Problems with standard algorithms

As older children are introduced to standard algorithms as in long division, multiplication and decomposition methods, more confusion can arise since they sometimes forget the procedures and have no strategy to fall back on. Children often abandon effective mental methods to do a calculation in the standard written way. The standard algorithm has been under attack and is accused of making students dependent and cognitively passive (Zarzycki, 2001). Zarzycki recommends that students create their own algorithms and compare them to standard methods. He found that children do not understand why the algorithms work and believes that the logic behind them should be taught. Others would disagree; for example, Merttens and Brown (1997) advocate that children should practise algorithms so that they become automatic: children then do not have to think about what they are doing, or why. Askew (2001) still has questions about the standard algorithm and invites other responses. The debate continues but the important point is that the standard algorithm is in question: it is not an absolute mathematical teaching method for solving equations. This then puts in doubt other standard procedures and the rightness of imposing them on children. We know that the algorithm is a recognised written mathematical language that children can work towards, but there is no need to hurry children into these procedures to the detriment of their own mathematics and understanding.

When do you teach sums?

Gifford (1997) raised the question of when to start teaching formal sums. Formal approaches have from the early 1960s given way to a Piagetian perspective of delaying any forms of teaching abstract mathematical concepts, until the children are 'ready'. Practical mathematics became the main focus of many Early Years classes. There has been and remains an abundance of commercially produced mathematical materials. Sorting and sets and matching – in Piaget's terms 'logico-mathematics' – created classrooms full of plastic bits and structured apparatus. The use of what are known in the USA as 'manipulatives' was an attempt to bridge the gap between the children's informal knowledge and the formalism of standard calculation (see Barratta-Lorton, 1976). This practical approach is now questioned (see Chapter 7) and Hall's review emphasises that: the cumulative evidence suggests that the value of manipulative materials in mediating understanding is at best unclear and may indeed be adding to the difficulties which children experience in making the transition from total dependence on informal knowledge to the use of the formal notation system' (Hall, 1998, cited in Maclellan, 2001, p. 75).

With the advent of the National Numeracy Strategy, teachers in England have now moved away from concrete to mental mathematics in the Early Years, with less emphasis on writing numerals or practical mathematics. The modelling of calculations by the teacher is encouraged. The teaching of mathematics in other countries such as Hungary and Holland have heavily influenced this (see Chapter 1). The role of 'the sum' and the question of when to introduce it is still unclear, but encouraging mental mathematics is a shift in the right direction, since we are encouraging children to move towards the abstract. There is also more of a link between children's mental methods and their own written methods.

The transition between mental methods and standard written algorithms is a difficult one because, it is argued, 'the mental approach to mathematics is almost diametrically opposed to the written conventions' (Holloway, 1997, p. 27). Unfortunately the videos and the materials produced for teachers of this phase by QCA (2002) focus on the teaching of mathematics in the narrowest sense. Play especially is misunderstood in these materials: for example, a teacher-directed cooking activity is described as play. Children's own methods are encouraged in the National Numeracy Strategy but there is little guidance on how to support children's own marks. The focus of this book addresses this difficulty.

The tins game

It has been well documented that the key to children understanding formal mathematics is to support children so that they make the transition from their own informal home mathematics to formally based school mathematics. As early as 1977 Ginsburg argued that the gulf between children's invented strategies and school-taught, formal written procedures was a very likely reason that children had difficulty with school mathematics. Hiebert (1984) had a similar thrust, arguing that making connections between the formal school mathematics and the children's own mathematics was imperative, if children were to become mathematical thinkers rather than mindless followers of mechanical rituals.

In 1986, Hughes's research heightened awareness of the gap between home and school mathematics. A host of literature followed this publication, that confirmed the belief that the answer to children's difficulties might lie in the role of children's own recording and mark-making (Williams, 1997).

Much of the literature has concentrated on explaining Hughes's 'tins game' (Montague-Smith, 1997; Pound, 1999). Some researchers have duplicated the tins game to find out if it brings the same results in different circumstances (for example, Munn, in Thompson, 1997). Yet this published research and these texts have failed to show children's own mathematical marks in circumstances other than the tins game or variations of the game (see Gifford, 1990). Atkinson's book included teachers' stories of children's own mathematics: this was the only reference we found that rooted the practice of children's own mathematics in real classroom situations with a variety of tasks which were significantly different to the tins game (Atkinson, 1992). Most of the research into this area has been of the clinical task type which claims a 'human sense' approach: however, we argue that in order to understand children's own marks then the research must make 'child sense' (Carruthers, 1997a).

Our study is based on evidence from our own teaching. This enabled us to see a wide variety of children's mathematical graphics in a full range of mathematical contexts, with children throughout the 3–8 years age range. The range of examples we gathered during a number of years helped us to develop our teaching. As we did so we uncovered children's meanings on paper and began to link theory and practice.

In this book we look closely at the development of children's graphics and the teaching to support the connections between informal and formal maths. We have placed our research in real classrooms, in authentic teaching situations, over a period of 12 years. In support of our premise that the translation between children's formal and informal maths is important we now explore the way in which second language learners make this transition.

Mathematics as a foreign language

Through our teaching during the past 12 years our research interest as teachers moved from a broad focus of different features which supported young children's understanding in mathematics to a focus on one aspect. During our discussion one day, the two of us talked about the fact that there had been almost nothing written that linked theory *and* practice about ways of 'bridging the gap' (Hughes, 1986). In our teaching we had experienced some wonderful insights from young children and had been thrilled by their highly original responses through their mathematical graphics. But in what way did their own marks support understanding of the abstract symbolism of mathematics? We discussed this at length and the following is part of one discussion:

> 'maybe it's a bit like learning a second language – you build on what you know in your first language to help understand a second language. It becomes possible to move between two different languages – with increasing fluency in the second.'
>
> 'And maths is a language – written as well as spoken – then the social aspect needs greater emphasis too.'
>
> 'Young children feel comfortable with their first mathematical language – the informal spoken and written marks of home. If they can gradually make sense of abstract symbols and written methods in their *own* ways, surely they would be developing fluency in both? They'd be able to move between the two languages with understanding – like being bi-lingual.'
>
> 'Bi-mathematical!'
>
> 'What about *bi-numeracy*?'

Mathematics has often been referred to as a language (for example, Burton, 1994; Cockcroft, 1982; Ginsburg, 1977). Pimm goes so far as entitling a chapter he wrote on this subject: 'Mathematics? I speak it fluently' (Pimm, 1981).

The issue of language and mathematics is a complex one. We use everyday language to talk about mathematics we are doing, for example, 'I'm counting how many cups we need'. We use everyday words and phrases in one way at home, such as the term 'take away' (of fast food such as an 'Indian take-away') and in another way in school mathematics when working out subtraction. There are also very specific mathematical terms that are rarely used in everyday contexts, such as vertex and angle. Children and teachers also may use language to discuss aspects of mathematics such as infinity.

From a different perspective, Oers argues that young children use language to help make the meanings of their marks clear to others (Oers, 1997). In his book Hughes pointed out that for many learners mathematics is 'more like an unfamiliar foreign language' (Hughes, 1986, p. 42), an idea that he extends, proposing that the difficulty is that children have to learn to *translate* between mathematical language and their everyday language.

But there is another highly significant aspect of language that has been largely ignored in the debate about the difficulties children experience in translating from home to school mathematics – the question of *how* children learn to speak a second language – and it is this perspective that we believe can make a huge contribution to the debate.

Halliday (1975) describes learning a first language as 'learning how to mean', a phrase that sits well with our emphasis on children *making meaning* through their mathematical graphics. John-Steiner reminds us that 'the Vygotskian perspective ... places the issues of bi-lingualism into the broader framework of the psychology of language and thought'. Thus learners draw on their 'internal meaning system while comprehending or producing language'; they 'are increasingly able to comprehend, condense and store information, they start the process of weaving two meaning systems together' (John-Steiner, 1985, pp. 357, 364–5).

Multicompetencies

In a recent and thought-provoking study of second language learning or *L2 learning*, Cook observes that the starting point for teachers of second languages is 'the learners' own language system' (Cook, 2001, p. 16). The descriptions of second language learners matches accepted understanding of early writing development and the few studies of children's early (written) mathematical development; they also match our own findings closely. Cook describes second language learners as inventing 'a system of their own ... curious rules and structures which they invent for themselves as they go along' (Cook, 2001, p. 16). These personal systems have been termed 'interlanguage' (Selinker, 1972). This interlanguage showed that learners were using their 'temporary language systems' (Cook, 2001, p.15).

However, Cook has challenged this assumption – widely accepted now in the field of second language learning – as not going far enough: 'on the one hand we have the user's knowledge of their first language; on the other, their inter-language in the second language. But both these languages co-exist in the same mind; one person knows both languages' (Cook, 1992 p. 16). Cook proposes that learners' first language and their interlanguage be viewed together as 'multi-competence': this leads to competence for learners in their second language.

It is not difficult to exchange the words 'first language' with the concept of children's early, informal mathematics and substitute the abstract symbolism of mathematics for 'second language'. Cook's perspective of second language learning links closely with the model of early mathematical learning we have developed. Deepening our understanding of bilingualism is, John-Steiner asserts, 'effective, additive, joyful and competent use of two or more languages – [and] is increasingly important today for growing numbers of children … [who] find themselves in alien lands with little knowledge of the languages spoken around them' (John-Steiner, 1985, p. 369). For many children mathematics can be an alien land.

Becoming bi-numerate

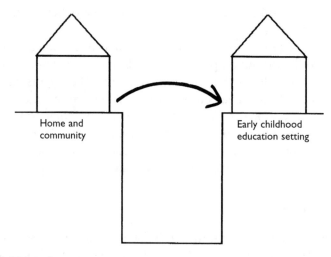

Figure 5.2 Bridging the gap

In our model (Figure 5.2) the gap that separates informal and formal mathematics is represented by the gulf between informal home and abstract school mathematics: this is both wide and deep. This symbolises the extent of the difficulty that must exist for young learners. In the literature children are seen as needing to translate between the informal and formal mathematical languages, though in practical terms there has been a dearth of guidance on how this might be achieved. However, recent literature has very much supported the idea of older children using their own written methods mathematics. For example, Thompson (1997) uses the term 'personal written methods' and Anghileri

(2000) writes about 'invented methods'. There is a lack of evidence from published examples of younger children's mathematical graphics, yet this is where most of the difficulty begins: children's confusion is ingrained before they might be given the freedom to try their own written ways in mathematics. We are arguing that teachers need to understand children's mathematical marks much earlier than current available literature explains.

We know the pressures that teachers experience, including tests, inspections and demands for 'results' and 'standards'. Some of these pressures can be interpreted as a need for children to achieve abstract symbolism rather than use informal mathematical graphics *in the short term*. The pressure leads to children being hurried on by recording in 'acceptable' (neat or standardised) forms such as worksheets. It can also include teachers' requests that children use a particular form of representation: this might include standard calculations, or that all children in the class use tallies or a pictographic form when working on a particular calculation.

In Figure 5.2 this shift is represented as a bridge, with children moving *from* their informal mathematics *to* the standard and increasingly abstract forms of representing mathematics in school. The implication in such a model is that the desirable movement is generally of one-way traffic, therefore it will follow that the most desirable position will be to move the children to the abstract mathematics without a transitional or *interlanguage* stage.

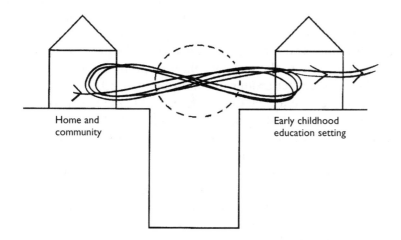

Home and
community

Early childhood
education setting

Figure 5.3 Infinite feedback loop

In Figure 5.3 we provide an alternative model. Using their own mathematical graphics and constantly moving between their own informal understanding and abstract mathematical symbolism in an infinite loop ensures cognitive feedback. This allows concepts to metamorphose: informal marks are gradually transformed into standard symbolism. Children become what we term 'bi-numerate' and like bilinguals they will come to use these two languages of mathematics fluently. Their understanding of the second language – the abstract mathematical language – will develop at a deep level since they will have constructed their own understanding of the role and function of the symbols themselves. John-Steiner observed that such 'complex and opposing relationships' were noted by Vygotsky, who suggested a two-way interaction between a first and second language (John-Steiner, 1985, p. 368).

The strength of this model is that whilst the most significant development occurs for children during the Early Years phase, older children can also benefit from using their personal mathematical graphics – at any stage or for any calculation or problem.

Cook outlines features of second language learning which we believe are the same in early mathematical graphics, including approximation, invention, re-structuring and falling back on the first language (Cook, 2001). Reflecting on the observation that learning mathematics is 'like an unfamiliar foreign language' allows us to see that children's own mathematical graphics supports children in developing their multicompetences and enabling them to become bi-numerate.

Using blank paper

The findings of our questionnaire (see Chapter 1), showed that whilst 79 per cent of the teachers of 3–8-year-old children who responded used worksheets, 82 per cent of the same teachers also either allowed or encouraged some use of blank paper for mathematics. At first glance these figures appear encouraging. The teachers who said they use blank paper provided 476 examples of the sort of mathematical marks children might make on blank paper. Of these almost 85 per cent were either when the teacher told the children what to do and how to record, or when the teacher produced what was, in effect, a copy of a worksheet.

Nine per cent of examples referred to the use of blank paper within children's role-play. This provides positive opportunities for children to use marks in the context of their play. Unfortunately in the current context in England, however, role-play is rarely found in classrooms with children beyond the age of 5. This effectively rules out the use of blank paper within any play situations for children once they move into their second year in school.

In only 6 per cent of examples of mathematics on blank paper did teachers refer to children 'making their own marks'; using 'emergent writing'; using paper 'in their own way' or making 'jottings'. This paints a disappointing picture, especially since most of these teachers used worksheets for a greater part of the time. Blank paper appeared therefore to be viewed as an extra to the teachers' usual activities or for occasional use.

We wondered what happened to the pieces of paper on which the children made their own marks. In our own teaching we have found that these pieces provide invaluable information that helps us assess, support and extend children's learning and build a constantly unfolding picture of their development. We explored additional questions through telephone interviews with a sample of the teachers in this study. When asked, 77 per cent of the teachers said that the children took home what they had done and several replied that they did not keep them. Of the teachers interviewed who did occasionally use blank paper, only 23 per cent kept examples with children's marks: these were used for the school records and only a sample of what the children had done, was saved. Blank paper was more likely to be used occasionally and therefore its use was of a different status to worksheets. The marks children made on paper during their play, for example, was generally not saved by teachers, suggesting that these marks were not seen as significant in contributing to the children's developing understanding. In mathematics it appears that a widely held view is that children's mathematics on paper is significant only when it is the outcome of a teacher-directed activity.

These findings point to written mathematics that is largely on worksheets or following the direction of the teacher. Furthermore, we believe that it must be almost impossible to trace children's development unless a comprehensive, dated collection of pieces is kept. It *is* possible to do this but clearly it is rarely done. In our work in visiting many Early Years settings we also seldom see examples of children's own mathematical marks displayed.

Teachers' difficulties

One of the problems teachers face is that young children's own mathematical thinking on paper is not always easy to decipher. It is quite easy to disregard children's mathematics on paper as incomprehensible or poor (Litherand, 1997). Even when children explain their thinking it still can present teachers with dilemmas because it may look wrong, or appear untidy. They may have crossed out things or chosen not to use the standard procedures. Teachers may feel that it takes too long to ask the child about it since it takes time to tune into children's thinking.

In classrooms where children are not given the opportunity to put their thoughts on paper, it never happens anyway. In such classes children's mathematical graphics do not fit the norm, and for many pressurised teachers it is too much to cope with: it disturbs the equilibrium. And teachers are often too busy to reflect on what the marks might mean. Yet a decision to explore further the meanings of their marks could render different perceptions. As Litherand contends:

> for the teacher who views learning as a process of development and construction rather than a process of association, knowledge could be seen as of personal and social construction rather than fixed and immutable, as dynamic rather than static. The impact of such differences upon the criteria by which teachers judge achievement is significant. (Litherand, 1997, p. 11)

Conclusion

Although the idea of bi-numeracy – the translation of informal (home) mathematics to abstract (school) mathematics – is a relatively simple one, the difficulty lies in the solution. 'Bi-directional translation' was a key feature in Maclellan's study, where teachers in the experimental group were constantly making connections in their teaching from informal mathematics to formal (Maclellan, 2001). This was a small study but it does add weight to the fact that the key feature indicated success in helping translate. She emphasises: 'informal knowledge serves as a powerful base on which to build more formal knowledge; and secondly, that by linking informal and formal knowledge the learner develops greater "power" to apply the formal knowledge (Maclellan, 2001, p. 76). And for teachers one of the strengths of encouraging children to use their own mathematical graphics – their thinking – in their own ways, is that it gives adults a 'window on to their thinking' that may otherwise be inaccessible to teachers.

In Chapter 6 we show how young children use their own marks to develop their understanding of mathematics. We introduce categories of forms of mathematical graphics and explore some early beginnings of number that children represent on paper, from numerals to representing quantities and counting.

6

Making Sense of Children's Mathematical Graphics

*How curious it must seem to a child beginning school, if so many of
her early experiments with print are not recognised and understood by
the adults in the class. Confusion must surely occur if what was
accepted as writing at home is not considered writing at school.
(National Writing Project, 1989, p. 18)*

The evolution of children's early marks

Introduction

In Chapter 5 we highlighted the difficulties young children experience when
they move from home to the increasingly abstract symbolism of school mathematics. Aubrey comments about children's early experiences of education when
teachers seem unaware of the 'rich, informal knowledge brought into school'
(Aubrey, 1997b, p. 138). Our evidence is that Early Years teachers often also fail
to recognise the value of children's early informal marks, including those that
may be mathematical. This difficulty, highlighted in the responses from many
teachers in our questionnaire, indicates something of the extent of the problem
(see Chapters 1 and 5). In this chapter we focus on the development of children's early mathematical marks.

Whilst early marks may sometimes be valued as the beginning of drawing and
writing, early mathematical graphics are rarely acknowledged (Matthews, 1999,
p. 85). For teachers and educators this may be in part due to the fact that so little
has been researched or written about children's early mathematical graphics. It
is almost as though young children never make mathematical marks: yet our
evidence, exemplified through the many examples of children's marks in this
book clearly contradicts this.

Most studies have so far concentrated on the analysis of children's number
representations in clinically set-up tasks (Hughes, 1986; Munn, 1994; Sinclair,
1988). Both Gifford and Pengelly, in two separate investigations, set up single
class studies. In doing so they identified the richness of children's own methods
in real teaching situations. However, both of these studies were of one task, in
one class and, because they were short studies, the researchers were unable to

analyse the development of children's mathematical graphics (Gifford, 1990; Pengelly, 1986).

Practical activities

From our questionnaire, teachers revealed that when they do give children opportunities to record mathematics most use worksheets (see Chapter 1). Many teachers did make some use of blank paper, though most gave examples in which they told the children how to record or provided outlines or directions for them to follow. The exception to this is that some teachers did say that they made blank paper available in the role-play area, for children to use if they wanted. Only 16 per cent of teachers in our study referred to children making their own marks, recording in their own way, choosing how to record or using their own jottings. This figure includes those teachers who referred to children making marks through their role-play. The picture is bleaker than these figures appear to show, when we analysed the type of marks children made and what the teachers did with the paper on which they were written (see Chapter 5).

Teachers tend to be overreliant on practical activities and miss out giving children opportunities to make their own mathematical marks. Many Early Years mathematical books written for teachers emphasise practical activities. For example, Lewis emphasises practical recording with materials and mathematics equipment, and suggests that children's own recording should be accepted. However, she does not give any examples or explain how teachers might support children in this way (Lewis, 1996). Threfall argues that 'the complete absence of sums in the Early Years is the only real alternative to concentrating on them. There is no viable middle way', and proposes practical alternatives (Threfall, 1992, p. 16). However, based on the evidence we put forward in this book we propose that there is a strong alternative.

Practical activities are proposed as the solution that helps children understand the abstract nature of mathematics. However, whilst we believe that practical activities are important, on their own they will not help the child come to use standard algorithms with understanding. Neither will they help the child understand the nature and role of abstract mathematical symbols.

As we have argued in Chapter 5, in order to help children translate from their natural, informal (home) mathematics to the later abstract symbolism of standard school mathematics, teachers need to support children's own mathematical graphics. Supporting their mathematical thinking by co-constructing and negotiating meaning helps children make connections at a deep level. It is through their mathematical graphics that children become bi-numerate.

Mental methods

Askew discusses the fact that it is not helpful to ask when a mental calculation becomes a paper and pencil method. He asserts 'any method involves mental activity' (Askew, 2001, p. 13). In England the National Numeracy Strategy (NNS) has stressed the importance of encouraging the teaching of mental methods (DfEE, 1999). Guidance for teachers in the NNS documents and on in-service courses encourages teachers to discuss children's own mental methods with the whole class and support all the children. This has been one of the main changes in the teaching of mathematics since the introduction of the National Numeracy Strategy.

The introduction of visual mental images to support the children's own mental facility has been a vital part of the new approach to the teaching of mental mathematics in England. Askew declares that while practical work with young children is useful, there must be an element of 'in the head' mathematics: if this is lacking, children may otherwise think that mathematics is always practical. Mental mathematics provides the children with images that they may explore on paper (Askew, 1998). As Harries and Spooner suggest, these images link together mental work and work on paper:

> it allows the children to operate between mental and written methods rather than feel that they are progressing through mental methods to written methods. What the images allow the children to do is to build up the bank of strategies from which they can choose an appropriate one for the task. (Harries and Spooner, 2000, p. 51).

Not only is mental mathematics vital for children's representations but the way in which the mental mathematics is taught is similar to the teaching we advocate for supporting children's own mathematical graphics and written methods.

Evidence from our observations of children of 3 to 8 years of age, during a period of 12 years, shows that whilst the youngest children may not be as prolific at 4 at making mathematical number symbols, they do draw and represent things in a variety of ways. As the examples in this book show, when adults really listen and observe the marks children make, they will see beyond the 'scribbles' and understand the child's intended meaning.

We have analysed almost 700 samples of mathematical graphics. These cover the entire 3–8-year-old age range of mathematical marks and work in which they used their own written methods. They cover all aspects of number and mathematics from the wider mathematics curriculum. They range from child-initiated marks within play to adult-directed sessions in which the children also chose what they wanted to put down on paper. All the samples have come from our own classes or classes in which we have been invited to teach. Based on this large sample of original children's marks from real teaching situations in real classes, our findings are therefore evidence based. We have grouped examples to show where some clear patterns emerged.

Categories of children's mathematical graphics

We have already shown how children select different forms of graphics to represent their mathematical thinking, both at different ages and for different mathematical purposes (see, for example, Chapters 2 and 3). In Chapter 4 we argued that there are some links between children's early (emergent) writing and their early mathematical graphics.

As members of the Emergent Mathematics Teachers' group, one of the important questions we endeavoured to answer was whether there was also a developmental pathway in children's mathematical marks and written methods. For many years the answer was elusive.

Mathematical graphics are more diverse, not only because children are not moving towards common forms of a written language such as English or Greek, but because the different mathematical genres often suggest quite different graphical approaches. In early written addition, for example, children usually begin with continuous counting before separating sets (see Chapter 7). In representing data, young children may use pictures and ticks and move towards increasingly clear layouts (see Chapter 8).

However, before we analysed children's own written methods of calculations we needed to focus on the range of different, graphical marks children choose and the evolution of children's early marks (for an overview of the development of children's mathematical graphics, see Figure 7.13 in Chapter 7).

Common forms of graphical marks

In analysing our examples of children's marks and written methods we have identified five common forms of graphics, including three of Hughes's categories:

- dynamic
- pictographic
- iconic
- written
- symbolic.

Dynamic

We use this term to describe marks that are lively and suggestive of action. Such graphics are 'characterised by change or activity (and) full of energy and new ideas' (Pearsall, 2001). We categorised Charlotte's 'hundred and pounds' (Figure 6.7) and Amelie's dice game (Figure 10.3 in Chapter 10) in this way. Both pieces have a freshness and spontaneity.

Pictographic

We have used Hughes's definition, 'that the children should be trying to represent something of the appearance of what was in front of them' (Hughes, 1986, p. 57). For example, in Figure 6.9 Karl was representing the tables that he had just counted in the classroom. In another example, Britney drew the strawberries that were on a plate in front of her, and which she subsequently ate (see Figure 7.6).

Iconic

These marks are based on one mark for one item when counting. Children whose marks are iconic use 'discrete marks of their own devising' (Hughes, 1986, p. 58). This can often be reflected in the popular use of tallies that are taught in some schools. However, when children choose 'marks of their own devising' we find that tallies are only one of many iconic forms. Scarlett used circles to represent one group of teddies and squares to represent another (Figure 10.8). Jennifer used stars to stand for individual beans in a set in her subtraction sum (see Figure 7.5).

When playing a game with two dice, Chloë drew stars, triangles and little lorries in place of the dots (not illustrated) and Kamrin drew some highly imaginative 'Tweedle birds' to represent the individual numbers in his division calculation (see Chapter 9, Figure 9.5). Since none of the iconic symbols that the children chose were suggested by us, it is difficult to know what their origin is. Scarlett may have used circles and squares since they were quicker to draw than separate teddies. These shapes then possibly suggested something else to her: by adding a few details she turned the circles into balls and the squares into presents. To adults, drawing balls and presents, stars, triangles, little lorries or 'Tweedle birds' in place of the items or numerals that were part of their calculations, may appear curious. But the type of iconic marks children choose to make are not important, provided they follow the one-to-one principle (Gelman and Gallistel, 1978).

Tallies may be one of the earliest forms of written counting with its origins in practical contexts stemming from holding up fingers as a temporary record of items. They may have links with traditional oral counting documented by Opie and Opie, (1969). Tallies pre-date the earliest forms of writing in the world (Hughes, 1986).

If they choose to use iconic marks, it is important to encourage children to move towards choosing increasingly efficient forms for their count rather than focus on beautifully embellished drawings.

Written

Using words or letter-like marks which are read as words and sentences are common in our examples and found elsewhere (for example, Hughes, 1986; Pengelly, 1986). In our culture written communication is evident everywhere and children come to see this as a meaningful response on paper. As the examples from Matt in Chapter 2 showed, children may begin to differentiate marks that carry meaning as words, from those that represent numerals or are drawings, before they are 4 years old. We collected many examples of children writing explanations and written methods entirely in words, as Figure 7.8

shows. In this example John wrote '2 grapes, there is (are) two. 4 grapes, there is (are) four. 6.' His addition calculation is a form of narrative, relating a sequence of events or numbers. We explore 'narratives' in greater detail in Chapter 7.

Symbolic

Children using symbolic forms use standard forms of numerals (for example '2', '7', '15') and gradually begin to incorporate standard (abstract) symbols such as '+' appropriately. In the examples from a group of children who were subtracting beans (Chapter 7, Figure 7.5), Eleanor decided to use standard numerals, the '−' operant and the symbol for 'equals'. Other children in the group chose graphical forms that were appropriate for them at the time. In the same chapter, Anna (Figure 7.10) used standard symbols (numerals and '+') for adding together the dots on the two dice she was throwing. This example contrasts with that of Amelie, almost a year younger, who represented the amount on each dice without adding, in a highly dynamic and personal way (Figure 10.3).

As we discuss in Chapter 7, before children reach the stage of using plus, minus and equals symbols, they often make their own sense of such abstract symbols in a variety of intuitive and individual ways.

Idiosyncratic or meaningful?

We have found the categories that Hughes developed to be a helpful starting point. Hughes's study helped many teachers recognise that children could use their own marks to represent numerals that they could then read. For teachers who understand and support early 'emergent' writing, this has resonance. However, after careful consideration, we decided not to use Hughes's 'idiosyncratic' category.

The term idiosyncratic was used by Hughes when the researchers 'were unable to discover in the children's representations any regularities which we could relate to the number of objects present'. Many of the idiosyncratic marks in Hughes's study, in which children's response was to 'cover the paper with scribble', could perhaps have related directly to the number of bricks the children counted (see Hughes, 1986, p. 57). However, it appears that the children had not been asked to explain their marks. In the clinical method of interviewing young children there is a flaw, in that young children may not wish to respond to a stranger. They might have responded more openly to a teacher or some other key adult in their life.

We argue that these idiosyncratic responses are significant and need to be understood by Early Years teachers in order that they can support children's written mathematical communication. It is easy to disregard scribbles and what appears to be idiosyncratic responses, if we are unable to readily understand their meaning. As experienced Early Years teachers we expect children's early marks and symbols to carry meaning for the child. Whilst we can only conjecture about the possible meanings of some marks, we do believe that young children's marks carry meaning.

Ewers-Rogers studied children's early forms of representation (for example, in party invitations and notes for the milkman). The most noteworthy finding from her study was that a highly significant proportion of graphical responses were those she also termed 'idiosyncratic' (Ewers-Rogers and Cowan, 1996). Like Saint-Exupéry as a child in *Le Petit Prince*, the marks the children make often fail to be understood by adults (Saint-Exupéry, 1958).

The five graphical forms discussed in this section (listed on p. 84), encompass the full range of marks we found. Whilst this is not a rigidly hierarchical list, children do appear to move from their earlier forms of dynamic marks and scribbles towards later standard symbolic forms of calculations with small numbers. These five categories refer directly to the type of marks – or graphics – that children choose to make. But whilst they are significant, the graphics alone do not represent the development of children's own written methods.

We have often found that children use a combination of two forms of graphical marks, for example iconic and symbolic, when they are in a transitional period. It appears that when they do this they are moving from their familiar marks towards new ones although they are not yet ready to dispense with non-essential elements. As their thinking develops, children appear to progressively filter out everything but what is necessary to them at the time.

Early development of mathematical meaning

In analysing almost 700 examples it became evident that, as they make marks on paper, the children's mathematical thinking and understanding supports their meaning. In turn, as their marks and representations are co-constructed and negotiated with others, this extends their ideas – not only about the form of their marks but about the mathematics. As we analysed the children's mathematical marks, we could see a development of both the children's marks and of their meaning.

Dimensions of mathematical graphics

From their early play and marks, through counting and their own written methods that children choose to use, we have identified five dimensions of the development of mathematical graphics. These dimensions span the period from 3-year-olds in the home and nursery, through to children of 7 and 8 years old in school.

1 Early play with objects and exploration with marks.
2 Early written numerals.
3 Numerals as labels.
4 Representation of quantities and counting.
5 Early operations: development of children's own written methods.

1 Early play with objects and explorations with marks

Making marks on a surface, for example with fingers or a pen, have a history. They arise from the infant's gestures that both precede and accompany a child's first marks (Trevarthen, cited in Matthews, 1999; Vygotsky, 1983). Children may be using 'their own body actions, and actions performed upon visual media to express emotion' (Matthews, 1999, p. 20). And, as Kress has documented, there are multi-modal ways of making meaning 'before writing' (Kress, 1997). Children's mathematical marks are only one of the ways they use marks to communicate and carry meaning.

In Chapter 3, the observations of Aaron's pattern of schemas indicate the rich and diverse ways in which he made meaning. As Athey revealed in her important study of schemas, action, thought and marks are interrelated (Athey, 1990). It is only later that children differentiate their marks in terms of the conventions of the school and its subject boundaries.

Melanie's ladybird

Melanie, 4:9, was exploring different layers of meaning through her marks and through cutting (see Figure 6.1).

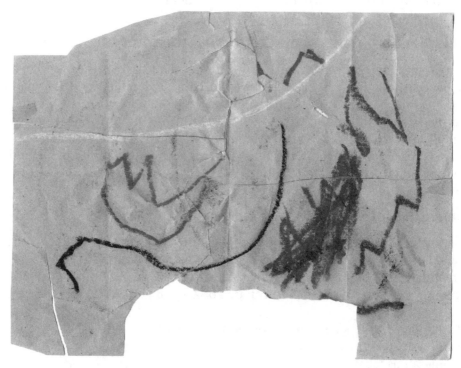

Figure 6.1 Melanie's ladybird

Having made various marks on her paper Melanie used some scissors to make cuts from the bottom of the paper and then removed a portion of it. She lifted the paper and moved it across the table top calling happily to other children 'she's dancing!' She added some more marks, telling the children nearby 'she's got a pretty dress' and then repeated her movements to make her paper 'dance'. Melanie explained that this was a 'lady dancing'.

At this point I was needed elsewhere to work with some other children. When I later asked the nursery teacher if I could talk to Melanie about her 'dancing lady', I discovered she had already left to go home. I was fortunate that Melanie's mother had kept what her daughter had made and the following day she returned with it. By now Melanie had again altered what she had done. She had cut across it in several places and her mother had 'mended' it. Melanie told her teacher 'it's a ladybird and it dances – (singing) la, la, la, la, la … '. Her teacher observed that she thought it was: 'significant that Melanie's representations can change. At first the split in the lower half of the paper had been reminiscent of legs, so it was a lady. The second time around possibly the "lady" bit got transferred (word association) to a ladybird' (Fiona, nursery teacher).

Kress points out that there is a strong 'dynamic inter-relation between available resources' (Kress, 1997, p. 22) – in this case the paper, crayons and scissors – and the 'maker's shifting interest … while it is on the page I can do "mental things" with it … when it is off the page I can do physical things with it' (Kress, 1997, p. 27). Melanie had transformed marks on paper (suggesting a pattern on a lady's dress) to a lady and subsequently a 'lady-bird' who danced. As Pahl (1999a, p. 23) argues, such objects have a 'fluid quality: they appeared to be finished and then the children would revise them'. In her study of making meaning in the nursery, Pahl proposes that such 'transitions from one kind of realism to another are particularly interesting when we look at the work of young children' (Pahl, 1999a, p. 27).

Melanie's ladybird is one of many 'modes' of representation. We include it here to indicate the significance of early, multi-modal ways in which children explore symbols and messages. What was Melanie's ladybird? Was it creative art or technology? Perhaps it might be described as small world play or a play with puppets? What are the links with early drawing, writing or mathematics?

One of the problems that teachers face, particularly once children move into school, is the apparent constraints of subject-led curricula which can require us to label learning neatly and put it in boxes. But young children do not make meaning in neat little parcels in such a way. Young children also make meaning through actions, thought, role-play, dens, cut-outs, models, marks, bricks and blocks (Athey, 1990; Gura, 1992; Kress ,1997; Pahl, 1999a).

Putting things in a bag

I was working in the nursery with a group of children and set out a selection of baskets with corks shells, conkers, coins and fir cones. Nearby I put small bags, different sized paper bags and a variety of small boxes. The following example is a transitional piece, linking play with objects and some marks made by one child about some of the objects. The child then used his paper with marks as an object in its own right.

> As the children filled and emptied containers they used mathematical language that I supported – 'inside; full; empty; enough; more' and number words. There were paper and pens nearby and of the ten children in the group, Cody, 3:5, and one other child decided to make some marks.
> Cody picked up several items and drew round them (Figure 6.2). As I watched, he then carefully screwed up his paper. Next he put the paper inside one of the paper bags which already held several bottle tops and a fir cone.

Figure 6.2 In a bag – Cody

Cody was making meaning about putting things *inside*: in the language of schemas we might say he was exploring *containing* and *enclosure*. First, he had drawn round some objects, directly 're-presenting' them on his paper. Then he put the paper with the marks of the objects that were in the bag, inside the bag. The marks on paper had been transformed into objects themselves and given new meaning. Kress advises that such 'successive transformations from one mode of representation to another ... need to be encouraged to do as an entirely ordinary and necessary part of human development' (Kress, 1997, p. 29).

We contend that teachers need to focus on all of children's meaning (here, in terms of their mathematical meaning), through their 'plethora of ways' (Kress, 1997). And early mark-making needs to be viewed as just one facet of this profusion. In her study of children's meaning making in the home and nursery, Anning found that 'children could move fluidly from drawing to modelling to small figure play at their own pace'. She writes 'in nursery classes adults are less concerned with the adult-led agenda (and) pre-determined outcomes' (Anning, 2000, p. 12). Such predetermined objectives and outcomes in schools often mitigate against such fluidity and multi-modal symbol-making in a variety of semiotic modes. As we have already argued, early mathematical mark-making on paper is just one of the 'hundred languages' of young children (Malaguzzi, 1996).

'The beginning is everything' – (Plato)
Early marks
Young children's first marks – sometimes referred to as scribbles – are a major development in a child's step towards multi-dimensional representations of her world. Malchiodi recognises that a child's first scribbles symbolise a 'developmental landmark', since they now can make connections with their actions on paper to the world around them (Malchiodi, 1998). Gardner (1980) found that the naming of scribbles occurs often in some children and not at all in other children. In the samples we analysed of children in this graphic stage, we found that many of them had actually attributed numbers to their marks (see, for example, Figure 2.1, 'Matt's numbers'; Figure 6.3, 'Molly's numbers'; and Figure 9.2, 'the number line', Jessie). We believe that when children do this, they have understood that numbers can be written down and communicated to another person.

Malchiodi suggests that if children are giving meaning to their scribbles then they may be moving forward in their development of representational images. Before the advent of speech many infants 'form in visual media a powerful expressive and communicative language' which is not recognised by many as being significant (Matthews, 1999, p. 29). Indeed, many of the studies on early drawings refer to scribbles in an almost scientific way (for example, Burt, cited in Selleck, 1997; Kellog, 1969). They address the scribbles as something that is useful for later drawing. Fein (1997) elaborated what she calls the 'visual vocabulary' to describe children's early marks, whilst Engle (1995) focuses on descriptions that stress meaning.

In his study of the development of children's art, Matthews observes that in almost all studies of children's drawings, a wide range of different marks are labelled 'scribbling'. These 'scribbles' are, he proposes, 'products of a systematic investigation, rather than haphazard actions, of the expressive and representational potential of visual media' (Matthews, 1999, p. 19). Scribbles are not careless accidents without worth but have significance for the child. 'At every phase in the development of the symbolic systems used by the child are legitimate, powerful systems capable of capturing the kinds of information the child feels is essential' (Matthews, 1999, p. 32).

After visiting the nurseries of Emilia Reggio, Selleck argued that 'scribbles' is a derogatory term for young children's art (Selleck, 1997). Children's first marks on paper therefore cannot be dismissed as a generic 'scribbles' stage because children are expressing in form and content; identities, structures, symbols, events, objects and meanings of their worlds.

Studies of mathematical marks

In Chapter 5 we referred to Hughes's categories of young children's early writing of numbers. In their separate studies Munn and Sinclair also identified and categorised a small range of marks (Munn, 1994; Sinclair, 1988). Atkinson, whilst not directly addressing the development of children's mathematical graphics, provides a range of teachers' accounts from classes of children from 3 to 11 years (Atkinson, 1992). None of these studies explored the relationship with children's early mathematical marks and other, multi-modal, ways of representing meaning, or with children's schemas.

In our own study the stunning range of children's mathematical graphics and their ability to make meaning constantly surprises and delights us. Pound emphasises 'children's truly amazing efforts to make sense of difficult symbolic languages' and observes that these are 'intelligent responses which reflect their incomplete knowledge' (Pound, 1999, p. 54). Nevertheless, in the nurseries and schools in which we have taught, we have found that these particular forms of mathematical graphics go largely unnoticed. In our interviews (see Chapter 5), less than 24 per cent of teachers asked said that they kept some examples of children marks and these they used for children's records.

Our conclusion is that children's marks do hold significance for them. Some marks will be very mathematical but, as Athey observes, 'without talking with children, there is little information on whether children are investing their marks with meaning' (Athey, 1990, p. 82).

2 Early written numerals

Children refer to their marks as numbers and begin to explore ways of writing numerals. Some children use personal symbols that may relate to standard written numerals. Children's perception of numerals and letters are of symbols

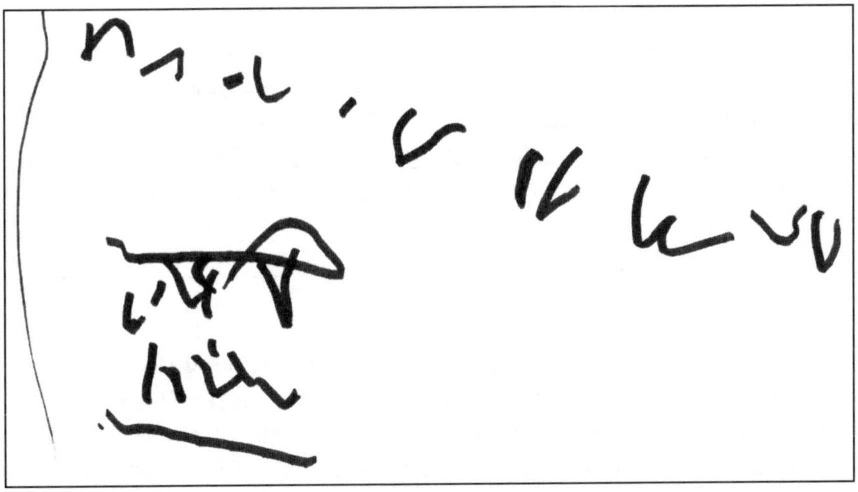

Figure 6.3a Molly

that mean something, first differentiated in a general sense, 'this is my writing', 'this is a number'.

Young children's marks gradually develop into something more specific when they name certain marks as numerals. At this stage their marks are not recognisable as numerals but may have number-like qualities. This development is similar to the beginning of young children's early writing (Clay, 1975). Children also mix letters and numerals when they are writing. They appear to see all their marks as symbols for communication and at this early stage their marks for letters may be undifferentiated from their marks for numerals.

Figure 6.3b Alex's numbers

Molly, 3:11 (Figure 6.3a) has made separate marks which are a development from Matt's linear scribbles which he named as a string of numbers (see Figure 2.1 in Chapter 2). Molly's marks are what Clay identified as letter-like and written from left to right (Clay, 1975). We would add that they are also number-like. Molly referred to her marks as numbers 'seven, six and number eight'.

Often teachers refer to a young child 'not knowing his numbers'. Alex, 4:11, has written his own symbols for numerals (see Figure 6.3b). This was self-initiated and did not appear to relate to any items that he counted: he used elements of standard letters (for example his '2'. '5', '6' and '7') and numerals (his '3' and '4') that he knew. He was consistent when repeating '5'. It is clear from this that Alex does know *his* numbers – it is adults' numbers that he does not yet know.

Jay, 3:8, (Figure 6.4a) was drawing and appeared to be interested in horizontal and vertical grids. As I watched, she added some letters though did not explain their meaning. Slowly she drew a curved shape which she joined. She paused, admiring what she'd done and said in a surprised voice, 'eight!' then turning to me adding, 'my brother's eight!' She again drew an eight, apparently enjoying the flowing movement and the resulting numeral. In beginning her final figure eight she took the pen in a different direction and abandoned her marks.

Visiting another class of 6-year-olds, I invited the children to hunt for numbers in their classroom. Before the children began we discussed the places where numbers are sometimes found and some of the specific reasons that they were used. The children made a number of suggestions including numbers on a radiator thermostat to control the temperature and on a clock. Michelle, 6:4b, went off with her clipboard and was very involved in what she wrote. When the children gathered together to discuss their findings, it was apparent that Michelle was unclear about the difference between written numbers and letters. She had copied the numerals on the clock (in the circle on the right), but had otherwise recorded letters and words from environmental print in the room (Figure 6.4b).

Figure 6.4a Jay's eight   **Figure 6.4b** Michelle's number hunt

Michelle's number hunt alerts us to the difficulty of differentiating between standard written letters, numerals and abstract symbols such as '+' and '−'. This difficulty may persist for some older children and is something one of us experienced when attempting to learn some basic Tamil in both spoken and written forms.

All forms of children's early written numerals have clear links to their early writing. They are personal responses and communicate meaning (Clay, 1975). For example the children know that:

- numbers can be written down
- they can represent numbers in different ways
- they can communicate with numbers.

Children use their current knowledge to make numerical marks and the following features are common:

- Young children make their marks first and then think of the numerals that they want to tell you about.
- Through their mark-making children may discover the shapes of numerals they recognise.
- Sometimes they have their own written number systems.
- They use marks and number- and letter-like shapes to represent the numbers they want to make.
- They very often use a left to right orientation as in early writing.
- Children will incorporate their current schemas in respect of their marks. They also use the numbers that particularly attract their attention (Athey, 1990; see also Chapter 4).

As we emphasised in Chapter 4, there are clear links between the development of early writing and of written numerals.

3 Numerals as labels

Young children are immersed in print as symbols and labels in their environment in the home, on television and from their community. Children often attend to these labels and are interested in how they are used: they can write in contexts which make sense to them (Ewers-Rogers and Cowan, 1996). Children look at the function of written numerals in a social sense. By the time children have entered formal schooling they have also sorted out the different meanings of numbers (Sophian, 1995). Their personal numbers can still remain at the forefront of their minds and in some cases, this can lead to confusion. For example, in teaching children that have just entered school, we sometimes initiate counting round the class. Often we do not get beyond 'four' as children say 'but I'm four, that's my number'! They are sometimes puzzled because they interpret the number 'four' in the count as a description of themselves rather than part of the set.

In our samples of children's written numerals we have evidence of their use of numbers in the environment as symbols or labels. This is significant because they have chosen to use numerals in different contexts: they know about these contexts and how to use the numerals within them. This shows the breadth of their understanding of the function of numbers and their confidence in committing this to paper. Knowing and talking about these numbers is different from actually writing them. When children choose to write these contextual numbers, they have converted what they have read and understood into a standard symbolic language. For example, Matthew, 3:9, drew one of his favourite storybook engines, 'James the Red Engine' and '5' which was the number of the engine (Figure 6.5). Matthew was very interested in numbers, not only on trains but in bus numbers and the destination of buses.

Tommy, 4:10, planned to copy numbers from a hundred square on the door of the classroom (Figure 6.6). He was very involved and carefully wrote numerals to 60. He then drew a hamster by the numeral '1' and drew himself above the numeral '4'. Finally he drew an elephant next to the numeral '60'. The previous day Tommy had been with his class for a visit to the zoo. When he showed me what he had done he explained that hamsters do not live very long and that he was 4 years old. He then drew on some new knowledge – 'elephants live a long time' (as much as 60 years).

Tommy had made a significant step in labelling, relating his knowledge about ages and the life expectancy of two animals, to the numbers he had written. He had combined his knowledge with his recent experience at the zoo and devised his own system of labelling.

Figure 6.5 Matthew – James the Red Engine

Figure 6.6 Tommy and the elephant

4 Representation of quantities and counting
Representing quantities that are not counted

Celebrating what he refers to as young children's 'unschooled minds' Gardner comments: 'the five-year-old is in many ways an energetic, imaginative and integrating kind of learner; education should exploit the cognitive and affective powers of the five-year-old mind and attempt to keep it alive in all of us' (Gardner, 1993, p. 250). The marks an un-schooled child makes can be unique, dynamic, energetic and exciting because they have many unrestricting influences. It is this dynamic form that teachers may see in children's mathematical marks when they enter school, for example Charlotte's 'hundreds and pounds' (Figure 2.2) or Joe's spider (Figure 2.3) where he represented something of his sense of the many legs of a spider. We also categorise Figure 10.3 as dynamic: as she played her dice game, Amelie's graphics show something of her excitement, enthusiasm and her mental energy. We are in agreement with Gardner who emphasises that keeping the spirit alive and thinking is crucial 'to educate students for understanding', in this case for mathematics. (Gardner, 1993, p. 250)

These young children either attend to the link between their early marks and meaning as a quantity in a general sense, or use the paper to arrange items and numerals in a random manner. Large numbers are not, however, undifferentiated by young children, since they clearly have the sense that there is a difference between larger numbers and smaller numbers. This was noted in Gelman and Tucker's (1975) study when they looked at the range of numerical estimates children gave for sets. They found out that even 3-year-olds showed a differentiated use of numbers from four into the twenties.

In representing objects on paper to count and to calculate, we will also show the way in which children's layout of items and operations is a combination of maturity and a learnt skill (see Chapters 7 and 10).

Representing quantities that are counted

During the same period that children represent un-counted quantities, they may also begin to count the marks or items they have represented and represent items they have counted. Whilst Matt, Charlotte and Joe represented their sense of quantities through the marks they made (Figures 2.1, 2.2 and 2.3), Amelie counted the dots she made on her paper each time (Figure 10.3). Although it is difficult for an adult to identify each separate instance of dots on a dice Amelie drew, she counted them out loud. Four-year-olds not only represent things they physically count, but also can often represent and count some things that they cannot see, such as Jenna's raindrops (Figure 6.8).

Horizontal and vertical arrangements

Next, children appear to represent items or numerals in a line, usually horizontally – as in his drawing of boxes of puzzles that William counted (Figure 7.3). Occasionally the items they draw are set out vertically, as in Jenna's raindrops (Figure 6.8).

Figure 6.7 Charlotte's 'hundreds and pounds'

Several researchers have demonstrated the vital importance of counting in the initial calculation strategies young children use (Carpenter and Moser, 1984; Fuson and Hall, 1983; Gelman and Gallistel, 1978). Gelman and Gallistel identified five basic principles that are guided by young children's implicit understanding. It is interesting to note that in their graphic representations, children's strategies do indeed appear to be governed by the principle of one-to-one counting: they invariably arrange items or numerals to be counted in a line, and then begin counting with the first item they had represented (Gelman and Gallistel, 1978).

Jenna, 3:9, began writing her name in the top right-hand corner. After writing 'J', she was obliged to continue from right to left to complete her name. She also drew and counted the raindrops from top right, counting each vertical column before proceeding to the next, in the same direction that she had written her name. Perhaps the coloured pens she's used reminded her of a rainbow and this suggested 'raindrops'.

Figure 6.8 Jenna's raindrops

Four dimensions

In the numerous examples we analysed, we found that these dimensions of early written numerals are not completely hierarchical: children will revisit earlier dimensions depending on what they are representing and their current concerns.

These four dimensions of early mathematical graphics provide children with rich foundations from which to develop early written calculations. At this point children can represent numerals, understand some of the contexts in

I had asked the children to help make an inventory of furniture and resources in the classroom to help the head teacher who was doing an audit. Karl, 4.9, decided to count the tables. He used a linear arrangement although the width of the paper meant that he had to continue his drawings of tables below the first ones he had drawn. Like Joe's spider (Figure 2.3), Karl has shown something of the appearance of 'lots of legs' which may have included the legs of chairs beneath the tables.

When he'd finished, Joe counted the tables and then re-counted, putting a mark on each table he'd drawn, with his pen. At the top he wrote his approximation of '10' and I wrote what he said beneath it (Figure 6.9).

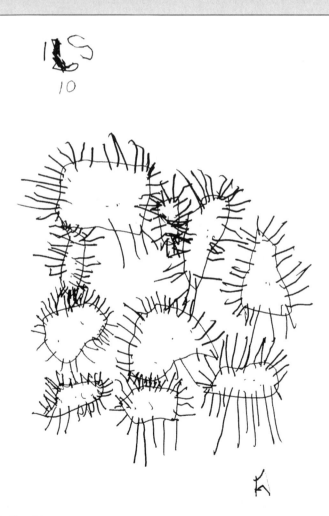

Figure 6.9 Karl's tables

which they are found and use them appropriately. They recognise a range of purposes of counting, and count real objects and objects that they have represented on paper. Now they are able to make use of these skills and understanding to explore early written calculations in ways that are meaningful to them.

In Chapter 7 we continue to explore the development of children's mathematical graphics. We focus on children's own written calculations, their growing understanding and use of operators and the development of their own written methods. In Chapter 7 we turn to the 'fifth dimension' – early operations: the development of children's own written methods.

Understanding Children's Developing Calculations

On the fourth planet a businessman was engrossed in counting:
  'Three and two make five. Five and seven make twelve. Twelve and three make fifteen. Good morning. Fifteen and seven make twenty-two. Twenty-two and six make twenty-eight ... Twenty-six and five make thirty-one. Phew! Then that makes five-hundred-and-one-million, six-hundred-twenty-two-thousand, seven-hundred-thirty-one.'
  'Five hundred million what?' asked the little prince. (Saint-Exupéry, 1958, p. 41)

There is one essential reason for teachers to encourage children to represent their mathematical understanding on paper that we discussed in Chapter 5.

It is through exploring mathematical graphics on their own terms that young children come to understand the abstract symbolism of mathematics. Using their own marks and making their own meaning – shared, discussed and negotiated within a community of learners – enables children to become bi-numerate. This allows children to translate from their informal, home mathematics to the abstract mathematics of school; to 'bridge the gap'. Being bi-numerate means that children can exploit their own intuitive marks *and* come to use and understand standard symbols in appropriate and meaningful ways: developing their own written methods for calculations is an integral part of this.

Practical mathematics

There is a view that 'practical mathematics' with the use of resources supports early mathematical understanding, for example Thompson argues that 'all calculations in the first few years of schooling should be done mentally, using whatever aids they need – counters, bricks, fingers etc' (Thompson, 1997, p. 98).

However, a study in 1989 confirmed that 'the link between practical work and the move to formal symbolic representation is often tenuous' (Johnson, cited in Askew and Wiliam, 1995, p. 10). Askew and Wiliam advise that results from this and other studies (for example, Hughes, 1986; Walkerdine, 1988) show that 'while practical work and "real" contexts need to be chosen carefully ... pupils' success on a concrete task should not be taken as an indication of understanding the abstract' (Askew and Wiliam, 1995, p. 11). Hall emphasises that the use of concrete materials has not necessarily made the links children need between procedural and conceptual knowledge (Hall, cited in Maclellan, 2001).

Thrumpston contends that 'children need help to form links between formal and concrete understanding, building on their informal methods of calculations and their invented symbolism in order to develop, understand and use more formal modes of representation' (Thrumpston, 1994, p. 114). These 'powerful modes' are, Pound explains, second-order symbols such as writing and numbers which 'must be based on a firm foundation of children's own invented symbols' (Pound, 1999, p. 27).

The range of children's informal methods and symbolism which we document in this chapter, is supported by the National Numeracy Strategy (DfEE, 1999) and is, Sharpe argues, one of its strengths (Sharpe, 2000b, p. 108).

Thompson comments that 'calculation takes place in the mind' (Thompson, 1997, p. 98). This is not precisely the same as mental calculations, but whether children (or adults) use paper for their calculations, thinking takes place. The type of thinking will not be identical for mental calculations as for those on paper but both will take place in the mind. Thompson proposes that calculations are only written down:

- as a record of mental activity involved
- as a means of support for the individual doing the mathematical thinking
- or as a means of communication to others.

These are all valid reasons and ones that we support. However, we return to our central argument, outlined at the beginning of this chapter and more fully explored in Chapter 5.

Thompson contends that in England 'we appear to be obsessed with written work in mathematics. It is as if no work has been done unless there is a written record to verify it' (Thompson, 1997, p. 78). This is not what we propose: what we recommend includes the type of examples within the pages of this book. But they will not be the same, for other teachers work in different contexts and children are all different. Neither do we believe that children should be using paper to explore their mathematical thinking every day – but when it may be appropriate, for the mathematics and for the child.

When we first started to give children opportunities to explore their own paper and pencil methods we found it was difficult to make an informed assessment of their mathematical recordings. Hughes had put his findings in neat categories which was helpful but we found many other variations (Hughes, 1986). Gifford gave 6-year-olds a calculation task and asked them to record in their own way. She also found it was difficult to interpret children's own mathematical thinking on paper (Gifford, 1990). The confusion over what these marks mean may lead to some teachers abandoning the idea of giving children opportunities to make their own mathematical representations. In this chapter we are therefore continuing to look carefully at children's marks and their meanings.

The fifth dimension: written calculations

For an overview of the development of children's mathematical graphics, see Figure 7.13.

In analysing examples of children's calculations a pattern of development appeared which we have grouped into categories:

5a: Counting continuously.
5b: Separating sets.
5c: Exploring symbols.
5d: Standard symbolic calculations with small numbers.
5e: Mental methods supported by jottings.

Representations of early operations

Beginning with counting

Before they begin formal schooling, research has shown that young children 'have some understanding of addition and subtraction with small numbers' (Baroody, 1987, p. 144). Carpenter and Moser (1984) found that young children first use counting strategies to solve simple (oral and practical) word problems involving addition and subtraction. They identified the following levels of strategies: counting all; counting on from the first numbers; counting on from the larger number; using known facts such as number bonds they know by heart and using derived number facts such as doubles, to calculate what they do not know (Thompson, 1995). Orton argues that whilst schools focus on combining and separating sets as an introduction to addition and subtraction, children's preference for counting persists (Orton, 1992, p. 145).

Studies of 5-year olds' calculation strategies have highlighted the range of procedures the children used that they had not previously been taught (Carpenter and Moser, 1984; Groen and Resnick, 1985). Such studies indicate that children 'tend to work towards more efficient strategies when given the opportunity to solve a variety of problems' (Nunes and Bryant, 1996, p. 60). Children do explore and use an ever-increasing range of graphics to represent number operations and some may be generated by individuals. It is important to encourage children to see the connections between the ways in which they represent their own ideas and the ways in which other people choose to do so. Egan writes that 'while we are encouraging children to be makers and shapers of sounds and meanings we will also give them many examples of other people's shapes' (Egan, 1988, p. 12).

The variety of graphical responses that children choose also reflect their personal mental methods and intuitive strategies developed from counting all. We explore this in the following section on the development of children's early calculations on paper.

5a. Counting continuously

In our study of young children's early calculations on paper we collected many examples of children's calculations through counting. Here we explore the extent to which the verbal and practical strategies for counting we have discussed are evident within children's early mathematical graphics (addition and subtraction).

We use the term *'counting continuously'* to describe this stage of children's early representations of calculation (addition and subtraction) strategies. Several studies have shown that young children can carry out simple additions and subtractions (with objects and verbally) and that they do this by using counting strategies: the most common strategy is to 'count all' or to count the final number of items (Carpenter and Moser, 1984; Fuson and Hall, 1983). Since the 'counting-all' strategy is not one that children are taught, Hughes suggests that we can infer that this is a self-taught strategy (Hughes, 1986, p. 35).

When young children are given a worksheet with two sets of items to add, they count the first set and then continue to count the second set. This is misleading for teachers since, because whilst such a page will be termed 'addition', children use it to count. As we show, counting is a valid and important stage in developing understanding of addition, but is not itself addition. However if the child chooses to represent addition like this (see Figure 7.1) then they have begun to understand the separation of the two quantities and are developing a sense of addition by combining the two sets. This is an important distinction and also a good reason to give children opportunities to use their own methods of recording. The teacher can then understand where the children are in terms of addition as opposed to the worksheet model.

Figure 7.1   Alison – counting continuously

One of the features of the early development concepts that Fuson detailed is when children use their counting to answer the question 'How many?' By doing this, they have begun to integrate counting and cardinality (Fuson, 1988). In addition to counting items (pictures or icons) continuously, in our study we found children often represented the objects to be counted as numerals, whereby each number in the sequence represented one object. In using numbers themselves as countable objects, this gives children a 'flexible means of solving addition and subtraction' (Fuson, 1988, cited in Munn, 1997, p. 11).

Comparison of strategies to add and subtract when counting continuously

Addition	Subtraction
5a Children can represent and count things they choose but cannot see, and also some things they physically count and then represent. *Features of counting continuously to add may include:*	5a They can represent and count things they choose but cannot see, and also some things they physically count and then represent. *Features of counting continuously, then removing some to subtract may include:*
• The pictures, icons or numerals representing the two sets are often arranged in a horizontal linear arrangement, or occasionally in a vertical arrangement *(see for example, Figure 7.1. The points in the remainder of this column also apply to Figure 7.1)*	• Horizontal or vertical layout as in addition, to show the total of the first amounts (before 'taking away') *(see for example Figure 7.3. The points in the remainder of this column also apply to this figure)*
• Where numerals are used, the two sets to be added are represented as one, the numbers continuing in sequence for the whole amount	• Where numerals are used, the first amount is shown in sequence beginning with 1, then children count back the amount that is to be taken away
• To add the totals of two sets, children count the items or numerals continuously, starting at one (or the first item they have shown)	• To subtract, children count the first amount and then use some means to show how they removed the second amount (see below)
• They count one-to-one	• They count one-to-one
• Children understand the need to count everything to arrive at a total	• Children understand the need to count everything to arrive at a total, then count those that remain after they have removed some

Additional features when representing subtraction

Children show that they have taken away some items by:

- rubbing out items or numerals they have represented (*see for example Figure 7.2, Louisa*)
- crossing out items or numerals, (*see for example Alice's flowers, Figure 7.2*)
- circling items or numerals to be 'taken away'
- using arrows – either to show which ones have been removed, or to show the direction of 'taking away' (*see examples in Figures 7.4 and 7.5 'subtracting beans'*).

An extension of this is when:

- some children begin to show the *action* of 'taking away', often showing the hand removing or holding some items or numerals (*see for example Figures 7.4 and 7.5*)
- some children begin to put the total that remains after subtraction.

In Figure 7.1, Alison, 5:1 was counting the children in her group and each child's toys, to work out the total who would be eating at the class 'breakfast café'. She counted both children and toys, representing these as a string of numerals. When self-checking she found that she had written too many numerals and put brackets round those she did not need. The last number in her count represented the total. The hand she drew may denote addition, though we cannot be sure in this instance.

As Figure 7.2a shows, subtraction requires more steps than addition. However, we have never found that this inhibited children in representing what they had done. If anything, the physical action of 'taking away' seems to be quite straightforward in terms of representation, and children use a variety of creative means to do so. Alice, 4:11, has drawn the total number of flowers in the two sets as a continuous count and then crossed out those she was subtracting. Louisa, 5:4, chose to use the computer to draw six grapes and then used the computer 'rubber' to remove three, see Figure 7.2b.

Figure 7.2a Alice

Figure 7.2b Louisa

John's strategy is similar to Alice's (Figure 7.2a). John, 5:4, represented the total number of grapes with numerals and in addition to crossing out those he wanted to subtract, he has drawn arrows pointing to the two he was physically taking away (Figure 7.3a). We discuss this 'narrative action' and 'narrative operations' below. William, 5.7, drew the total amount of books in two piles that he wanted to add and then drew his hand linked to the one book he wanted to keep to read (Figure 7.3b). The remaining grapes and books that these children had drawn could then be counted to arrive at the answer.

Figure 7.3a John **Figure 7.3b** William

Narrative actions

At this point, children often represent their graphic calculations as *narratives*. There is a sense that the children are recounting a story, providing a strong sense of introduction, sequenced narrative and conclusion. The operants '+' and '−' could be said to act as 'verbs' and the numerals or objects as 'nouns'. But this is not a 'number story' in the traditional sense, as for example when teachers ask children to make up a 'story' for the calculation 3 + 8.

These narratives appear similar to drawings described by Oers – either representing imaginary or real situations – or, in a mathematical context, abstract or concrete 'they are symbolically representing a narrative'. To make sure that all the features of the narrative are understood, children use talk (or sometimes add writing) to qualify their representations. In his research of the way in which children use speech as an 'explanatory function' to help adults understand the meanings of their drawings, Oers argues that most of the children's explanations 'refer to the *dynamic aspects* of the situation (what really happens), which they apparently feel is not clearly indicated by the drawing alone' (Oers, 1997, p. 242 and 244). These findings are relevant to young children's written calculations: in addition to verbally explaining, children often use symbols of their own devising to indicate their action – usually something they have done in a concrete situation. These symbols include drawings of hands holding an item or numeral (implying adding or 'taking away'), and arrows pointing away from the calculation to signify removal or subtraction: we term this 'narrative action' (see, for example, Figure 7.3).

The 'melting pot'

At this stage we can see a wide variety of different representations of operations which we refer to as a 'melting pot'. Carpenter and Moser studied the range of strategies children use to add and subtract and found that a variety of informal counting strategies persist through the primary years. Children's choices of ways to represent operations do not remain static since discussion, modelling and conferencing alters individuals' perspectives and continuously introduces them to further possibilities. Negotiation and co-construction of meaning is taking place. The melting pot period therefore covers a huge range of representations through an extended period of time. Some children in this period may choose different ways of representing their calculations as they refine their ways and ideas of representing addition and subtraction.

Subtracting beans

The following account is included to show something of the range of strategies children in one class chose, and their use of narrative action, when representing their subtraction calculations.

Working with my class of 5 and 6-year olds, I decided to use some surplus beans and flowerpots left over from science, for subtraction. Although we had explored subtraction in practical contexts, this was the first time that the children had represented what they were doing on paper.

Early in the session the children spent time playing with the beans, adding and removing small amounts of beans from their pot. I introduced a game to play with a partner. First one child in each pair counted (out loud) a small number of beans which she put in a pot. The other child then removed one or more beans and her partner worked out how many remained in the pot. Finally, they both counted the beans that remained in the pot, in order to check.

After a while I put some paper and pens near the children and suggested they put something down on paper to show what they had done. Barney (Figure 7.4) began writing '10 take 1 is 9', then changed his mind after he had written '2 take I is I'. Next he drew the flowerpots and beans, using arrows drawn in an arc above the one bean he removed. The arrows point to the second pot in which he has shown the total remaining. This narrative action is a very powerful way of representing what he has done. Using successive shorthand he next simplified this written method by reducing pictures of beans in pots to numerals and using the word 'is' to stand for the equals sign. This example shows that Barney had a very good understanding of the operation and that he is beginning to explore the use of abstract signs. It may be logical to use the word 'is' in a narrative.

In the same session he explored further written methods (see Figure 7.5). Next he again used numerals but this time experimented by drawing a hand instead of arrows, to show his own action of taking away one bean.

The other children in the group used a range of strategies. Alex also drew hands to show the operation (action) of taking away but Emma used drawings of hands to different effect. In her first example she has represented '5 −1 = 4' (she forgot to represent the one bean removed) using arrows pointing to the final amount after she had removed one. In her second example Emma included the bean that she removed. Kristian used arrows in a similar way to Barney, but used tallies to represent the beans. Like Barney he is beginning to explore the use of the equals sign in his own way.

Matthew used a simple means of showing the amount subtracted that is similar to Louisa's (Figure 7.2). Jennifer has combined iconic and symbolic representation and used the standard subtraction sign, whilst Francesca used iconic symbols combined with both the standard plus and equals signs. Finally, Eleanor chose to represent her calculations in a standard symbolic form, apart from the final calculation. The beans were all in use so she used some counters, writing '4 counters take I = 3'. This variety of written methods is found within one class when children have been used to choosing how they will represent their mathematical thinking on paper and have seen a variety of mathematical graphics modelled (see Chapter 10).

Supporting children's own mathematical marks

It is important to emphasise that as teachers we constantly assist and guide children as they move towards increasingly efficient processes and standard use of symbols. Supporting and extending children's mathematical understanding through their graphic marks can sometimes cause misunderstanding amongst teachers. Teaching in classes where children are unused to representing their ideas in mathematics in their own ways, we have found that during our visit some children spend time on drawings and colouring-in, viewing the task as a drawing exercise. This view may originate from classes where children have been

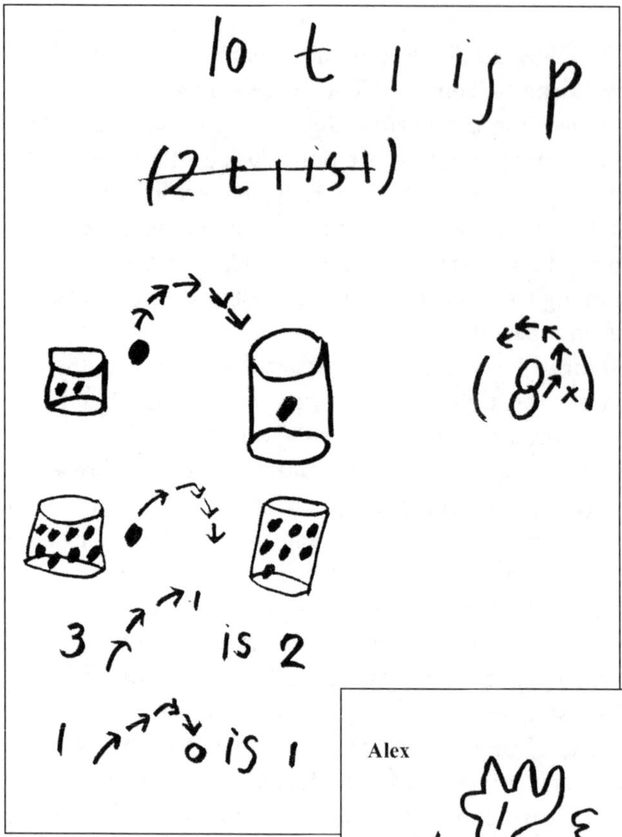

Figure 7.4 Barney's beans

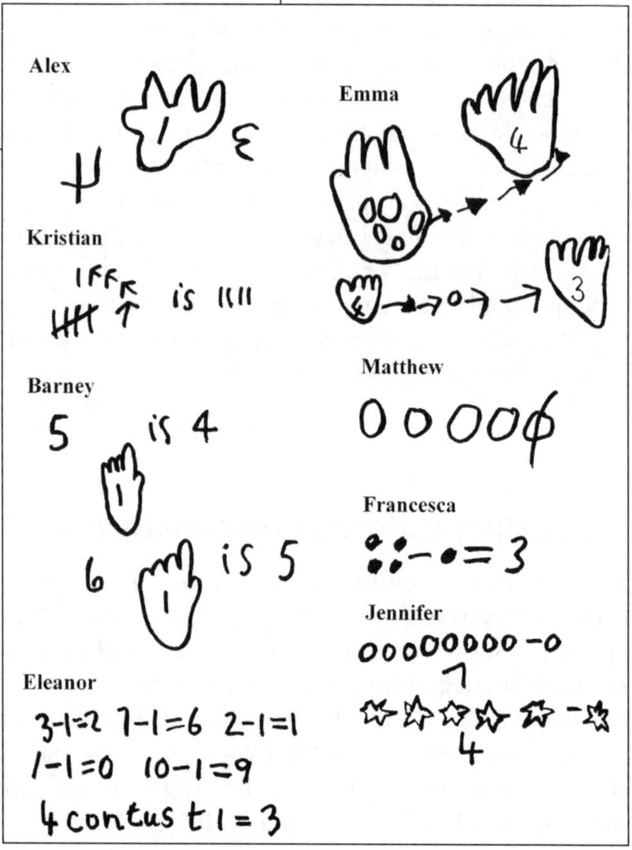

lo t l is p

(2 t l is 1)

3 is 2

1 o is 1

(8 x)

Figure 7.5
Group – subtracting beans

Alex

Kristian
IFF
HHt is IIII

Barney
5   is 4

6   is 5

Eleanor
3-1=2 7-1=6 2-1=1
1-1=0 10-1=9
4 contus t 1 = 3

Emma
4

3

Matthew
0 0 000

Francesca
:: - • = 3

Jennifer
00000000 - 0
7
☆☆☆☆☆ - ☆
4

used to using worksheets or adding a picture to their work after they have completed a piece of writing. In mathematics lessons it is children's mathematical understanding and written methods that are important. Whilst some children may use a pictographic form of representation, teachers need to help children understand that their thinking (of mathematics) is of far greater importance in this context than pretty pictures.

Another problem we have met is of children being expected to represent some mathematics which is insufficiently challenging, for example asking 6-year-olds to draw a story representing an addition for the number seven. There is a danger that children's own recording is only of teacher-suggested number stories. There is an abundance of literature supporting this kind of 'story' calculations, including Whitin, Mills and O'Keefe (1990) and Hopkins, Gifford and Pepperell (1999). We believe that these kinds of stories can be useful for mental mathematics because they help children quickly visualise a calculation in their heads. However, they are of limited value in terms of children's own representation since children tend to spend more time drawing pictures than focusing on the mathematics.

Ginsberg argues that 'young children are engaged in the spontaneous learning of economical strategies for counting. As children develop, many of their activities tend towards economy and efficiency' (Ginsberg, 1989, p.20). These are termed by Court as 'stages of abstraction' (Court, 1925, cited in Hebbeler, 1981, p. 153). Our study has shown that this tendency is evident in young children's early graphical mathematics: children move through different forms of recording, using a variety of strategies to help them calculate and discarding the forms and strategies they had previously used. However, when they move on to a more demanding level of calculations they often return to earlier strategies for reassurance. The strategies that children choose to use cluster into some common processes although there are numerous variations and often unexpected and highly individual responses, some of which are invented strategies for solving problems (Groen and Resnick, 1977; Leder, 1989). Significantly, Askew and Wiliam argue that whilst studies such as Aubrey's (1994a) and Munn's (1994) concentrated on mathematical content knowledge, they paid 'little attention to children's ability to solve problems through choosing and using appropriate mathematics. Competence involves not just the knowing of content, but also its application' (Askew and Wiliam, 1995, p. 7).

5b Separating sets

Children use a range of strategies to show that the two amounts are distinctly separate. They do this in a variety of ways including:

- grouping the two sets of items to be added either on opposite sides (to the left and right) of their paper, or by leaving a space between them
- separating the sets with words
- putting a vertical line between sets
- putting an arrow or a personal symbol between the sets.

Separating sets

Addition	Subtraction
Features may include:	Features may include:
• Children represent items to be added, in separate sets	• Children show two separate sets or numbers and a third set or number for the answer
• Use of word 'and' to represent '+' (*see, for example, Louisa and Scarlett in Figure 7.7*)	• Use of words 'take away' to stand for '–' . We have seldom found this: at this point children seem more likely to use some of the strategies shown in Figures 7.4 and 7.5
• Use of words to represent the total, for example '6 all together' or 'there are 7 now' (*see, for example, Figure 7.7*)	• Use of words to represent the total
• Use of a hand to show how many have been added to the first set: we come across examples of this less often in addition than in subtraction (*for an example see Figure 7.8 – Fred*)	• Use of a hand to show how many have been taken away from the first set. The hand is now drawn in the centre of the calculation, so that it can be 'read' in a standard way (*for example, see Figure 7.5*)
• Some use of invented signs, for example a single line for '=': (*see, for example, Jack, Figure 7.7*)	• Some use of invented signs, for example arrows in place of '–' (*as in Figure 7.5*)
	• Use of the word 'is' to represent '='
• The calculation written as a narrative, in words (*for example, see John, Figure 7.8*)	• The calculation written as a narrative, in words

Britney, 6:0, has drawn three distinct bowls of strawberries with different amounts of strawberries in each to be added (see Figure 7.6). She appears to have combined *counting continuously* and addition (of items in three sets), when, at the foot of the page she wrote:

$$1 + 1 + 1 + 1 + 1 + 1 + 1 + 1 + 1 + 1 +$$
$$1 + 1 + 1 + 1 + 1 + 1 + 1 + 1 + 1 + 1 +$$

Once again it appears that when children use these strategies they are using skills with which they are already familiar as they move into new ways of working. We do not know if children are counting or adding when they do this, but if they write '1 + 1 + 1 + 1', then we suggest that they are beginning to use the addition sign to good effect. Repeated addition is a strategy that they will later be able to use in the early stages to work out multiplication problems. Furthermore, it appears that as children move through increasingly efficient and economical strategies, they revisit their already familiar strategies in which they already feel secure.

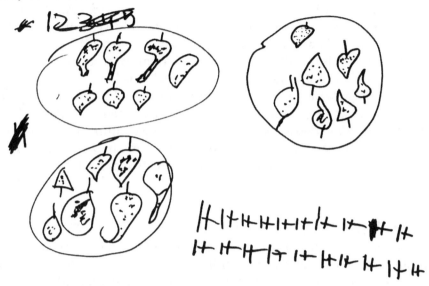

Figure 7.6 Britney adds

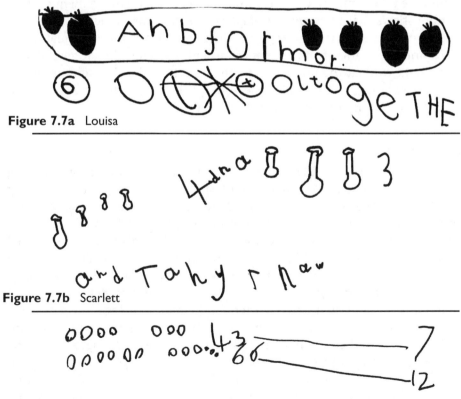

Figure 7.7a Louisa

Figure 7.7b Scarlett

Figure 7.7c Jack

Louisa, 5:1, like Britney, was adding strawberries (Figure 7.7a). She has combined pictorial and written graphical forms with symbolic (the numeral '6'). There is another narrative that reads '2 and four more all together 6'. She uses words as she experiments with the role and function of symbols. Scarlett, 5:6 (Figure 7.7b), and Jack, 5:3 (Figure 7.7c), were adding grapes. Scarlett's calculation is similar to Louisa's although she added a numeral next to each group of grapes she has drawn. She concluded 'and there's 7 now'.

Jack is exploring abstract symbols in a different way. He has drawn two separate sets of grapes, leaving a gap that allows this to be read as '4 *and* 3'. Gifford (1990) provides a similar example. Following this he confirmed the amounts to be added by writing the numerals and then drew a line between these and the final '7' (his answer). The line functions as an equals sign for Jack (see 'Exploring symbols', below).

5c Exploring symbols

As we have shown in some of the examples above, children explore both the role and the appearance of symbols. Some children who have begun to make explicit use of symbols may move on to increasingly choose to use standard symbols.

Other children show that they have an understanding of '+' or '=', but have not represented the symbols: the marks they make, or their arrangement of their calculation, shows that the symbol is *implied* and that they understand the calculation in their head. At this stage children may 'read' their calculation as though to include written features that are absent: speech is therefore used 'as a means to make explicit the implicit dynamic aspects of the children's intended meaning' (Oers, 1997, p. 244). We believe that this represents a highly significant point in children's developing understanding.

Code switching

This term is used in second-language learning and originated from teaching methodologists (Cook, 2001). In terms of spoken language, code switching occurs when a speaker switches from one language to another in mid-sentence (for example, from her native language of English, to French as in the spoken statement: 'J'ai mangé du fish and chips aujourd'hui'.). This has been observed in studies of the speech of bi-lingual children (for example, Drury, 2000 and Murshad, 2002). Significantly, examples of code-switching within the writing of young bi-lingual children has also been found (Mor-Sommerfield, 2002). Our research findings in children's own written mathematics therefore are supported by published research of both adults' and children's learning of a second (spoken) language and children learning to write in a second language. For the children whose marks we have studied for the past twelve years, these research findings support what we have found when children learn their second (abstract) mathematical language. For the speaker, a condition of code switching is that both speakers know the two languages used (Cook, 2001). In children's developing understanding of abstract mathematical symbols, we repeatedly see examples of code switching as children switch between different forms of mathematical graphics. The most significant switches occur when they use either:

- implicit symbols
- their own symbols

or when they begin to experiment with

- standard symbols.

Exploring the role and appearance of symbols

Addition	Subtraction
Features of this stage may include: • The use of '+' but '=' is implied rather than written. Children who do this appear to introduce the standard '=' symbol at a later stage	Features at this stage may include: • The use of either '-' or '=' are implied rather than written as the abstract symbol *(see, for example, some children's methods in Figure 7.5)*
• Children choose a combination of icons and numerals *(see, for example, Fred, Figure 7.8)*	• Children choose a combination of icons and numerals
• The use of personal symbols, to represent '+' or '=' *(for example, see Figure 7.7, Jack)*	• The use of personal symbols to represent '−'
• Interestingly, whilst children at this stage often use icons to represent the amounts to be added, they generally use a numeral for their total *(see, for example, Jack, Figure 7.7)*	• Again, whilst children often use icons to represent the first two sets in the calculation, they use a numeral for the total *(for example, see Francesca and Jennifer in Figure 7.5)*
• The use of implicit symbols *(see, for example, Mary, Figure 7.9)*	• The use of implicit symbols
• Some children have begun to show the operation in three steps (the two amounts to be added and the total *(see, for example, Peter, Figure 7.9)*	• Most children show the operation in three steps
• A 'box' or circle drawn around the calculation: children who do this appear to understand that each calculation is separate and complete in itself *(see, for example, William, Figure 7.9)*	• Children may draw a box or circle around their calculation

Figure 7.8a Fred

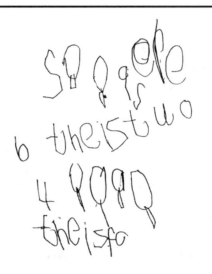

Figure 7.8b John

Fred, 5:8 and John, 5:5, were also adding grapes (Figure 7.8a and 7.8b, respectively). Fred has separated the two sets with a line (drawn above one finger of the hand). The plus and equals signs are implied since the whole can be read as '5 plus 1 equals 6'. Fred wrote the numerals '5', '1' on the left and, finally, wrote the total of '6' below.

John chose to use a written response, writing '2 grapes there is two, 4 grapes there is four'. It is interesting to note that John wrote both the numerals and words for both amounts. Finally John also wrote the total '6' (to the left). We have often found that children choose to use a written response (see Chapter 6 and Pengelly, 1986).

In Figure 7.9a, Jax, 5:2, also implies symbols, using dots (an iconic form) and numerals (symbolic). This can be read as '6 and 4 = ten': Jax wrote the initial 't' of the word 'ten'. Mary, 5:4 (Figure 7.9d), has also used a combination of iconic and symbolic responses, with the minus and equals signs implied. William, 5:7 (Figure 7.9c), moved from working out some calculations with small numbers to trying (for the first time), two with larger numbers: he also implied the plus and equals signs. Peter, 5:9 (Figure 7.9b), has used his own shorthand which, provided we know the context, can be read as '4 –3 = 1': from this it is clear that Peter could work this calculation out mentally.

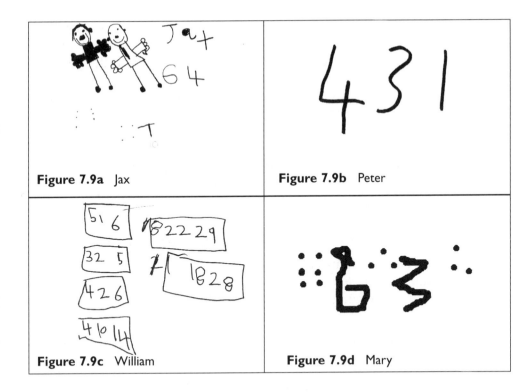

Figure 7.9a Jax

Figure 7.9b Peter

Figure 7.9c William

Figure 7.9d Mary

In his study of 6-year-old children's addition based on the 'box task', commenting on the findings, Hughes noted that the most common response was when children wrote the total, rather than their written method and answer. Observing that the findings were 'quite striking', he suggested that the pictographic or iconic strategies children used in the 'tins game' would have been far more useful (Hughes, 1986). Hughes concluded that the most obvious explanation was that the children 'were actually asked to make written representations whilst working on a mathematical problem, and so were presumably *set* towards adopting the inappropriate strategy of using numerals (Hughes, 1986, p. 130). Yet our evidence, illustrated by some of the examples in this section, is that when young children represent only the total with numerals, this is in fact an intelligent response since these children were clearly able to do the calculation mentally. Furthermore, whilst *asking* children to make *written* representations is something we would avoid, we often find that some children choose to write (in words). The point we wish to make here is that the children's methods in such instances may have been *implied*. The children in Hughes's research project may have used strategies that were appropriate to them, though it is difficult to ascertain this when children are unused to representing mathematics in their own ways. As we show here, when children put down part of a calculation, the numerals without the signs or only the answer, what they have omitted may be implicit.

In the story of the *Little Prince*, the pilot was asked to draw a sheep. Finding this difficult to do he finally drew a box explaining, 'this is only the box. The sheep you asked for is inside'. The little prince understood the drawing and bending over the drawing observed, 'look! He's gone to sleep' (Saint Exupéry, 1958, pp. 10–11). It is possible to see in children's mathematical graphics, the meaning children have *implied* but not shown, like Saint-Exupéry's sheep in a box.

William, 6:2, has shown his confidence in these addition calculations by challenging himself with larger numbers (Figure 7.9). He used a combination of known facts (number bonds for numbers to ten), and counting continuously although he was confused with adding larger numbers of '8 + 22' and then '11 + 8'. Once again the operator '+' and the equals sign are implied. William was obviously very interested and wanted to know how to calculate larger numbers, so this was a real chance for me to explore these calculations with the whole class.

5d Standard symbolic calculations with small numbers

This stage arises directly out of the preceding ones. All their previous knowledge combines to support simple calculations with small numbers. Calculating with larger numbers is challenging. There can be a problem here since children:

- may not know how to use their previous strategies
- are unable to make approximations (do not have a feel for larger numbers)
- cannot manipulate several steps.

Children should be continuously handling larger numbers that they may not be confident in but find challenging. This is the reason they need to write down their calculation, since it is too large to deal with mentally.

In the concluding chapter of his book, Hughes suggests that 'work could be done with children's own representations of addition and subtraction before introducing them to the conventional plus and minus signs' (Hughes, 1986, p. 177). This could be misleading, like suggesting that in supporting children's early writing, teachers withhold standard letters, printed texts and punctuation. What is important is that we provide children with the *whole* picture – and for addition and subtraction this will include the standard symbols (see Chapter 10 on 'modelling' mathematics). It is clear that teaching early writing and early mathematics can pose difficulties for teachers, and that misconceptions are often perpetuated (see Chapter 4 on early writing and Chapter 5 on the difficulties teachers face).

Hughes's final comment on the findings of his studies shows that they differ from ours. He observes that they showed 'a striking reluctance on the part of school-age children to use the conventional operator signs of arithmetic' (Hughes, 1986, p. 78). We do have examples of some children from 5 years of age choosing to use standard symbols, although we do not suggest that doing so should be a goal for all young children. The examples in this chapter show that whilst children often use other marks, words or strategies in place of symbols, they may also use implicit symbols and others use the standard symbols by choice. As we argue throughout this book, children should be able to choose the graphical form and written method and be supported in their developing understanding.

Standard symbol use when adding small numbers:

Addition	Subtraction
• The use of standard numerals and symbols in a horizontal layout *(see, for example, Anna, Figure 7.10 – and for the features below)*	• The use of standard numerals and symbols in a horizontal layout
• The operation is shown in three steps	• The operation is shown in three steps
• Often calculations are separated from each other by a line, circle or box	

Anna, 6:3, chose to represent her calculations in a standard symbolic form (see Figure 7:10). The context of this was of the 'dice game' that Amelie (Figure 10.3) also played. These children were in a class of 4 to 6-year olds and Anna was a little over a year older than Amelie. As we showed in Figure 7.5, there can be a wide variety of graphical responses from children in one class. Whilst Amelie represented the dots on individual dice in a dynamic and highly personal way, Anna used the opportunity to add the amounts on the two dice thrown each time, shown in Figure 7.10, and represented what she had done in a standard form. She also chose to draw a 'box' or circle around each calculation, a feature that she had copied from her peers though which had not been teacher-modelled or taught. This separation shows her clear understanding of the separate calculations.

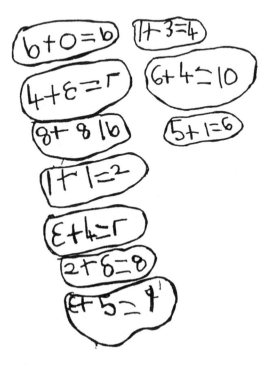

Figure 7.10 Anna

5e Calculations with larger numbers supported by jottings

In a study of children's arithmetic Steffe (1983) found that children who 'derived or deduced solutions rather than trying to recall taught procedures were more able to adapt their methods to cope with new problems and anticipate solution strategies. It seems that pupils with access to *both* recalled and deduced number facts make more progress because each approach supports the other' (Askew and Wiliam, 1995, p. 8).

At this stage children still use a variety of ways of representing their mathematical thinking. The mental methods that children use tend to cluster together and often reflect approaches that have been introduced by their teacher. Often children can use these mental methods to help them visualise and work out the calculations, and at other times children put down some of the stages of these 'mental methods' on paper, to support their thinking.

Calculations with larger numbers supported by jottings

Features for subtraction are very similar to addition on all points. *Many of the features listed below can be seen in the examples in Figures 7.11 and 7.12.*
   Addition features may include:

* using known number facts
* counting on from the larger of the two numbers
* using a number line with points marked on it
* using an 'empty number line'
* partitioning numbers
* exploring alternative ways of working or checking a calculation
* the use of derived number facts
* some understanding of commutativity (see Figure 10.6 'super-zero').

Darryl, 7:3, decided to work out this addition calculation by partitioning the numbers before adding (partitioning numbers is a taught strategy). He noticed that he had made an error to begin with and reworked what he had done, lower down. Working in this way allowed him to go beyond the hundred boundary (Figure 7.11a). Although at first Stefan, 7:7, had added 8 and the 4 rather than 80 and 40, he was soon able to see that this did not make sense and reworked this part of his calculation (Figure 7.11b). Stefan used his jottings to help him arrive at an answer which he finally resolved mentally.

Examples of subtraction with larger numbers using mental methods or jottings

The empty number line is also a taught strategy introduced in England by the National Numeracy Strategy (DfEE, 1999). It is also used in Holland (see Chapter 1). In England this is one of several forms of notation that are termed 'jottings', although these are not intuitive methods. This term 'jotting' is ambiguous.

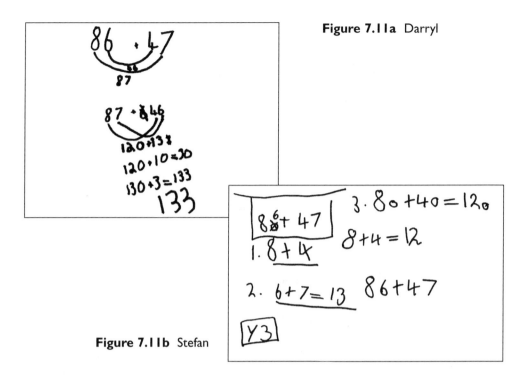

Figure 7.11a Darryl

Figure 7.11b Stefan

Jotting something down is something most adults would be familiar doing when, for example, estimating rolls of wallpaper for a room – our jottings aid quick calculations. Sean, 7:6, (Figure 7.12a) also partitioned 86 and 47 in order to combine them, checking by re-working the calculation in a different order beneath what he'd first written. At the foot of his page he used a drawing of a number track to check part of his calculation.

In England the term 'jottings' now includes taught methods such as the empty number line. There is potential for children to adapt this number line model in flexible ways dependent on their need, as Miles, 7:5 did (Figure 7.12b). Miles's class were about to leave for a residential trip; we used a pack containing three nectarines to calculate how many packs would be needed for the whole class (see Chapter 9). Using a piece of A4 paper Miles began by drawing a horizontal line across the width of the page. Because the way in which he had chosen to orientate his paper restricted the number of jumps he could make, Miles adapted his method of subtraction, changing from jumps of 3 to jumps of 6 several times. Reading from right to left, he wrote beneath the jumps the cumulative number of packs of nectarines that he was calculating for 26 children to have one nectarine each, to arrive at his answer. This signifies that Miles has discovered a more efficient method.

Increasingly children self-correct part way through a calculation, for example as Darryl in Figure 7.11 and Miles in Figure 7.12. When children do this it shows that they are considering their strategies and what they have written.

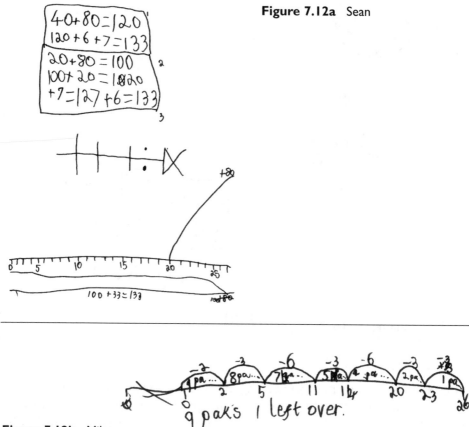

Figure 7.12a Sean

Figure 7.12b Miles

Dialogue

In all the examples in our book, the sort of dialogue that allows for meaning to be explained, negotiated and co-constructed was an important feature. It is language (discussion) that Oers asserts 'gradually moves the child into more abstract forms of semiotic activity ... This might be a very important stage in the process towards more abstract thinking especially in the domains of literacy and numeracy' (Oers, 1997, p. 244).

It is interesting to note that researchers found in Japanese classrooms, 'emphasis placed on communication between pupils ... [which] meant that Japanese children were having to explain their thinking – and in some cases, other children's thinking – on a daily basis' (Hughes, Desforges and Mitchell, 2000, p. 113). As a teacher of six-year-olds remarked to one of us at the conclusion of a numeracy lesson, 'I had never thought of asking a young child to explain (i.e. to read and interpret) what another child had done'. Doing this allows other children to interpret another's written methods and the child to whom they belong is able to see if what they have done makes sense to someone else. In data collection an addi-

Adrian was sitting in the writing area. He took an envelope and attached six 'Post-it' notes to the outside of the envelope. On the first four he wrote a '+' and on the fifth he wrote a 'y' saying 'yes'. Finally, on the sixth piece of paper he wrote another '+'. When he had completed his marks he touched each one saying 'No, no, no, no yes, no'. A few minutes later Adrian gave the envelope to me, telling me 'it's for you'.

He watched carefully as I removed the brass fastener he had used to secure it and, as I was about to remove the little notes from the envelope he said 'they're not kisses'. I laid them out on the envelope as he explained 'they're plusses'.

tional strength is that this is an early form of analysis, allowing others to interpret data in order to draw conclusions from what has been written.

There is another sort of dialogue that accompanies the children's marks as children 'make sure the observer sees the meaning of the drawing *as it is meant'* (Oers, 1997, p. 242). Oers comments that their findings indicated 'that not just things are represented in children's drawings, but meanings ... so speech has an *explanatory function* with respect to drawings' (ibid., p. 242). We had come across such explanations many times but were excited when, a few days before we were due to send in the manuscript of this book, one of us observed Adrian, 6:2, do just this in our classroom.

Within the space of a few minutes Adrian had explored three possible interpretations of the symbol '+' that he had written – 'no', kisses and 'plusses'. He was exploring these multiple meanings of one ambiguous symbol in ways that he could understand and wanted to make sure that I understood his meaning 'as it is meant' (Oers, 1997). That this example occurred at this moment was even more surprising, when we reflected on what we had just written about the ambiguity of such symbols as '+' and 'x' (see Chapter 5, p. 70).

As our examples of young children's calculations in this chapter show, their understanding and their written methods develop over time. Children should not be hurried into written calculations with standard symbols before their intuitive understanding has developed through their own mathematical marks and written methods. Building secure foundations in this way, children's understanding will develop at a deep, rather than at a superficial level. Education needs to appreciate that, as Vergnaud noted, 'conceptual fields' such as addition 'develop slowly from 3 to 14 years and beyond' (Aubrey, 1997b, p. 150).

As Thrumpston stresses, 'schools can train children to become skilful operators, to perform well in the short-term but this does not develop the network of connections, symbolic representations and meanings which extends the power of thinking and hypothesising' (Thrumpston, 1994, p. 12).

Figure 7.13 Dimensions of mathematical graphics

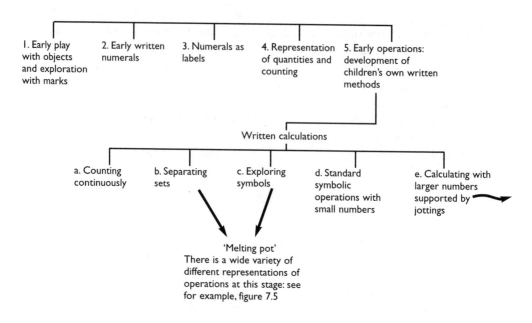

The development of children's mathematical graphics: becoming bi-numerate

Figure 7.13 represents the development of children's mathematical graphics from approximately 3 to 8 years, as explored in Chapters 6 and 7.

Conclusion

We have tried to show something of the level of challenge and thinking that children experience when working in more open ways and when selecting their own written methods. This is, we have argued, 'provocative maths, that is to say it inspires, motivates and challenges children's minds' (Worthington and Carruthers, 1998, p. 15).

In this chapter we have concentrated on children's methods of representing addition and subtraction. We have also found that young children do represent division and multiplication in their own ways (see Chapter 9). We believe that the links between the operations can be seen in children's own thinking through their representations. Studies of young children's own representations of division and multiplication are needed to inform us how to further support children's mathematics.

The development

As children develop mathematically beyond what we have described here, continuing support for their own methods is vital, otherwise their confidence and cognitive integrity are sacrificed. This 'focus on the pupil's own thinking has the benefit of encouraging autonomy in tackling problems but if personal confidence is to be maintained, there needs to be progressive process of negotiation as more formal calculations methods are introduced' (Anghileri, 2001, p. 18). There is no point where there is a definite separation of intuitive and standard methods. Children will adapt from the models they have been given and use what makes sense to them, if they are encouraged to do so. Anghileri (2000) and Thompson (1997) both give examples of older children's own methods of calculation. In many ways they have had some similar insights into how children use their own methods and how this is helpful to their understanding of mathematics.

Children's understanding of the abstract symbols of mathematics and their role in algorithms is not immediate. Claxton has identified time as a vital element in problem solving. He suggests that it is not really a question of *quantities* of time, but rather of taking one's time. He writes:

> the slow ways of knowing will not deliver their delicate produce when the mind is in a hurry. In a state of continual urgency and harassment the brain-mind's activity is condemned to follow its familiar channels. Only when it is meandering can it spread and puddle, gently finding out such fissures and runnels as may exist. (Claxton, cited in Pound, 1999, p. 49)

In the following chapter we focus on practical aspects that teachers may wish to consider developing in their Early Years settings, in order to support young children's mathematical literacy.

8

Environments that Support Children's Mathematical Graphics

Rich mathematical environments for learning

Inside one classroom

Karen teaches 4 and 5-year-olds: her classroom is in the heart of a very large Victorian building in a London school. As I walked into her classroom I could feel the positive and calm nature of the setting. The room was well ordered: children could see what there was to do and all was easily accessible. However, the room was not clinically tidy. There was a sense of industry: the classroom was alive.

Children were actively engaged and involved in all kinds of play inside and outside the classroom. Harriet and Muna selected large pieces of paper to draw and think together on the carpet. Children's own drawings and writings covered every space on the walls from top to bottom. All about the classroom the displays beckoned children to respond. Children had made their own signs, for example, 'Don't splash me it's not nice'. Kirsty and Leojon picked up the teacher's counting stick and started counting. The teacher asked them if they wanted to put numbers on it and they agreed. The teacher gave them an unopened pack of bright orange 'Post-it' notes. Kirsty opened them and gave Leojon some and they both wrote numbers and put them on the stick.

Above all, I noted that there was a sense of respect shown to the children: they were listened to seriously and their ideas and contributions were acknowledged. It is in such an enabling environment that children's own mathematics can thrive.

The open classroom

Central to classrooms that support children's own mathematical marks on paper, are the conditions that foster this; the atmosphere that gives opportunities for children to feel that they can put their own thinking on paper. The psychological environment is equally as important as the physical environment.

What the child initiates and makes sense of on her own or with other children is equally as valued as the adult-directed or adult-led sessions. In an open classroom adults will encourage the children's initiatives. This encouragement is important for the child to feel strong enough in herself to take further risks and opportunities.

The balance between adult-led and child-initiated learning

In the open classroom there will be a balance between adult-directed activities and child-initiated activities. Both will be valued and, at times, come together to provide a strong connection to support the child in her learning. There is a state of energy balance within this understanding. Energy is known by the Chinese as 'Tao'. Chiazzari (1998) observes that Tao is manifest in all things through the dynamic interaction of the two polar energy forces, yin and yang. When these are in perfect balance then total harmony exists. The balance is not necessarily an equal balance but one that promotes the health and well-being of the whole child. This is rooted in the theory that one supports the other. For example, an imbalance of a very formal academic curriculum does not necessarily ensure that children will gain academic excellence. The balance for young children in Early Years settings is better weighted in favour of child-initiated learning. The careful planning and consideration of this needs to be thought through.

In adult-led learning contexts, the adult knows what she is moving towards in terms of what she wants the child to learn. The adult usually has a specific aim in mind, perhaps even a written objective. The task does not necessarily need to be closed and the children can actually be given a good deal of autonomy within the prescribed task. Below is an example of an adult-led session.

Adult-led learning: nursery class – ages 3 and 4 years

The adult has invited four children to bath dolls. Each child chooses a doll and a bath. The baths and dolls are different sizes so the children think carefully about which bath and doll they would like. The children watch the teacher fill up her bath with water. She asks the children if they think there is enough water to bath the doll. The teacher carefully tests the water with her elbow to see if it is too hot. One child shouts out 'that's what my mummy does when she baths my Ben'. The children then fill their baths up with water and test to see if it is too hot. The teacher continues to talk and listen to the children as they bath the dolls. She asks them questions and their opinion about bathing babies. The adult has an aim in mind to give the children scientific and mathematical experiences, though in a child-friendly way. The adult leads the discussion but encourages children to take over and talk about their meanings and interests in bathing dollies. Paper, writing and drawing implements are available should the children choose to put their experience on paper.

In child-initiated experiences the child directs and leads the activity. It belongs to the child. The child chooses the equipment, the length of time, the space and the outcome. Child-initiated learning is usually a part of what Bruce (1997) describes as 'free flow' play.

An example of child-initiated learning

> Jason, 3:11, has chosen to play outside with the large blocks. He places two blocks on the ground, a distance apart. He then places a plank across so that he has made a kind of platform. He adjusts the blocks so that they fit better. He tests his structure by walking and jumping lightly on it. He smiles and seems pleased with his efforts. Carly, 4:1 joins him and walks on the platform. She then uses another block and plank to add to the existing structure. They both select other blocks and planks and make networks of platforms in the outside play area. Other children join and play with them, testing the platforms that they have made.

In this learning experience we can also see the mathematical and scientific learning that might take place but there are no planned adult outcomes: the plans are in the children's heads and unfold as the activity takes place. The adult's role is crucial in this experience. The adult has provided the materials, the time and the space. The adult has carefully observed the child's play and made notes of this session. She has asked the children if she may try out their platforms. She asks them if they will remember what they have done and suggests they sketch their network. She helps one of the children to take a picture. Two children decide to sketch the network. The adult takes notes of this session back to the planning meeting for the next week. The staff in the setting discuss ways they can extend the children's building interests and ideas about platforms and supporting structures.

It is important to understand the distinction between adult-led and child-initiated learning, otherwise the teacher might plan what she believes is a play session when it is really adult directed. The children might in such circumstances end up with an imbalance in their learning opportunities where there is no free-flow play. The reverse of this can also happen. When there is no adult-directed input in children's learning, children then do not have the opportunity to see adults modelling mathematics and the learning might not be sufficiently scaffolded (Bruner, 1971). In such situations the children do not have the full benefit of the teacher as the 'knowledgeable other' (Vygotsky, 1978). In Early Years settings where there is an open culture an atmosphere of enquiry and discussion exists.

Figure 8.1 illustrates the features of both adult-led and child-initiated learning. Fisher sees this in three ways; teacher-initiated, teacher-intensive and child-initiated (Fisher, 1996). The teacher-initiated learning arises from the teacher's

FEATURES OF ADULT-LED AND CHILD-INITIATED LEARNING	
YIN	**YANG**
Adult-led	**Child-initiated**
• The adult has the agenda	• The child has her own agenda
• The adult chooses what the children do	• The child chooses
• The adult asks most of the questions. These can be open questions	• The child has her own questions to ask.
• Experiences can be in small or large group times	• These points (above) are usually a feature of free-flow play, when children are independent
• Adults motivate children to ensure that they are involved	• The child is usually deeply involved in what she has chosen
• Adult's assessment is based on the adult's criteria	• Assessment is based on observations of the child's actions, representations and thinking (including talk)

Figure 8.1   Features of adult-led and child-initiated play

planning, but is very open so it could be something the teacher started and the children could carry on in their own way.

The teacher-intensive session is a focused group, where the teacher stays with the children and has objectives to teach. The teacher-initiated and teacher-intense learning are both adult led and neither is play. Fisher (1996, p. 105) reminds us 'that the minute an adult has a predetermined task or goal in mind, then the activity cannot be play'. In the adult-directed learning spectrum there are different levels of adult involvement:

- where children lead after the adult has an initial input
- where the adult provides open problem-solving questions but guides and supports the responses
- where the whole class is teacher-directed; this is usually seen in older age groups and is not a sufficiently good model for younger children.

The significant feature is to be clear what play and child-initiated learning is, compared to adult-directed and adult-led learning. Studies have documented the difference between teachers' espoused theory of play and what actually happens in their classroom (Bennett, Wood and Rogers, 1997; Pascal, 1990). Some teachers' rhetoric about play can suggest that their practice matches what they say. The reality is often very different. For example, whilst one teacher firmly stated that choice was important in play, in her actual classroom practice choice was very limited. The children had choice what they did in the play area but had no choice of play area or with whom they were playing with in that area. In an even narrower understanding of play, the well-intentioned teacher had turned the role-play into the 'Three Bears' Cottage' and then proceeded to tell the children what they would play. In terms of children's mathematical marks the role-play area can offer rich learning environments but it must be in a sense of free-flow play or the opportunity to make marks through their own thinking is lost.

Role-play and mark-making

In their role-play children are making sense of characters, relationships, behaviours and responsibilities. When they use writing for their own purposes in play this can demonstrate their knowledge of what writing can do (Hall and Robinson, 1995). In the same manner we have often found, provided that the culture of the setting supports mathematical marks within their play, children will integrate their mathematical purposes in an authentic way. This is demonstrated by the examples of children using mathematical meaning, marks and writing in this chapter, in their 'library van' play (Chapter 9) and in the 'garden centre' and 'Omar's dog' (Figures 8.5 and 8.6). Atkinson also makes reference to opportunities for writing mathematics in role-play 'at the hairdresser's' and in 'the baby shop' (Atkinson, 1992).

In England by the time children are 6 years old they have fewer opportunties for play in school. In Denmark there appears to be a better understanding of children's play and it is common to observe several groups of children playing in classes of 6-year-olds (Brostrom, 1997). However, it is interesting to note that until recently literacy materials have been deliberately excluded from play in Danish schools: it was generally thought that children would get confused if literacy materials were combined with play. This, teachers thought, would impede the children's development. Recent research findings advocate that the opposite is true – connecting literacy to play will support rather than hinder the children's literacy development. Nevertheless, it is crucial to reflect that pressurising children into producing something based on the teacher's expectations will stifle the imaginative and creative aspect of the play. Elkonin cautions against an educational use of play (didactic play), for example by playing 'grocer's shop', in order to try to teach children to give correct change (Bostrom, 1997, p. 20).

Office box

Visiting the school office one day we discussed the secretary's work and the resources we'd seen her use. It seemed natural to add a few additional resources for role-play and the children had lots of ideas: the box in which they were

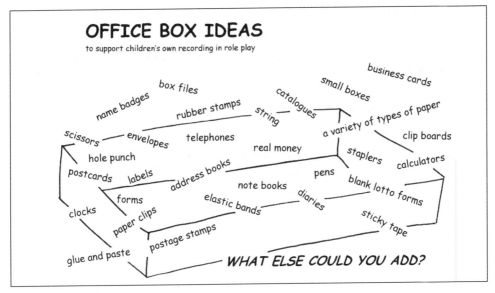

Figure 8.2   Office box

stored was soon named 'the office box' by the children and included the resources as shown in Figure 8.2.

The children incorporated these resources into their play in ways that were meaningful within the contexts of roles they assumed (see 'Marina and the library van' in Chapter 9).

BED NUMBER	PATIENT'S NAME
Bed 1:	
Bed 2:	
Bed 3:	
Bed 4:	
Bed 5:	
Bed 6:	
Side room:	
Waiting for a bed:	

Figure 8.3   List of patients

Other resources

Blank paper offers the best background for children's marks in mathematics, writing and drawing. However, occasional use of computer-generated forms based on children's own ideas arising from their play can provide additional resources in a similar way that a few officially printed forms do. The examples in Figures 8.5 and 8.6 are from two different classes of 4- and 5-year-olds.

Patient's name:	Number of spoons of medicine:	Time to give medicine:

Figure 8.4 List of medicines

The physical environment

There are many practical opportunities for writing and making mathematical marks that can be accessed in an Early Years setting. It is helpful if writing and drawing implements and paper are freely available at all times in different areas of the classroom and outside. Different sizes, colours and shapes of paper add to the scope of the mark-making. There need to be places to draw, sketch, write and make all sorts of mathematical marks. Large paper with space to make marks, perhaps on large carpeted areas, provides the children with freedom to explore large movements on paper. Clipboards are useful for travelling to different areas

The garden centre

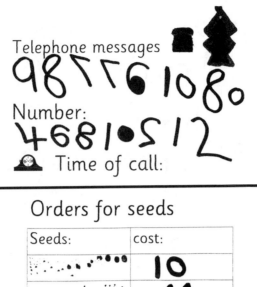

Figure 8.5 The garden centre – telephone message and orders for seeds

in the school and for outside work – and young children love the feeling of importance when they collect information with the help of a clipboard.

The way in which the environment is shaped is also significant. For example, whilst we advocate that children have opportunities to mark-make, we are also saying that there needs to be freedom of movement within this. We are not saying that children should be sitting down holding a pencil at a table for most of their day. A classroom full of tables and chairs would not be conducive to young children's own mathematics.

The setting has also to be accessible to the children. It is hard for children to take notice of labels and displays if they are near the ceiling and adult orientated. Displays and signs are better placed at children's height starting from the

PETS FOR SALE THIS WEEK

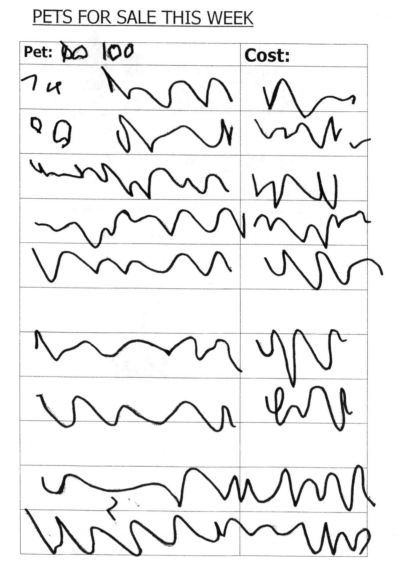

Figure 8.6 Omar's dog

The pet shop

Omar, 4:6 used the form to reflect on the pet he'd like (Figure 8.6). At the top he wrote '£100 for a dog, £10 for a hamster'. Then he read 'I haven't got a dog and my mum might be thinking about it,' adding 'dogs cost a lot of money'. At 4 years of age Omar understood the difference between £10 and £100 shown by his estimate of the cost of the two animals. He also understood the financial implications of keeping a dog.

floor up and not the ceiling down. A useful thing to do is to get down on your knees and look at the classroom from a child's eye view.

When environments are mathematical, mathematics happens

Hall (1987, p. 19), states that:

> children should never need to ask if they can engage in purposeful literacy acts. If a classroom provides an environment where the state of literacy is high, where there are powerful demonstrations of literacy and where children freely engage in literacy, then children will take every opportunity to use their knowledge and abilities to act in a literate way.

A purposeful literacy act:

Kate, 4:9, and Naomi, 4:11, had decided to paint a picture in the art area. When they had finished Kate decided she would give her painting to her aunt. She went to the writing area and wrote a letter saying to her aunt: 'this is for you. Love from Kate'.

If we substitute the word 'literacy' with 'mathematics', then we can see that Hall's statement can also be true for mathematics. The mathematical environment is important because of the value placed on child-initiated learning. The actual physical environment is less important in a purely direct instruction model of learning: in this the teacher with the knowledge is 'telling' it to the child. The environment is vital in a balanced learning setting because the emphasis has moved away from the teacher as sole giver of knowledge. The child has time within this environment to choose and notice the mathematics around her and uses that mathematics to make meaning in 'child sense' ways.

A purposeful mathematical act:

Josh, Josephine and Ellie (3:1 to 3:7) are playing in the home corner. They decide that Ellie is going to a wedding and she needs a dress. Josephine is going to make the dress with Josh and he goes to the writing area where he borrows a tape measure. Josephine puts the tape measure around Ellie's waist and shouts 'twelve'. They choose material from the scrap area. They have a discussion about how long this needs to be for Ellie. They choose some length of pink netting and Josh says that Ellie could be the bride. Josephine agrees and they return to the home corner very excited.

Hall et al. wrote about a conventional nursery class where there seemed to be no evidence of children's writing and it would be easy to assume from this that children were not interested in writing (1986, cited in Hall 1987). However, the authors of this study changed a non-literate home corner in to a 'literate' home corner. When they added writing materials and utensils in everyday writing contexts (e.g. a notepad was placed beside the telephone in the role play area), the children became prolific writers and engaged in a lot of reading behaviours. This we believe can also be true for mathematics. In another study one of us added additional resources that offered potential for encouraging writing, mark-making and talk that was related to mathematics. The outcome was dramatic: whereas no reference or use of mathematical symbols had previously been observed, children now self-initiated mathematical behaviours – including talk and writing – within their play. My observations showed behaviours such as leaving notes for the milkman, reading the time from a clock or using a tape measure and writing down a child's height. If the children are used to writing mathematics, for many different purposes, they will become proficient at exploring their mathemtical thinking on paper.

Practical steps
Morning books

Parents and carers accompanying their children to school every day can provide the perfect opportunity to share mark-making and writing opportunities. Some settings welcome parents into the classroom as soon as they arrive in the morning. A question is posed on the board for parents and carers to respond to with their children. It provides an opportunity for a discussion and a talking point, and gives the parent a chance to join in with part of the school day with their child. Involving families offers the child different styles of mathematical writings. It also offers the parent and teacher time to talk, to share cultural perspectives and to get to know each other. It gives the child the chance to share school mathematics with their parents. It gives the teacher a chance to listen to what might be happening in the home. When done sensitively and in an open way, families really appreciate this start to the day and often younger siblings will join in with the mathematics. A good way to encourage the younger siblings to be welcome is to have a basket of toddler toys available for them to play with. There are many ways to share the start of the day this way with parents.

- *Morning books* – a question or statement is written on the board for parents and children to answer together in any way. This is an open question to stimulate discussion, for example:

> Look around the room, estimate what objects are about five centimetres long. Write down your thinking.

> ## What do you know about money?

Morning books can of course have any title; one teacher I worked with changed the name to 'sunshine books' because she had an afternoon group.

- *'All aboard'* – on a large writing board, questions can be posed for children, parents and carers to write on the board. For example, in a nursery class of 3- and 4-year-olds I wrote:

> We are collecting birthday dates. Please write
> your name and your birthday date below.

This was very popular and the parents compared and discussed the dates with each other. For example one parent told another, 'my brother Johnnie's birthday is one day after your birthday on the eighth of June it is the ninth of June'. The children of course were listening to this conversation and watching as the parents wrote their dates. Real conversations have a meaningful power to children.

When we have provided a model such as the morning books for the children we have found that they are very keen to write their own questions for other children to answer. Parents often provide interesting questions and are keen to share ideas, and this often develops into a fun time where questions are puzzled over and laughed about. The fear of mathematics goes, as a safe environment develops. The families take the questions back to the home to discuss with other family members.

During a discussion about shapes with 4 and 5-year-olds, two of the children had suggested that irregular shapes were not 'real' or 'proper' shapes. Another child suggested that they could 'make up' shapes that no one had previously drawn. Later she wrote a question in our large morning book: 'Can you make up a shape?'

At first children and their families drew irregular 'blobs' and some regular shapes combined. In their descriptions some children used mathematical terms: some of their labels were often more precise descriptions, e.g. 'roundy-tri' for the circle with a triangle attached. In contrast, labelling an invented shape 'a thingy' did not tell us about its properties. After discussion the children added the request that everyone should give their shape a mathematical name.

A wealth of invented shapes filled our morning book and each day we discussed the names they had assigned to their shapes. The children became rigorous in their evaluation of terms. Increasingly, they extended their vocabulary so that it became more precise: 'corners' sometimes became 'right-angles', 'straight-sides' included reference to 'parallel' and words such as pentagon and hexagon were used in context.

It was interesting to note that in a class with 4 and 5-year-olds, at first children related their invented shapes to something familiar such as a sun (a curved shape) or a rocket (for a shape with a definite point). As their language developed during the year, children were increasingly likely to use mathematical descriptions. When exploring invented shapes later with children a year older, most of the children described and named their shapes using specific mathematical language.

Displays

Displays give children a model for mathematics. It is important to put up the children's own representations because it is saying you value the child's ideas. Displays that children have taken part in are the most useful. This can be a risky business because in some settings the rule is tidiness. Children's work does not always appear to be tidy to a visiting adult. This is where the teacher's knowledge in explaining the graphics and the educational soundness of the children's mathematics is necessary. One of the best kinds of displays are those in which the children can engage, for example where the children can respond to a question, a drawing or an idea.

> This giant is 2.5 metres tall. What age do you think he is? Write your answer below.

> Alex's rule is that all the numbers that end with 2, 4, 6 and 8 can be shared equally. Is this always true? Add your comments below.

> Lakshmi says that her Dad said that one million has six zeroes in it. Do you think that is right? Try writing one million in numerals below. Try to discuss with a partner if you think one million has six zeroes.

Displays can be time-consuming so they need to be useful. Displays also can be put up with the children's help and input in a day. These can be quick response displays. For example, you can ask the children to pin up all their ideas about shapes that have more than three sides. Displays that show 'work in progress' are a useful point of discussion with children: for example, a chart or a list to which children are going to add information.

Noticeboards

Shearer (1989) talks about noticeboards outside of educational settings being dynamic and meaningful. They often are haphazard and display a range of items. The items grow and grow until old out-of-date things are removed, replaced by more urgent notices. Noticeboards at home reflect the lives of the people in that home. There can be dates of notable happenings, reminders of events, photographs, receipts, bills to pay, dental and doctor appointments, shopping lists, school letters and children's drawings. Noticeboards provide a communication vehicle that is purposeful and interests everybody in the household in some way. Providing a noticeboard for children in the classroom gives them a further means of accessing literacy opportunities but it can also provide a way of promoting mathematical communication.

Noticeboards are usually best if they are put up in a focal point of the classroom. It is vital that they are at children's height so the children can easily display anything they wish to communicate with others. Explaining the function and modelling how the noticeboard works is essential to get the idea started: for example, the teacher may start to put up notices and explain them to the children.

JACK HAS A DENTAL APPOINTMENT AT 2.OO ON FRIDAY.

SPECIAL ASSEMBLY THIS WEEK ON MONDAY AT 10 AM

REMEMBER 50P MILK MONEY, TOMORROW

Once the children find ownership of the board then they will post a variety of pieces from pictures to brochures. They will remind the teacher to put up current events and they will remember to look every day.

> Because it was part of the classroom culture, children often used the noticeboard for their own purposes. Matthew, 5:8, decided to try to teach some of his friends to play chess and to help them, he made his own book of rules of how to play chess, although other children found it difficult. Soon Matthew had an idea of starting a 'maths games club'. He wrote a message about this and pinned it on the noticeboard, inviting children to sign their names if they wanted to join. For most of the summer term the club flourished, other children introducing their favourite games and several children inventing games of their own.

Graphics areas

Graphics areas provide a range of resources for a variety of literacy purposes. For many teachers the objectives for the graphics area are usually literacy based and so you may see a predominance of literacy-related resources. By adding mathematical equipment one can give the graphics area a different focus.

Mathematical equipment to add:

- rulers
- calculator
- calendar
- measuring tape
- number lines (different lengths)
- stamps
- shapes
- tickets
- cheque book
- cut out numbers
- clock.

The size of this area is important. In ideal conditions when space is no object it is worth providing sufficient room so that at least six children are able to use it. If the area becomes popular, make it larger. This is recognising the flow of children's play.

A board is essential for children who wish to put up their pieces. Once I saw a whole length of wall devoted to the children's own writing including their mathematical writing. If there is very little space for a writing table you could think about supplementing this with an 'office box' which takes up very little space and can be used anywhere (see Figure 8.2). This area will be used if the teacher highlights the purpose and shows the equipment to the children. Sometimes a graphics area becomes old and needs revival: then a theme may restore some interest. Here we suggest some themes that give a mathematical focus:

- calendars
- cheque books
- birthday cards
- petty cash receipts
- raffle tickets
- recipes.

Observations of this area are important to see what the children write and how they are using the area and these can be added to their records and also be used for planning. Do children use mathematics in their own self-initiated learning? This is a useful assessment point. If children freely put their mathematics on paper then they are beginning to make connections between practical and more abstract forms of mathematical thinking: this will help them move into standard forms of maths.

Max and Alex, aged 7, in the graphics area – self-initiated maths activity

Max and Alex invented what was later termed 'a multiplication roll'. Max cut out a long strip of paper. He wrote three at one end and rolled it up so the three was hidden and then he wrote another three and rolled it up and repeated this until he had run out of paper and he had made a complete roll. He undid the roll and rolled it backwards adding the threes in his head and he ended with twenty seven which he put on the other side of the paper. He then 'tested' Alex by giving him the rolled up paper and explaining you have got to add the next number 'and you keep going until you get to the end'. Alex tried and retried, eventually they did it together. Alex then made one for Max to try. He chose the numeral one to use in the multiplication roll. Max laughed and suggested that they could make that really long and so they 'taped' several strips of paper together and wrote I + I + I + I + I and so on. They tested the strip on Nicholas who found it fascinating. At the review session they shared what they had been doing with the rest of the class.

This started a craze at the writing table of making multiplication rolls in all lengths and a variety of numbers. I used this opportunity to discuss repeated addition and the connection to multiplication: this reinforced work on multiplication the children had been engaged in previously in the term. It also presented an excellent link to the repeat function on the calculator.

Creating opportunities in a nursery setting

Munn (1997) in her study of nursery classes found that the adults provided many literacy experiences but few numeracy experiences for children. The teachers seemed not to be as aware of the mathematical possibilities as they were of other subject based opportunities. On finding the provision of mathematical writing materials in her nursery was not sufficiently stimulating, Mills (2002) supported the children's interest in mathematical marks and set out to provide more mathematical experiences for the children:

over the remainder of the autumn term I gradually introduced resources into the setting. Number lines were placed in the graphics area along with diaries, lottery slips, raffle tickets or any 'numbered' pieces of paper. A small play table in addition to the graphics area had a calculator with large number keys and a large LCD display. A note pad was placed beside a telephone. A large dice was provided and a set of laminated number cards which children could handle, write on and play with. Numbers were displayed at eye level including number line up to 30 and a number square up to 25. At every opportunity numbers were counted up and down the number line. Certain play situations were set up to encourage the use of number in their play.

In her observations of the children she found that the children were using more mathematical language and engaging in mark-making with a mathematical intention. Children played 'taking registers', made up number games, jotted down 'numbers' as they spoke on the telephone and self-initiated 'practised' writing numbers. Below are some of her observations of children in the graphics area.

> Bradley, 3:5, played with the calculator for about 15 minutes at the writing table, writing as he looked at the keys. He said 'my dad's got one of these'. Sam, 3:6, was watching as Bradley used the calculator. He also made marks on paper (see Figure 8.7a).
>
> Sophie, 4:2, played with the telephone at the writing table. She said 'I know Jade's telephone number' and wrote it down (see Figure 8.7b). Sophie was very interested in numbers and was very confident in writing numerals. Alex listened to Sophie and started copying what she was writing.

In both these play situations the children were interested in each other's mark-making and what each other had to say. This social exchange will help them develop confidence in their ability as mathematical writers. The adults in this situation were keen to understand the children's graphics and how they could support them. Not only did they provide the materials but they listened to what they said about their marks and noted this down for future planning and for the children's records.

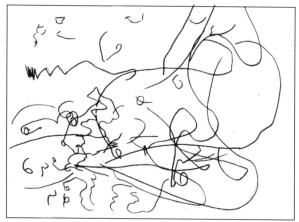

Figure 8.7a Sam's marks

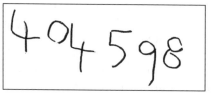

Figure 8.7b Sophie's marks

In order to create rich mathematical environments we need to put on our 'mathematical glasses' to see the possibilities. Young children need environments that encourage use of mathematics in purposeful contexts and ways that have meaning to them. By providing mathematical experiences these nursery teachers supported and developed children's natural mathematical interest.

In another class of 4- and 5-year-olds one of us had observed the use children made of the graphics area and the range and purposes of their marks. Part way into the term I offered to add some mathematical resources and this triggered a wider range of marks. Of the marks the children made during one session, over a quarter were mathematical.

Form-filling is always popular in writing areas – children of 3 often make marks over pictures, symbols and writing on forms whilst 4- and 5-year-olds fill in the boxes with their own writing and with numerals.

On one form James, 5:7, wrote his name in one box followed by a reversed 'N', '9' and '1' in the next, which he referred to as 'number'. Below this he wrote that his favourite object was a train and drew a train in the 'comment box' at the bottom of the sheet.

This passion for form-filling extends to form-making, relating to children's grid schemas (see Chapter 3).

Kacie, 4:9, drew a grid with ten boxes which she filled with writing like marks which she called a 'holiday list'. It was a checklist with features that were important to her and could be ticked off. They included 'packed lunch, look for seaweed, toy boat, climb on rocks' and 'starfish (blue)'. Madison, 4:10, covered a sheet of paper with a grid which she filled with a variety of numbers that included a series from 1 to 11, 222 and 1010. Sometimes children made registers which they completed with their own or copied symbols. Other popular activities in classes with children from 4 to 6 years are filling envelopes and making books – both relating to *containing*, *enveloping* and *connecting* schemas (Chapter 3). Raj, 4:5, drew many little grids on small pieces of paper that he had cut out and then attached them to pages with sticky tape throughout a book he'd made.

Some graphics can be seen to relate to the current class culture. A 'garden centre' role-play area made Emily, 5:2, draw a vase with three flowers in and beneath it she drew four coins – the price of the flowers for sale. Emily drew this the day after I'd added a box of real coins to the graphics area.

Many homes and early years settings have wall clocks and children often draw clocks in the graphics area. Jessica, 4:6 (see Figure 8.8) selected a piece of paper at the graphics area and she drew a clock attempting to fit all 12 numerals around the clock. In her first and second attempts Jessica could not fit the 12 numerals in but in her third drawing she had managed nearly all 12 numerals. She was pleased with her drawings and told the adult that 'it is nearly milk time'.

Jessica knows that there are 12 numerals on a clock. She was persistent with her learning and challenged herself: getting the feel for layout, space and shape. On this occasion she was playing with a piece of knowledge and connecting it to a real context, i.e. milk time at the nursery. Jessica carried around her sign to show the other children in the nursery. Woods (1988) talks about children being the 'architects of their own learning'.

Figure 8.8 Jessica's sign

Other clocks go through a period of transformation when children add move-able hands and cut their clocks out. Louisa, 4:9, took this a stage further by creating a dial for the children to select play activities in their class (Figure 8.9).

In the graphics area, Louisa, 4:9, made what appeared at first glance to be a clock face, but which she intended to use for a different purpose. In this class the children in each group had certain options for play from which they could choose each day. When she explained how to use her dial, she assigned an activity to the numerals 1–5: bricks, puzzles, role-play, reading and painting. She paused with her finger on '6', unable to think of other possibilities: then smiling, explained 'then you have a sleep'. As she moved the hand of the dial she stopped at the letters 'fo' and pointed out that this was 'where you turn it off'. Louisa had related what she knew about analogue clocks to that of her classroom culture: perhaps she was making links with her home culture too, where, after finishing what she plays with at the end of each day, she goes to sleep.

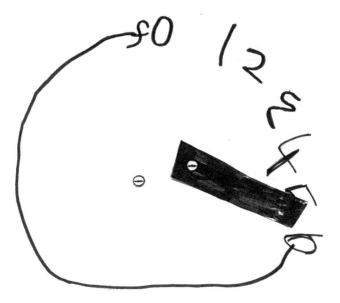

Figure 8.9 Louisa's dial

Scarlett, 5:0, drew a shop till (Figure 8.10) which may have also been influenced by the class 'garden centre'. She wrote and cut out numbers for the different amounts which she attached to the till. At the top of her till she had drawn an LCD screen with more numerals explaining 'that's what you have to pay'. Finally she cut out her till so that it became an object she could use in her play.

Both Louisa and Scarlett had moved from purely representing their objects to cutting them out so that they became objects with which to play. In Pahl's words they were making them 'more real' (Pahl, 1999a, p. 35). Kress highlights the significance of cutting out: 'there is then a continuum for the child, between things on the page – one kind of distanced, intangible reality; and things here and now, another kind of reality, not distanced but tangible. The two kinds of realism are linked through the actions of the child' (Kress, 1997, p. 27).

When children wrote lists, made books and filled in forms they had no need to cut them out since these things were already objects which were symbols in their own right.

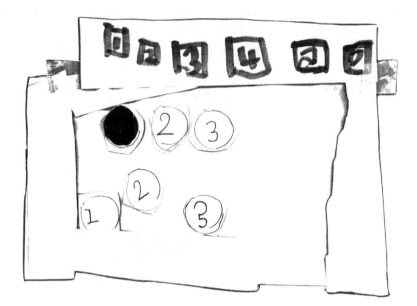

Figure 8.10 Scarlett's till

Rose, 5:4, and Stephen, 5:1, were interested in the numbers of shoe sizes: their interest had arisen from one of the children proudly showing his new shoes. Stephen explained that numbers 'go on forever' and that there were just 'too many things to count in the world' but agreed that he would see how far they could count. They chose some strips of paper in the graphics area and each began to write on a separate piece of paper, eventually agreeing that each strip should have no more than the 20 numerals. When they had a total of five strips covered with numbers they were unsure how to arrive at a total.

Rose's response (Figure 8.11) shows how she was able to link her previous knowledge of counting in tens to this new problem, by grouping pairs of tens. She read the numbers as '10, 20, 30, 40, 50, 60, 70, 80, 90, 100'. She explained that the numbers between each line represented the numbers (20) on each of the five strips of paper

Building on their knowledge of counting in tens, together the children were able to count in twenties. The following day Stephen added two further strips of 1–20 and confidently wrote '10040' (140) for the total number of their seven strips.

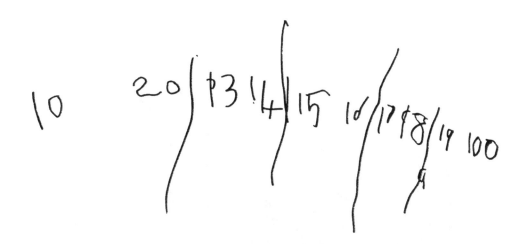

Figure 8.11   Rose's counting in twenties

The maths explored here included estimation and adaptation of known rules. Building on their partial understanding they used repeated addition and were able to arrive at a total. Young children have a fascination for larger numbers and, provided they can see a purpose, will grapple with complex and challenging ideas. Allowing children to explore and practise skills in ways they have chosen permits them to enter a task at their own level: it also allows learning to be differentiated to learners' needs (Worthington, 1998).

One day Natasha, 4:6, brought a piece of paper and a pen when I did the dinner register and this led many other children to choose to make their own during the term. Gemma, 4:4, used marks with some approximations of symbols ('0' and '+') and Natasha focused on the concept of a list including some ticks and circles (Figures 8.12a and 8.12b, respectively). Alice, 5:3, used only two symbols (one for each type of lunch) and refined her layout (Figure 8.12c).

These examples show a progression in the way in which the children have chosen to represent data and in their layout. Other children drew lunch-boxes or plates, drew children's faces or wrote names. Afterwards they 'read' their registers, allowing them to see the different ways others had represented data. These frequent opportunities provided the children with useful models of data representation from their peers and they were often able to suggest ways in which they could add information to help someone else to read what they had written.

8.12a Gemma

8.12b Natasha

8.12c Alice

Figure 8.12 Dinner registers

In one setting of 3 and 4-year-olds, children were responsible for collecting the choices for mid-morning staff drinks. The children took a clipboard to collect the drink choices of the staff. They then read their information to the member of staff who made the drinks.

There are many other regular opportunities for collecting and representing data in Early Years settings including session registers and lists for different purposes. The key significance of such events is that they provide opportunities for representing, reading and discussing meaning. Such examples provide powerful foundations for later formal data handling in mathematics.

Graphs

The graph or chart is an easy and potentially purposeful mathematical representation. It is useful to provide a range of graphs that children can read. These can be commercially produced graphs and also those that have been drawn up by the teacher about the children. These are then displayed on the walls for children to read. It is important to note that the graphs displayed reflect a range of layouts and that they do not always need to be done by the children. Graphs and tables provide models for discussion and, if purposeful, children then can see the application of data handling,

EGG/SPOON	CLOTHES	HOPPING	BACKWARD	BALLOON
Kenny	Lilly	Famidah	Nick	Stuart
Nick	Glynis	Kenny	Lilly	Zak
Ben	Max	Oliyemi	Zak	Alex
Rose	Famidah	Shabana		Joseph
Shabana	Ginny	Max		Sanjay
Famidah	Susie	Susie		Alice
Alexis	Ginny			
	Jason			

Figure 8.13 Chart of races chosen for sports days

Number lines

There are many different kinds of number lines that can be displayed in the classroom. They are used for different purposes: as a reference for the children to use if they need to; as a teaching tool; for the children to construct their own number line (Carruthers, 1997a). Number lines are an essential part of helping children develop visual mental images of numbers. If we want to help children with their understanding of the position of numbers then the importance of number lines cannot be underestimated, and it is vital to have effective number lines. Through the year a change and a growth of numbers on the line help the children focus on them. To help children see the pattern of numbers it is vital to have number lines beyond 30. When we look at numbers in the outside world they are not always horizontal: it adds another dimension if you suddenly add a vertical number line, especially when you are talking about scales.

As the year progresses, put up an empty number line where children can add their own numbers (for example, see Chapter 9, p. 158). Sometimes start with other numbers such as 30 or 100. Children find it interesting to work out what comes next and add it to the line. Negative numbers are also a source of interest and a challenge for young children. To encourage the children to write their own number lines put strips of paper in a pocket beside the number line. Once you have modelled the use of the number line then the children can challenge other children by starting at different numbers they have chosen. Children as they progress through their understanding will choose to use the empty number line as a method of calculation.

Outside

The outside environment in a setting can promote children's marks just as much as inside. Here they can have the space and freedom to make large marks with an exciting variety of tools. Large paintbrushes with water buckets provide a stimulating invitation to paint on walls or large rolls of paper. Here children like to experiment with large shapes and it is especially liberating for children who find finer pencil control difficult.

Teachers can set up a large chalking area either on the ground or on walls. One nursery I worked in had a large piece of ground painted in black. They had also put a border around the black square. It became one of the most popular outdoor activities. Easels with the usual painting tools are an ideal way to use outdoors and the space to create. Children also like to use clipboards outside and the 'office box' can also prove a useful addition to the outside area.

Labels and signs

If we think of the mathematical environment that is outside the setting in the real world, then what we are trying to do is to bring that kind of mathematics into our setting. Think of the labels that we see that are communicating mathematics, for example:

- 30 MPH
- OPEN AT 5 0'CLOCK
- BACK IN 5 MINUTES.

In the setting we want to reflect this variety of number signs: for example, 'tidy up time' provides a good opportunity to use a sign.

> 5 MINUTES FOR TIDY UP TIME

A child can carry this sign around and depending on how much time you have, you can alter the times. Often children will start making their own signs and a culture of sign-making will follow.

Figure 8.14 Mark-making outside

Conclusion

We have shown the importance of giving children daily opportunities for child-initiated play and learning. Well planned and valued by the teacher, this time can provide children time to explore aspects of learning that are of significance to them personally. Provided the choices are wide and the environment offers mathematical possibilities, children will often choose to explore aspects of mathematics. The examples in this chapter show some of the ways teachers can provide opportunities for mathematical choices. We have also discussed features of an open classroom where in adult-led situations the children can also explore their own mathematical representations.

Implications for teaching

- It is useful to take an audit of your environment; how mathematical is it?
- Identify an area that you might develop.
- It is better to start with just one thing you would like to change and observe this for future development.

In Chapter 9 we include case studies of both child-initiated play and mathematics lessons which provided opportunities for children to use mathematical graphics in their own ways. The children are aged from 3 to 8 years.

9

Case Studies from Early Childhood Settings

University lecturers, researchers, advisers and even head teachers can forget all too easily what it is like to be a classroom teacher. Nothing that any of these people say or do is profitable unless it can be used by teachers in their classrooms. (Davis and Pettitt, 1994, p. 157)

The following case studies are of authentic classroom practice. This is a small sample to represent the age range from 3 years to 8 years. We begin with observations of children initiating their own learning through play. We have also selected a mixture of teacher-directed small groups and whole-class teaching. There is no one set way to support children's learning in mathematics or in any subject. We offer these examples for your reflection and as a discussion point with others. Sharing what we do as educators may give us a stepping stone to refine or rethink our own practice.

The birthday cards

THE MATHEMATICS	number knowledge as a function in society
AGE	3- and 4-year-olds
CONTEXT	free representation in the writing area – individual responses
FEATURES	providing opportunities for mathematical representations within a nursery setting

Birthdays are something young children identify with and that excites them. The changing of their age is very important to them. To enhance our graphics area for a birthday focus we asked the children to bring in old birthday cards from their family. We discussed with each child the card they had brought in and then they put it up on the writing area display board. As well as a discussion tool the birthday cards gave the children models to create their own birthday cards for other people. We added plastic, cut out cardboard and shiny paper numerals to the writing area, as well as decorations for the birthday cards. The children made lots of cards for themselves and other people. Children chose to come to this area if they wanted to. There was sometimes an adult there to discuss with the children anything they wanted to do. We carefully observed this area and noted down our findings. The children showed ownership of their cards: Stacey, 4:2, showed the birthday cards she had made for her sisters to her granny; Thomas, 3:9, showed his to his sister; Daniel, 4:5, showed his to his mum. There was always somebody at this area and all the children were able to discuss for whom they were making the birthday card. Some children just felt the numerals and others glued as many numerals as they could on a piece of paper. A parent helper aided the children's experimentation with rulers and folding the paper and card to make the birthday cards. The children chose the paper carefully, selecting the colour and size that would suit them.

Figure 9.1 Nikita's birthday card

Nikita, 3:4, made a birthday card for herself (Figure 9.1). She looked through the different colours of paper and finally decided on pink. She looked through the box of cardboard numbers and selected the numeral three, which was her age. She glued the numeral on to the paper and wrote in black pen. She was very quiet and whispered to me that the card was for her – 'I am three' she said. Nikita showed her understanding of birthday cards. She knew her own age and was able to select the appropriate numeral to put on her card. Her marks look very much like writing and the crosses might be kisses, although she never gave me this information.

Evaluation

The birthday card area showed children at different stages of their knowledge of birthday cards. Some of the children had a strong idea about birthday cards – they made them for other people or for themselves. Some of the children liked to touch the numbers: they either did not want to make a card or did not understand. The action of putting numbers on the cards was the focus for some children. They may have been in a connecting schema (see Chapter 3). Some children knew that birthday cards had one number on them and you gave them to other people. Birthdays for some were more personal: Daniel put number four on his birthday card and gave it to his mum. This was his own personal age number and it was special enough for his mum. It was also the numeral he recognised and was familiar with. The birthday writing area facilitated acceptance and understanding of each child's growth and concept development of birthday cards. It is important to give children opportunities to explore different mathematical genres.

A number line

The following extract is adapted from Carruthers, E. (1997) 'A number line in the nursery classroom: a vehicle for understanding children's number knowledge', **Early Years**, Vol. 18, No. 1, Autumn.

THE MATHEMATICS	number recognition and order, social and personal numbers, problem-solving and self-initiated mathematics
AGE	3- and 4-year-olds
CONTEXT	interacting individually and with others in constructing a number line
FEATURES	understanding children's number knowledge

In setting up an environment that encourages and supports children's mathematics in my nursery setting of 3- and 4-year-olds, I decided to put up a number line with the children's help. This number line was planned to grow in accordance with the children's interests. The number line was going to be a 'touch and feel' number line and the numerals would probably be approximately half the height of a 4-year-old. The number line was based on discussions with children who volunteered to take part. I explained what a number line was and asked the children what number they would like to start to make. They decided to begin with number three. They probably knew more about three than any other number: some of them were three, some of them had been three, so we started with a very personal number. It took two months to accumulate numbers to ten and beyond. Eventually the number line went as far as 22. At one point zero was put up because there was a space next to the one and that prompted discussion. Each time a group chose a number they had to estimate where it would go in relation to other numbers. We had to leave spaces for numbers not yet done. Personal numbers were first chosen; for example, after three, four was chosen because some of the children were four. Toby, 3:9, chose number eight because that was his brother's age. Toby loved to feel that number and showed his mother that number. Amy, 4:6, initiated a circus game using the number line.

I decided that because the children were so interested in this number line I would invite them to make their own number lines. I provided long strips of paper and pens beside the number line. The children then could freely use this if they wanted. Several children took the opportunity to do their own number line.

Jessie, 4:3, is centring on her 'J'. This is the most important letter to her at the moment and she uses it for number symbols as well as writing symbols (see Figure 9.2, top). In her teaching of reading, Ashton Warner reasons that the letters in a child's name are personal to them (Ashton-Warner, 1965). Jessie's dots may be representations of other numerals and 'line' may be a literal translation of line because she often heard us refer to the number 'line'.

Donna, 3:6, talked about the numbers as she did them. She moved from left to right as she wrote. She has one number very firmly at the beginning of her line (see Figure 9.2, centre).

Daniel, 4:8, has mixed up letters and numbers. Again, like Jessie, he is using letter symbols for numbers (see Figure 9.2, bottom). In her observations of children writing, Clay (1975) also noted that this two way use of symbols happened. Daniel has used four as his first number on his line because it is his age number and it means something to him.

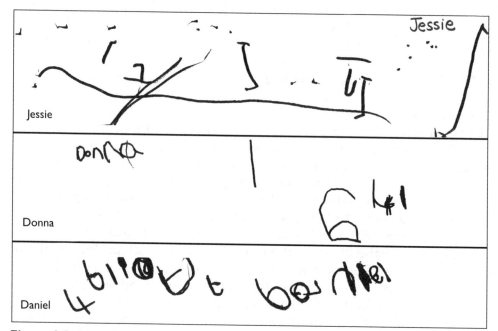

Figure 9.2 Number Lines

Evaluation

Usually number lines are hardly noticed by children but I believe this one was popular because the children had ownership of it. It was not a piece of wallpaper but a 'living' number line that they could engage in if they wanted to. Children made their own meanings from their experiences because they were empowered to guide the learning and receive appropriate teacher responses at relevant times. The number line was an excellent evaluation tool and informed me what the children knew. The children learned from each other as they listened to discussions about the numbers. The language used and received was important for their growing understanding of number lines and number sense.

Carl's garage

THE MATHEMATICS	counting
	using numerals in play
	the use of numerals for real purposes in society
AGE	3- and 4-year-olds
	Carl, 4:5 years
CONTEXT	in the nursery
	child-initiated play
FEATURES	opportunities to make mathematical marks in play
	adult interaction in play
	informal observation of one child

Role-play and small world play

I was spending an afternoon in a local nursery school and this provided an opportunity to observe some 3- and 4-year-olds at play. Carl had decided to play with the big wooden blocks and began constructing a house with Danny's help. Part way through their play I joined in, making pens and paper available: this encouraged Carl to use a great deal of mathematical mark-making. I picked up an imaginary telephone:

Teacher   Ring, ring. Ring, ring.

Carl looks surprised and turns to look around the room. I hold out my imaginary phone.

Teacher	Phone call for the builders.
Carl	Oh – yeah, right. Hello?
Teacher	This is the builders' yard. I've got some cement to deliver – do you want anything else?
Carl	Blocks – three blocks.
Teacher	Right – I'll bring them round on my lorry.

I arrive with imaginary delivery.

Teacher	You'll have to sign for them. Three blocks and one bag of cement.

Carl, Danny and Sam make some marks on the paper.

Figure 9.3 Carl's delivery note and parking tickets

Mathematical mark-making through play

Carl 'read' what he had written on the delivery form (Figure 9.3a) saying, 'if it breaks, fix it'. Daniel read 'three blocks' and Sam said nothing when he made his marks. The construction continued for a few minutes until the roof was complete. Next Carl decided to build a 'car-park' for the house which he soon developed into a public car park, repair garage and car sales.

Using small wooden blocks Carl began to arrange cars in rows on the floor and put two long blocks at right angles to form a boundary for the parking. He talked about where the cars should park, commenting 'You have to have a ticket or you get done!'

I noticed that there were no mark-making materials in the block play area so I put paper and pens near Carl. I was sensitive to the fact that this was his play and I did not expect him to use them unless he decided to do so. After adding a few more cars Carl started to make some marks, then fetched scissors and cut out tiny pieces of paper for 'parking tickets'. He 'read' each ticket as he placed them in turn on top of a car '40p, 40p, 40p, 50p, 70p, 80p, 90p' (see Figure 9.3b).

Having paper and pens to hand triggered many more ideas. The ideas flowed from Carl and none had been suggested by me. Next Carl wrote a sign – which he referred to as a 'label' – saying 'no parking'. Then he made a '£50' sign on a car for sale and a 'closed' sign to go on the brick which he'd used as a gate to close the car park.

The children talked about 'broken' cars and said they would 'fix 'em': Carl referred to several cars as 'G-reg'. After a while he looked across to me and asked if I wanted to buy a car, offering one he said was £40.

Teacher   No thanks – that's too much money.
Carl   This one's £50.

Teacher	Oh dear – that's too expensive – I haven't got enough.
Sam	Here's some more money from the bank!

Sam gave me a handful of money.

Carl	This one's £10.

I agreed to buy this cheaper car and counted out ten coins. Carl dipped his hands into a box of toy cars and handed me a yellow bulldozer.

Teacher	Oh dear! I can't have this – it's a bulldozer! I can't take my children to school in a bulldozer.
Cerrie-Ann	Here's one for £30. You can take your children to school in it and it's got petrol and it doesn't need fixing – it's G-reg.
Teacher	That sounds good. But it needs a registration number plate!
Carl	OK. 0665 G-reg.

Evaluation

Carl referred to his dad's lorry several times and appeared to have a great deal of knowledge about cars which he explored through talk and the marks he made. Making paper and pens available widened the opportunities for him to include mark-making if it arose within the context of his imaginary play.

Through closely observing Carl's play it was clear that he had a well-developed understanding of the use of numbers – for the price of a car, number plates and the cost of parking tickets. For most of the parking tickets Carl used the first letter of his name to stand for the number, but for '70p' he wrote '17' and wrote '8' for '80p'. At first when I explained that I thought £40 was too expensive for a car, he offered an alternative but dearer one for £50: later he adjusted this and found one for £10. Drawing on his knowledge of cars and lorries from his home experience, he was also able to use a string of numbers for the car registration plate and knew the special term used to describe the registration by a letter for the year it was first sold.

Additionally the observation illuminated other children's understanding. Cerri-Ann especially had listened to the features of cars that we discussed and integrated them in her sales pitch for a car, offering one cheaper than Carl's original offer and incorporating several features I'd wanted. To make the deal attractive she confirmed that it had a full tank of petrol and that it 'doesn't need fixing' – a point Carl had repeatedly made. Finally, she added Carl's boast that her car was a 'G-reg'.

Young children think division

THE MATHEMATICS	problem-solving
	division by sharing
AGE	4 and 5 years
CONTEXT	whole class and groups
FEATURES	the variety of responses

The main part of this session was a whole-class introduction to the concept of division through sharing. I wanted to provide the children with several models of this while emphasising they chose their own model to write down their findings. I demonstrated models throughout the session so that children could take those aspects with which they currently identified and then make them their own. As this was only a single session of one visit I was unable to model a variety of possible ways of recording over a period of time (see Chapter 10).

I introduced division through sharing by telling a story which I had invented. Stories are wonderful ways of bringing some sense to difficult concepts in maths. In brief the story is about twins who like everything the same. 'If Rosy has two sweets then Kathy also has two sweets. Rosy and Kathy like numbers that share equally. What numbers are sharing numbers?' The children and I discussed how we might find this out. I asked one child to choose a number out of a bag. 'How could we tell if you can share that exactly?'

Most children of this age that I have taught understand the 'one to you, one to me' way of sharing and when asked how to share quantities, one child did suggest this. I had some cubes and a child demonstrated this and we agreed that five cubes shared between two children, left one cube over, so five was not a sharing number. The importance of vocabulary and the 'one left over' is crucial to develop understanding of remainders. At this point, therefore, I had presented two ways of working out the 'sharing' numbers. I then went on to discuss images in their heads. Could we work out if it was a sharing number without actually using cubes? This helps the mental process in mathematics: if children can do it in their heads, they should do so. Some children were able to have visual mental recall with small quantities but this seemed generally more difficult to them.

The children went to tables to choose numbers for themselves to work out. I had put a tin of numbers on the tables from which they could select. I encouraged them to put their findings on paper 'so you can remember'. Blank pieces of paper and pencils were available on the tables. Some children chose to work on the carpet. On this occasion there were three adults available as some children needed more discussion and encouragement of their own ideas. Although I suggested that they work in pairs, most children worked on their own. This class had an open culture where children were not apprehensive to try things out. The teacher had moved away from the premise that mathematics is either right or wrong: she was much more interested in their thinking and how to support and encourage them. I was impressed by their independent thinking: no two children produced the same response on paper. Every child was willing to discuss their ideas.

A variety of responses

Harry, 5:4, remembered the twins story and used that to represent his findings. He used cubes to divide the amounts out. On his paper he had drawn two very large figures with their arms extended and he had written the numeral nine between them. He explained 'nine is not a sharing number. It makes one of the twins get more, so that is not fair'. He said 'two is a sharing number': he worked this out mentally. Harry had understood the concept of sharing and was able to represent that on paper. He was able to express his opinion about the situation and had worked out that one of the twins would get more. He also knows mentally two can be shared. Harry has a good knowledge of numbers to build his ideas of division. He was concerned with the inequality of the situation, which I helped the children explore at the end of the lesson. Although he did not talk about 'one left over', in future sessions he may be interested in discussing this. This will help him form ideas of remainders which, in turn, will ease his way into more difficult division concepts.

9.4a Elliot   9.4b Charlene

Figure 9.4 Young children's division – Elliot and Charlene

Elliot, 4:11, took three cubes and shared them between three people. He drew the number three and made some other marks beside it (see Figure 9.4a). Elliot did not wish to tell his teacher about it. He has taken the task and has made his own meaning from it. It seems Elliot is focused on the quantity and attaching a numeral to it. He made sense of the task by sharing the cubes, one to each person. In future sessions Elliot's interest in quantities and counting will be the focus and this will be extended in everyday sessions and in the play areas.

Charlene, 4:10, made sense of this task by focusing on the writing and naming of numerals (see Figure 9.4b). She has chosen to write lots of numbers and in discussion with an adult named the numerals she had written. She is not yet quite clear about the names of some numerals and this is why she is focusing on them. She is experimenting with the shapes of numerals. For example, she could not name the eight she had written but she said 'this is a round one' and 'this is another round one'. She also said she was trying to find the same numbers. Charlene needs more opportunities to write numerals as this is where her interest lies. Extending the writing area to include numerals and more mark-making equipment including numeral stamps will interest Charlene. She might also be interested in such self-initiated opportunities such as writing down phone numbers in a play situation.

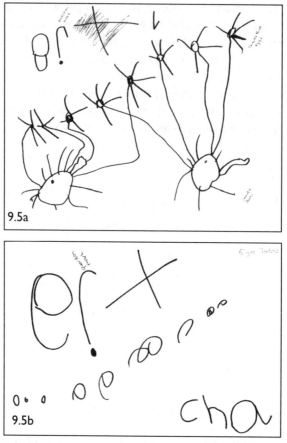

Figure 9.5 Kamrin's division

Kamrin, 5:7, invented his own system of checking. He worked through three examples consistently using his checking method (see Figure 9.5a and b for two of these). He depicted different stories. On his first paper he made up the 'Tweedle' birds and each bird has four eggs. He then wrote the numeral eight and a question mark. He put a tick to show that eight could be shared. On the second paper he drew two faces depicting two people at a bowling alley. He drew the skittles and linked arrows and the symbols '1, 2, 3' to the faces. In this example he also put a tick and said 'a tick shows us that six is a sharing number'. In the third example Kamrin moved away from pictorial narrative graphics and used iconic/symbolic. This is much more efficient for him as he understands the symbols he is using. He wrote nine, a question mark and a cross sign to show us nine is not a sharing number. His own symbols mean something to him and he understood the sharing concept through them. In this one session it was significant that Kamrin realised that there were quicker ways to represent his mathematical thinking and was able to use them.

Elizabeth, 4:9, chose the numerals four and 11 and used cubes. She said 'four is a sharing number but not 11'. She put a heart beside four to show us it is a sharing number and a sad face beside 11, to show that this was not a sharing number.

Evaluation

The examples of the children's representations on paper show a wide range of responses. All the children's marks were respected and accepted because the adults viewed them as intelligent responses. Many tasks teachers set children are not always fully understood by the child but they make their own sense of them. In this session because the children's choice of marks were accepted and analysed carefully, the teacher understood more about the children and their thinking.

In the last part of this session children shared their marks with each other. I wrote on the board the numerals zero to 15. I asked them to tell me what they had discovered about each one. I put a line beside the numerals that the children indicated shared equally and a cross beside the numbers that did not share. We also discussed other symbols that could be used instead of ticks and crosses, for example, Elizabeth's hearts and sad faces. They could see a pattern and some children were able to predict the numbers that shared. I introduced the class to the words 'odd' and 'even'. Their teacher asked them if their age was odd or even. This prompted a very lively and interesting discussion.

A zoo visit

THE MATHEMATICS   data handling
AGE   4-year-olds
CONTEXT   adult led group
FEATURES   range of strategies chosen

A class of 4- and 5-year-olds had just returned from a visit to a local zoo. Bursting with excited talk about their favourite animals I used this opportunity for some data handling. Each child chose their own way to put down three or four of their personal favourites and, armed with clipboards, they circulated among their friends checking one another's preference.

In the two examples below, their layout shows different understanding and each is appropriate for the individual. The children were free to use any means to record children's choices of animal: some chose to write individual names, some crosses and others used personal marks or tallies.

Bianca, 4:5, was interested in her personal favourites (Figure 9.6a). She wrote her name in the lower right-hand corner to show that she likes lions best and wrote two other children's names nearby, using the only available blank space. For someone else reading what she'd done, other children's choices are not clear but Bianca could recall what they had said.

9.6a   Bianca

9.6b   Tommy

Figure 9.6 The zoo – Bianca and Tommy

Tommy, (4:7): Tommy's layout allows easier reading of the number of responses for each animal since he decided to leave spaces between each animal (see Figure 9.6b).

Evaluation

At the end of the session we read and discussed the outcome of the information the children had collected. Because they had chosen their own means of recording their data, what they had done made good sense to the children. The children had used different ways of representing information, of recording their friends' choices and of layout. Our discussion provided valuable opportunities for constructive criticism and peer modelling that would provide support for future data handling.

Mathematics and literacy in role-play: the library van

THE MATHEMATICS	counting
	exploring letter and number symbols and amounts to pay
AGE	4- and 5-year-olds in school
CONTEXT	child-initiated role-play
FEATURES	play grounded within real experiences
	schemas
	mathematics, reading and writing within role-play
	exploring the way in which adults use writing and mathematical graphics in society

Our class of 4- and 5-year-old children visited one of the city libraries during a school 'Book Week'. Two weeks later we visited the mobile library van that came to the village, to change a box of books. The outcome of the second visit was totally unexpected. The space inside the van was very restricted and made a huge impression on the children: as they squeezed past each other and reached over to lift books from the shelves, they were exploring *enveloping* and *enclosing* schemas (see Chapter 3). This first-hand experience of a narrow confined space provided a stimulus for some rich play.

Child-initiated role-play

On their return to school, a group of eight children led by Marina (whose fifth birthday it was on that day) set about creating their own 'library van' (Figure 9.7). They used the big wooden blocks to create a narrow, enclosed space and Marina was their self-appointed 'chief librarian'.

Figure 9.7   Marina and the library van

Exploring mathematics and literacy through role play

During their play, the children arranged the books we had borrowed and pretended to stamp the date on them.

Marina and Frances were especially concerned about library fines and wrote a number of letters demanding huge fines for overdue books, using paper, envelopes and stamps from the office box. They used calculators to work out fines due on several books and real money to give change. Their calculations may not have been 'correct' but the children were using tools and resources in appropriate contexts and for purposes that made sense. They remonstrated with readers who argued about the amount of fines and Marina spent a long time on the phone complaining to borrowers about overdue books: clearly this aspect of libraries had left an impression.

Marie-Anne made a road safety poster which she attached to the front of the 'counter': in the city library she'd seen a road safety poster in the same position. The children filled in forms with titles of books and recommended particular books to 'parents', drawing on their own experience. They counted how many books each borrower took. One of the children instructed a 'new' borrower to fill in a form with her name and age in order to join the library.

Evaluation: using mathematical language

Observing this rich episode of role-play it was clear that the children had integrated their experiences and understanding from their visits to both libraries. The mathematics they used allowed them to explore language related to time: 'today', 'tomorrow', 'next week'. They referred to the duration of time books could be borrowed, advising 'bring it back soon', 'not too long'. They were able to relate 'too long' to the penalty of having to pay a fine and use the language of money including 'pounds, 'not enough' and change' when taking money. They counted and re-counted piles of books involving numbers up to fifty.

This play was grounded within the children's first-hand experiences. I had arranged the visits and the resources were always available, but the play itself was entirely the children's. Having the 'office box' (see Chapter 8), contributed to the development of the mathematics language and graphics and to writing: this allowed them to write within their play and to link their play directly to the two library visits.

Aaron and the train

The following case study is based on an article by Worthington, M. (1998) 'Solving problems together: emerging understanding', *MT* (The Journal of the Association of Teachers of Mathematics) Vol. 162, March.

THE MATHEMATICS	problem-solving
	using repeated addition as a basis for multiplication
AGE	4- to 6-year-olds in school
CONTEXT	teacher-led group
FEATURES	children's own line of enquiry
	differentiated learning

A school trip

One autumn term we took two classes by train to visit a covered market in a country town some distance away. Our focus was the stalls and the goods sold in the market: our aim was to use the visit as a stimulus for creating an 'autumn market' for our Harvest Festival in school. In the market I saw the potential for mathematics such as measuring ingredients to make biscuits, weighing bird seed into small bags, counting equal number of bulbs into flower pots and paying and giving change. However on our return it was clear that something unexpected had excited Aaron: the crowded train on which we'd travelled on our return journey had really impressed him.

Aaron's question

When we sat down to chat about our visit the following day Aaron remarked 'I bet there's a million seats in the train!' We discussed how we might find out the number of seats and the children offered several suggestions – the library, computer, headteacher – and then one child suggested we 'phone the train people'. Once I had helped Aaron dial the correct number for the local railway station he was able to ask for the information he wanted. Returning to the classroom, Aaron proudly announced that there were 75 seats in one carriage and seven carriages on the train on which we had travelled home. A group of ten children subsequently explored this question in a variety of ways that were appropriate to them.

Differentiated responses

- Several of the youngest children drew random shapes, some drew squiggles and one child drew a person: all were able to talk about Aaron's question and contribute ideas.
- Some children used iconic responses based on one-to-one correspondence. They drew circles or squares, sometimes checking their count by making a mark inside the shapes they had first drawn. One child used tallies and another used dots – also icons – to represent the seats.
- Several children drew either seats in a carriage or people on their seats – pictographic responses – including Aaron (Figure 9.8). He drew some seats with a thick pen and then counted them: finding he had only drawn 22 seats, he added more with a thinner pen in the remaining spaces, only stopping when there was no more space on his paper. He then counted the total number of seats and beneath his drawing he wrote '32 seats in the carriage' and then said 'it's full'.

Figure 9.8 Aaron's train

- Marina and Rachel chose ten scallop shells and into each they put two wooden beads (see Figure 9.9). By choosing their own ways of representing the problem and selecting their resources and their method, they explored repeated addition (early multiplication). The children connected their first-hand experience of the rail journey and simplified the question by reducing the number in each carriage. In this way the question was essentially the same (multiplication), but was matched to a level appropriate to them. They were then able to work out an answer for 'two people in each carriage and ten carriages' in a way that made real sense to them.

Figure 9.9 Marina and Rachel's scallop-shell train

- Frances used a range of responses and was the only child to use standard (symbolic) number symbols as a part of her working out. She began with a drawing of a carriage with seats. At the top she wrote '75 seats' although she only had room to draw seven seats in her carriage.

  Next Frances wrote '75', seven times (Figure 9.10a). In the lower half of the page she wrote 'There's five in the carriage. There's seven carriages'. Frances then collected a tray of plastic bricks and put five in each of seven trays and counted them. Returning to her paper she drew five people and wrote '35' beneath them: Frances had calculated 'seven lots of five'. By doing this she appeared to have been calculating (by repeated addition) with the '7' and the '5' of '75'. She may also have worked with the smaller numbers to help her understand how to then work on the problem using the larger numbers.

  Next Frances drew squares to represent the seats within the carriage (see Figure 9.10b). On re-counting she found that she had drawn 76 rather than 75 and crossed one out.

Insightful mathematics

I was impressed by Frances's ability to represent and check the 75 seats. Although I did not expect her to multiply 75 × 7, I wondered if she saw any possible next steps to solving this problem. Smiling, I remarked 'but there were seven carriages'. Frances looked puzzled: after pausing, she burst out excitedly

Figure 9.10 Frances and the train

'the photocopier!' She explained that she'd need 'six more'. When the six additional copies were laid out across the floor with her original drawing, the children were very excited to see the complete 'train' with equal numbers of seats in each carriage.

   This had been a tremendous insight for Frances and was also a very powerful representation for the children. Several children then offered to count all of the seats but they found this difficult: none was yet at a point where they could add or multiply seven lots of 75 as a calculation – something I was certainly not expecting them to do. Later that day I displayed all the children's written methods with Aaron's original question and during the following weeks children were often seen counting the different representations of seats or people and carriages displayed and talking about Frances's seven carriages with 75 seats in each.

Evaluation: developing personal skills

In this setting children had access to an extensive range of resources including the photocopier and telephone. Within a genuine context Aaron's question had provided many possible ways of exploring a challenging mathematical question that encouraged talk and the use of a range of practical and graphical responses. It also encouraged the children to meet challenges, to take risks and to be adaptive.

I think that we all know that those features of adult planned trips we intend children to focus on, are often not those which are the most significant to them. In this instance, interest in the train journey and the crowded carriage superseded our planned objectives of the goods for sale in the market. It can often be more worthwhile to extend children's own line of enquiry rather than exclusively following pre-planned adult mathematical activities.

Multiplying larger numbers

THE MATHEMATICS	multiplying larger numbers
	problem-solving
	working from known facts
AGE	7-year-olds
CONTEXT	whole class and small group
FEATURES	children need number fluency to tackle problems

For the main teaching part of this session there was a discussion on multiplication. The children had already been thinking of this in terms of an array. The children knew the two and ten times table. They displayed ways of showing two times three on the board. Jane made a set circle and put three dots on one side and three dots on the other side. James wrote the numerals two, four and six , counting up in twos from two.

Ayesha wrote 2 + 2 + 2 thus using a repeated addition model. I emphasised that there are also other ways of tackling multiplication especially with larger numbers. 'Obviously with two times three we can do it in our head, we know it, but what if we did not know it? Can you do the nine times table?' Two children said 'yes'. 'Can you do the 99 times table?' Everybody laughed and said 'no'. We had previously reviewed the ten times table and the 100 times table. The class agreed that the 100 times and the ten times table were easier than the two times table. I said that ten and 100 are 'friendly' numbers because they are easy to work with. I then said I thought 99 was a friendly number: there was puzzlement about this. Then Sophie asked 'is it because it is near a friendly number?' but she did not explain further. I wrote 99 times three on the board. 'How would we work out this? Could we use our knowledge of the 100 times table?' Thomas said that three times 100 is 300, then you take one away – which is 299. We considered that answer and I wrote it on the board. Tom had carefully thought this through but he needed to reflect further. The children did not respond but there appeared to be a lot of thinking. I asked them to consider the repeated addition model.

Dervla wrote '99 + 99 + 99' on the board and stopped. I wrote '100 + 100 + 100' and asked the children what the difference was between 99 and 100. We established that instead of taking just one away from 300 we needed to take three away. I then asked them what knowledge they would use to work out the nine times table.

The children worked alone or in pairs on multiplication calculations with larger numbers. Blank pieces of paper and pens were on the table so that if they needed, they could work out their ideas on paper.

Alison first chose two times 99 and then wrote, after much crossing out, '99 + 99 = 20098' (Figure 9.11). This is a logical way to write 298: children often write the hundreds like this. It shows that they are really being resourceful because they have never written numbers beyond 100. Alison then went on to choose 99 × 5. At first she used an iconic method of writing a stroke 99 times in a set ring and then she proceeded to carry on with this method for the other four lots of 99s. Alison found this method difficult with such large numbers because she often lost the count.

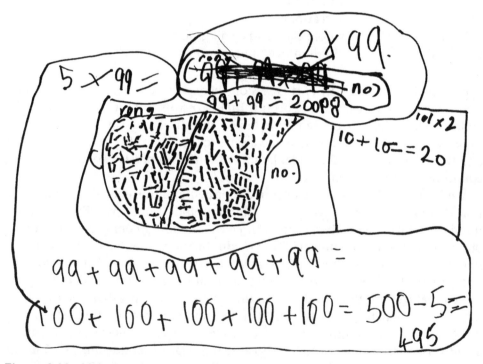

Figure 9.11 Multiplying larger numbers – Alison

In discussion with Alison I asked her if there was anything else she could put down to show 99. She seemed to be perplexed, so I said, 'think about repeated addition'. This seemed to be a 'eureka' moment for Alison because she had made the connection between counting out 99 five times and substituting that method for the symbol. Alison had moved through the iconic to the symbolic response which was much more efficient and less error prone. She used repeated addition for 99 and for 100 and was able to subtract the amount needed to come to her final answer.

Ben, 7:4, first chose to use repeated addition to work out nine times seven (see Figure 9.12) . He later abandoned that idea and used his mental skills because he did not need to see the numbers repeated. He easily moved on to the 99 times table.

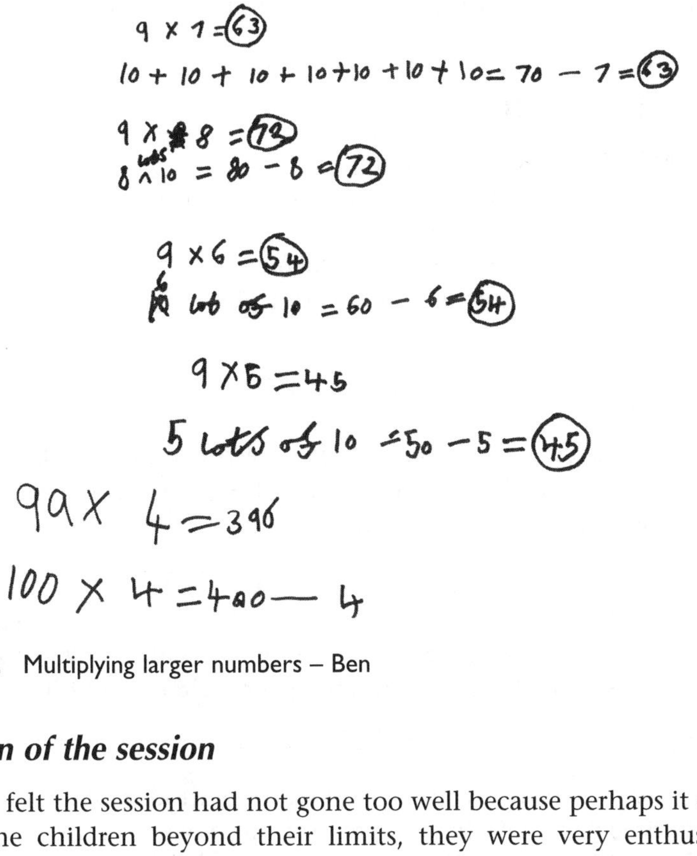

9 x 7 = 63

10 + 10 + 10 + 10 + 10 + 10 + 10 = 70 − 7 = 63

9 x 8 = 72
8 x 10 = 80 − 8 = 72

9 x 6 = 54
lots of 10 = 60 − 6 = 54

9 x 5 = 45

5 lots of 10 = 50 − 5 = 45

99 x 4 = 396

100 x 4 = 400 − 4

Figure 9.12 Multiplying larger numbers – Ben

Evaluation of the session

Although I felt the session had not gone too well because perhaps it challenged some of the children beyond their limits, they were very enthusiastic and shouted out how great they thought it was. I felt that a lot of the children did not apply their knowledge of multiplication, for example of repeated addition. Generally the children found working with multiples of 99 a difficult concept to grasp. Some of the children seemed to struggle to get the sense of larger numbers because they were only used to working with numbers up to a hundred. Counting back from larger numbers and knowing how to write the number was not an easy task for some of the children. The teacher found it a great assessment tool and remarked that the children concentrated very well on what they were doing. Many were working in the zone of proximal development (Vygotsky, 1978): this means they were thinking just beyond what they could do to form new thinking. Discussing their graphic responses on paper helped the children think again and change some of their representations.

I felt most of the children could work out the nine times table using what they already knew. The next steps that I would take are within the environment of the classroom. I would display larger numbers in context and put up a number line to 1,000. I would also introduce a variety of counting strategies within a thousand and beyond. Working within hundred squares beyond 100, for example 500 to 600, would extend the children's knowledge of numbers beyond 100. The children also need more opportunities to write larger numbers within lessons and independent learning opportunities, for example through role play.

Nectarines for a picnic

THE MATHEMATICS   problem-solving
                              using division and multiplication
AGE   7 and 8 years
CONTEXT   whole class with teacher
FEATURES   supporting taught strategies or 'jottings'

Real problems

The children in this class were about to go on a residential trip and were planning to stop on the way for a picnic. I used this as an opportunity to solve a problem relating to fruit they would take.

> Twenty six children are going to Salcombe. Mrs Hammond has brought some nectarines. There are three nectarines in each pack. How many packs will be needed so that 26 children can have one nectarine each?

The younger children used a variety of written methods that included drawing squares with three dots in each, then crossing out one dot in the final pack (this was 'one left over'): this was an iconic way of representing repeated addition.

Lewis wrote 'nine packs are needed for 26 children so 3 × 9 = 27 and one nectarine is going to be left over'. He had recognised the link between his repeated addition and multiplication and used both the '+' and the '×' symbols. Liza concluded by writing 'you have to have nine packs of three because you can't get packs of two'.

Grace and Chang counted in threes. Grace (Figure 9.13a) first considered dividing and then multiplying by three but appeared unsure of this. She then counted in threes and then put numbers from one to nine alongside. She worked out that there was one left over by counting back from her total of 27 nectarines to 26 (the number of children). This left her with 'R1'. Several other children wrote out a string of multiples of threes as in Chang's example (Figure 9.13b).

Finally, several children drew 'stick people' in threes as in Harriet's example (Figure 9.13c). Several children used a way to show that only two of the figures in the last group would be counted, as Harriet did.

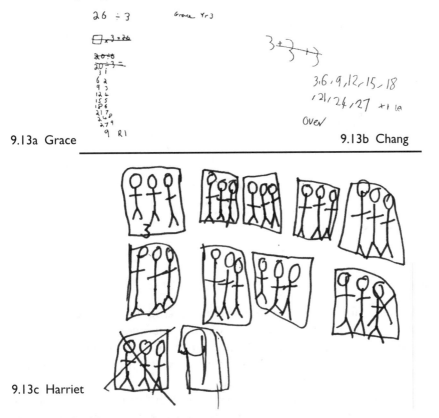

9.13a Grace

9.13b Chang

9.13c Harriet

Figure 9.13   Nectarines for a picnic

Ann used various methods to self-check (Figure 9.14). To begin with she wrote '3 × 26' but was clearly puzzled by this. She then wrote multiples of three followed by icons of boxes with three dots in each apart from the final box. Finally, she used an empty number line on which she counted in jumps of three to 27 and then back one to 26.

Evaluation

These children have incorporated methods they have learnt in the classroom but are able to select from a range those that make sense to them. Counting in multiples of three and using an empty number line have helped them to work on this problem in ways that make sense to them.

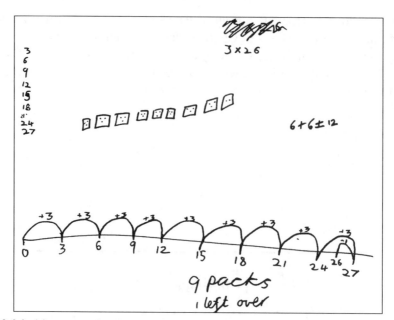

Figure 9.14 Nectarines for a picnic: Ann

Conclusion

In their play the availability of resources for making marks, and sensitive support, resulted in some rich and very relevant mathematical marks. The teacher-led examples were planned to be sufficiently open to allow children to decide how they would respond and, if they chose to use graphics, which written method would be the most appropriate.

These case studies show the range of marks – both informal and some more standard symbols – that they chose to use. They also show that these children were never afraid to use their ideas and to change direction if what they had started was not useful to them. Because each child had chosen their own graphics and ways of working they understood what they had done. The important point is that in supporting children's own marks, they will develop independent techniques to not only use standard methods of calculation but to understand the methods. As the range (children from 3 to 8 years) in this chapter also demonstrates, their early informal marks do develop over time to the standard 'school' mathematics.

In Chapter 10 we look at ways in which teachers may support children's understanding through effective assessment and modelling of written forms including the use of abstract symbols.

10

Developing Children's Written Methods

The process of assessing children's learning by looking closely at it and striving to understand it, is the only certain safeguard against children's failure, the only certain guarantee of children's progress and development. (Drummond, 1993, p. 10)

The assessment of children's mathematical representations on paper

Introduction

The assessment of children's mathematical marks on paper is as complex as the assessment of any part of children's learning. It is complex because we are actually trying to tune into children's thinking. Carr (2001) gives the analogy of an iceberg. Imagine an iceberg; what we can see of it is the same as what we see of children's minds and what we do not see of the iceberg and of children's minds is the far greater part.

Assessment is also difficult because we cannot be totally objective. In her observations of the children in her class, Paley had to rethink her original assumptions time and time again (Paley, 1981). However, as she scrutinised her transcripts she learned so much about the children and their thinking. She also said she was learning from the children.

Looking beyond the superficial helped us assess almost 700 samples of children's own mathematical marks that we had collected over a period of twelve years. If we look closely at children's own marks we uncover much more about their learning and how we might help them develop their understanding and our understanding. As Drummond states 'a desire to understand can enrich our powers of seeing' and as we looked over the variety and diversity of our samples we were intent and inspired. As a result of this we became more insightful, not only because we contemplated, revisited and revised but because we were driven by a deep motivation to understand. We saw new meanings in these marks that children make and we knew that this was the key to children's understanding of their mathematics. This will help them make the connections into more abstract forms of mathematics. If they are allowed this empowerment they will be active in their thinking of mathematics. The teacher's role in this assessment is crucial because this is what will inform her knowledge of where children might be in their thinking and how she can support and extend this.

Torrance (2001) identifies two kinds of assessment. In 'convergent assessment' the major emphasis is to work out if the learner can do a task that has been previously set, the features of which are detailed planning with no flexibility and the questions and the tasks are closed and restricted. This kind of assessment is teacher and curriculum dominated and the child's meaning is not taken into consideration. The other type of assessment highlighted by Torrance was 'divergent assessment' which focuses on the child's thinking rather than the teacher's agenda. It is about not taking a testing mode but a finding out and uncovering what the children know, so that the teacher can work from there. Torrance's study made the distinction between 'help' questions and 'testing' questions. In testing questions the children gave the answer that they thought the teacher wanted to hear. Some classrooms are dominated by testing questions. This makes it difficult for children to reveal what they know and work out their own meaning because they are too busy trying to work out what the teacher means. Testing questions do not help the process of learning. Testing questions look for right and wrong answers, they are intent on the product not the process.

If we only look at children's written mathematics in terms of right and wrong answers then it will tell us nothing to support the child in her understanding or aid the teacher in her teaching. If we believe that mathematics is not just a set of rules to remember then we must also respond to children's mathematical representations in a more flexible way. Divergent assessment is a more suitable tool to analyse children's mathematical marks than convergent assessment. It is, therefore, this kind of assessment we are proposing to analyse children's mathematical graphics and written methods.

Divergent assessment *(adapted from Torrance, 2001)*

Assessment which aims to discover what the learner knows, understands and can do. This is characterised by:

Practical implications
  1 Flexible planning or complex planning which incorporates alternatives.
  2 Open forms of recording e.g. children's own ways of recording their representations.
  3 An analysis of the learner and the curriculum from the point of view of the learner and the curriculum.
  4 Open questioning, open tasks and following children's self-initiated enquiries.
  5 Focus on aspects of the learners' work which will yield insights into their current understanding and help them think about their learning.
  6 Descriptive rather than negative judgements.
  7 Involvement of the pupil.
Theoretical implications
  8 A sociocultural view of learning (see Chapter 2).
  9 An intention to teach in the zone of proximal development (Vygotsky, 1986). This acknowledges children's partial knowledge (Athey, 1990).

10 A view of assessment as accomplished jointly by teacher, child and family.

The problem with worksheets

Mathematics worksheets have dominated and still do dominate many classrooms from pre-school upwards. They come in all shapes and forms from being teacher-made to workbook pages in published schemes. They are popular in nearly every country that can afford paper. The USA uses the words 'ditto sheet' and there they have special shops called 'Parent Teacher Stores' that are abundantly stocked with copy masters. Worksheets are seldom used in some European countries. Selinger argues that schemes have controlling material that decides what should happen next and what pathways of learning should be encouraged (Selinger, 1994). They generalise for all children and they provide a dependent culture for the teacher as well as the child. Anghileri is concerned that schemes often introduce set pro-cedures and formats (Anghileri, 2000). The children see calculations as 'rituals' which leads to little understanding of the signs and symbols used.

In our large-scale study of teachers' beliefs and practice concerning children's 'written' mathematics, we investigated how Early Years settings (3–8 years) sup-ported children's mathematical representations. We found that, of the sample of 273 responses, worksheets were used by 77 per cent of teachers. It is alarming to note that of these, 72 per cent of teachers with 3–5-year-olds used worksheets. Once children reach 6, 100 per cent of teachers in this study use worksheets (see Chapter 1).

Pound discusses the prolific use of worksheets in Early Years settings. She puts the view that 'worksheets are seen by many Early Years workers and parents as being an indication of a formal and somehow more productive educational process going on' (Pound, 1998, p. 13). She says that the suppliers suggest that amongst other things, the sheets may be used to introduce the child to record-ing. Pound strongly refutes this idea by saying that the restricted format of the worksheet does not encourage the children's own meaning but sets a 'tight jacket' which hampers their own drawing and writing (Pound, 1998). Fisher agrees with this: 'worksheets restrict what a young child can tell you about what they know and understand. If children devise their own ways of recording knowledge and understanding, then they will select ways which make sense to them and give all the information they want to share' (Fisher, 1996. p. 59).

Our questionnaire study of the way teachers supported early written mathe-matics and children's written methods revealed the reason that some teachers used worksheets was for assessment purposes. We would question the value of worksheets as an assessment tool because:

- the children have no ownership of the content of the worksheet
- they are also confined by layout; the child has to fit into the worksheet organ-isation and way of doing mathematics
- most worksheets have closed questions and only one answer; this may make the situation a testing one for young children

- worksheets do not tell what a child knows about mathematics and the way they are thinking
- worksheets do not reveal what the child can do but often what they cannot do
- young children can often get bewildered in finding the sense in a worksheet
- the match of worksheet to child is difficult and children can work below their actual ability
- worksheets that claim to be 'teaching' mathematics have sometimes very little mathematics in them to assess; for example, the typical worksheet with the numeral two in dots for the children to go over, accompanied by two large balloons to colour in. The child might respond to the teacher's question, how many balloons? This takes three seconds and the child traces around the numeral and colours the balloons. The colouring-in takes 20 minutes or more. The exercise is really colouring-in and not mathematics!

Importantly, both published and teacher-made worksheets prevent children from making meaning through their own early marks and written methods. They also deny them opportunities to translate from their early informal marks to later abstract symbols. As we have argued in Chapter 5, developing their own early marks and written methods is the way in which children become bi-numerate.

A worksheet

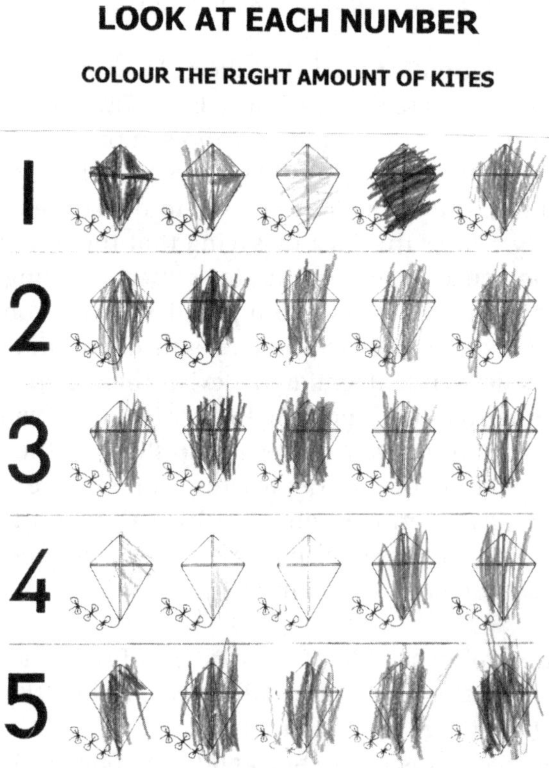

LOOK AT EACH NUMBER

COLOUR THE RIGHT AMOUNT OF KITES

Figure 10.1 Susie's worksheet

Figure 10.1 is an example of a worksheet done by Susie, a 4-year-old in a reception class (Carruthers, 1997). This was Susie's second week in school. What can we assess about Susie's knowledge of mathematics from this worksheet? This worksheet was given to a group of children as a 'holding task' while the teacher worked with another small group of children. The teacher shared his concern with us, over the child's response to this task. We might ask ourselves if the child understood the task? If we presume that she did understand, then we could say she got it wrong. If you look, Susie coloured in all the kites. She started colouring in neatly but by the end we could deduce she got bored. The task's main objective was counting to five but the child did more colouring than counting. If we take Susie's mathematics from the evidence of the worksheet, then our assessment would be that she could not count quantities to five.

What did the child say about the mathematics she did in the worksheet? As she rushed out of school, into the backseat of the car, her mother enquired about this worksheet that Susie clutched. Susie said with a frown on her face 'I got it wrong'. Her first taste of written school mathematics was negative. When Susie was at home, before she started school, she rode on the highway of curiosity where there were no right or wrong answers: she was accepted into the mathematics world of home. She used numerals daily in meaningful contexts. She counted with her mum, dad and sister. She knew the function of numbers in many contexts, e.g. time, measurement and money. She liked to count out apples into a bag when she went shopping with her mum. She also liked to share things, like sweets between people. She has a sense of fairness. If there were any left over she suggested that everybody have a half each. She was therefore coming to understand fractions through natural problem-solving. She liked to play a game with ages: for example, she said 'when I am seven Daddy will be forty-three'. She enjoyed finding out about larger numbers and counting up to 100 and beyond. Her mother told me that one of their last conversations together before Susie started school was about infinity. Susie had posed the question, 'What is the last number?'

Susie's home mathematics is in sharp contrast to the worksheet she had to complete at school. The worksheet told us little about Susie's number knowledge. Perhaps the teacher could have asked Susie's group an open question for initial assessment. If Susie had been given the opportunity to make her own marks she would have made more sense of them. It is vital to ask parents and carers about the mathematics children do at home. There is an increasing number of studies that show there is great discrepancy between the mathematics of school and home. Many young children come to school with a sense of mathematics which is never truly uncovered by their first teacher (Aubrey, 1994b; MacNamara, 1992).

In our study of teachers' beliefs and practice, some teachers responded with statements that they do not use worksheets but they wrote on blank pages in the children's mathematics books for them to fill in. This, they said, was very time-consuming but suited their purpose more than worksheets. Using blank paper in this way has the same pitfalls as worksheets but may be more personal to the class and the curriculum objectives. This kind of recording lies in the same category as teacher-made worksheets. We would argue that this again does not give a true account of where the children are in their understanding of written mathematics.

From our own experience of teaching every age group in the Early Years, children are pleased and eager to share their own mathematics. This is partly because we are interested in what they have to say. It is difficult to get excited about a worksheet! It does not belong to the child, there is only one way to do it: the worksheet way. We would like also to state that just as it is difficult to get away from using worksheets when using them is part of the school's culture, we also have used worksheets in the past because at that time we knew of no better alternative.

From our survey, the use of worksheets in mathematics seem prolific. Yet there are many who question their quality in supporting the young learner including Fisher (1996), Pound (1999), Anghileri (2000) and Selinger (1994). We will never see the demise of worksheets in mathematics teaching if practitioners do not support children's own ways of putting their mathematics on paper.

Assessing samples of children's own mathematics

What assessment of children's own written mathematics needs to recognise

The context

It is important to know how a piece of writing evolved since this gives us a clearer understanding of the focus the child might be having when making the marks. This might tell us about how the child acts in certain contexts. A sample of writing taken in a free-flow play situation may appear very different to a teacher-directed task or a teacher-led task. For example, does the child choose to use mathematical marks if not directed or supported in some way by the teacher? When children are 3 years old or younger they may seldom choose to write or draw anything mathematical. When they do, we might be able to see some connections they are making. For a child of 3, the significance may be that they now choose to represent their mathematics on paper and this may mean that they understand mathematics can be written down. They can translate what they think on paper: this development cannot be underestimated. It is like their first step or spoken word and, although it is not as noticeable, it represents a huge sign that they are aware of this written form of mathematical communication.

What the child said

Listening to what children say about their marks is important because what we think they are writing is not always what they mean. Sometimes children talk to themselves or others as they write and you may be fortunate enough to catch these moments. At other times it is useful to say 'can you tell me about this?' This helps to get an accurate connection between their thinking and their graphics. It is better to ask the child as soon as possible after they have finished recording. At other times the children change the meaning of their marks completely. Sometimes they forget some of the details if there is too much time between recording and explaining what they have done. Some children choose not to say anything about their mathematics on paper and this should be respected. This usually happens with younger children and less confident older children. When they do feel confident and choose to speak then it is an important growth point. It shows they are beginning to explain their thinking and this reinforces their own ideas. Building up this relationship with the child leads to extended dialogues. Children appreciate this one-to-one attention in an atmosphere that is non-threatening.

What the child did
Looking at children's actions tells us their intentions through certain kinds of graphics, usually in schemas, dynamic and action representations. We have found children who use any of these three are in a highly experimental stage and when they visit new concepts they revisit these features.

The mathematics
In what mathematics is the child engaged? This could be any aspect of number or calculations, measurement, space and shape, problem-solving or data handling.

Parents' and carers' comments
Parents play a vital part in this assessment. They will be interested in their own children's representations and may be able to add comments about what they do at home. Samples of children's home maths adds to the profile and gives us a more holistic view of the child's understanding.

Assessment
We recommend a positive model of assessment. Every child's mathematical marks are treated as 'intelligent responses' (Pound, 1999). Good-quality assessment takes time to work out and quality assessment of children's learning goes beyond the superficial: it probes further.

All of the above help to build up a picture to make a real and useful assessment of children's mathematical thinking through their own representations.

The next step
The next question is how are we going to develop and support the children's own mathematics. By working through the above points closely, we have now gathered useful information to support and develop the child's understanding. At this stage we need to consider carefully what the child needs, to continue their development so we can plan accordingly. Figure 10.2 is a model to show the cycle of assessment planning and teaching.

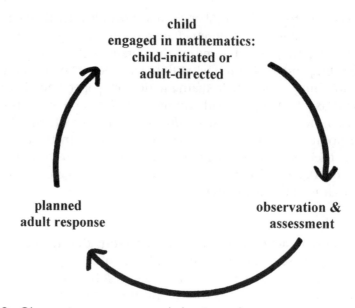

Figure 10.2 Observation, assessment and planning cycle

Figure 10.2 illustrates the way in which observations can be used to inform teaching that supports deep levels of learning (Worthington and Murchison, 1997).

Assessment needs to be manageable

Teachers cannot do this kind of assessment for every piece of written mathematics, all the time. It may be possible to assess all pieces of graphics from young children, from about the age of 3 or 4, as they seem not to be so prolific in their mark-making. Young children may be representing mathematics in multi-model forms, for example through schemas, art forms, construction and technology (see Chapter 6). They also produce less at one time but their marks may be more complicated and for some teachers less easy to decipher. The explanations in Chapters 2, 3, and 6 may have helped explain some of these very early mathematical marks and representations.

Looking at and assessing children's graphical representations with another adult gives a more objective assessment of the marks. We also learn how another person views the children's graphics and learn together: our understanding expands upwards and outwards. Often another adult aids and challenges our thinking and the more we do this, the more proficient we become. We find ourselves assessing more and more samples quite naturally. Some you will select for in-depth analysis, others you might put in a file for children to look back at. Children may want to take them home and, of course, photocopying is useful. We have found it particularly helpful to look at what appears to be 'growth points' for the child: this may be something that they have not done previously. In other examples you may find the child has focused on more complex thinking than before.

Examples of assessment of children's mathematics

We have selected three example of children's mathematics to discuss. The samples are from school settings and, like all the samples we have collected, they differ from each other. No two pieces of children's thinking on paper are the same because no two children's minds are the same: we all have different experiences to form our thinking. Think of snowflakes – each has a different pattern, and all are so beautiful. It is the same with children's own mathematics on paper: as the children get older they slowly refine their skills to more efficient strategies and integrate the standard forms of symbols on paper with understanding.

The first sample (Figure 10.3) is provided as an example of an assessment form with all the relevant sections we have discussed previously (Figure 10.4).

Figure 10.3 Amelie's dice game

Whole-class assessment

A very open question is useful for whole-class assessment purposes. An open question is much more personal and infinite compared to an 'open-ended' question which seems in some respects to have an end. Take the question 'how many ways can you make 20?' This may show us how many ways a child can make 20 but it does not show us what else a child knows. The question itself is a very useful investigation-type question and can show us many aspects of a child's thinking, but we

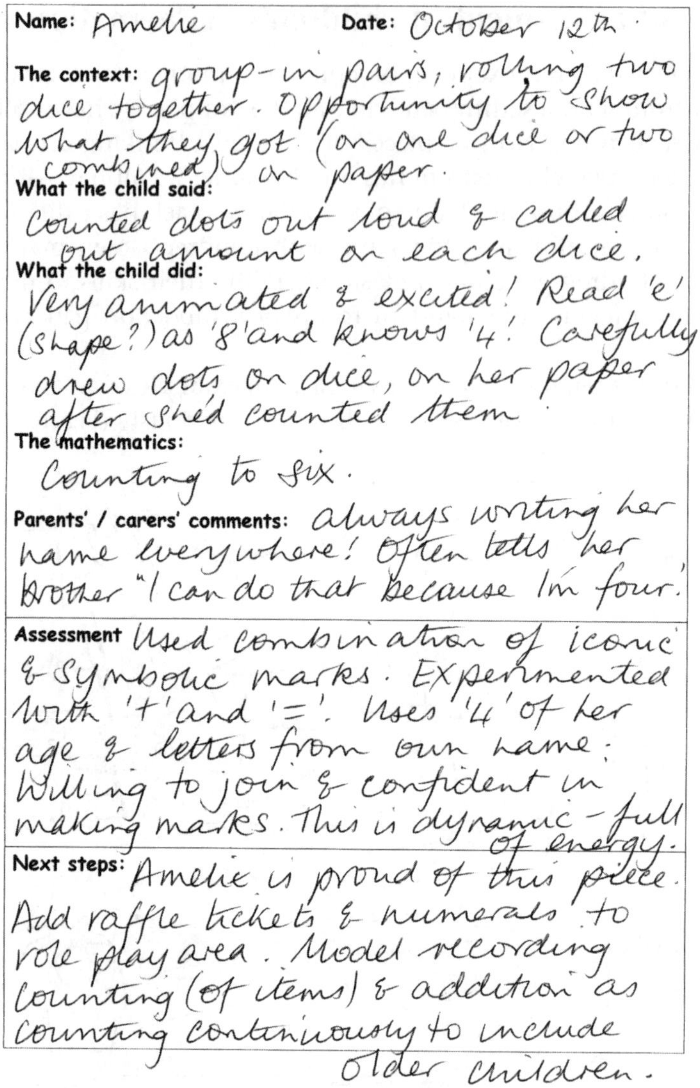

Name: Amelie   Date: October 12th.

The context: group-in pairs, rolling two
dice together. Opportunity to show
what they got (on one dice or two
combined) on paper.

What the child said:
Counted dots out loud & called
out amount on each dice.

What the child did:
Very animated & excited! Read 'e'
(shape?) as '8' and knows '4'. Carefully
drew dots on dice, on her paper
after she'd counted them.

The mathematics:
Counting to six.

Parents' / carers' comments: always writing her
name everywhere! Often tells her
brother "I can do that because I'm four."

Assessment Used combination of iconic
& symbolic marks. Experimented
with '+' and '='. Uses '4' of her
age & letters from own name.
Willing to join & confident in
making marks. This is dynamic - full
of energy.

Next steps: Amelie is proud of this piece.
Add raffle tickets & numerals to
role play area. Model recording
counting (of items) & addition as
counting continuously to include
older children.

Figure 10.4 Assessment form

limit knowing what the child wants to tell us she knows about mathematics. Open
questions are useful to use when you actually do not know what the children
know. This might happen at the beginning of a new school year or when you
begin a new mathematics topic. The following assessment on a child's mathematical marks came from a class who had been asked by the teacher in the second
week of school 'What do you know about numbers?' She wanted to know what
they knew about numbers before she planned her teaching sessions and her learning environment. The teacher encouraged children to choose what they needed.
In this example Jason had chosen to use a combination of materials (see Figure
10.5). As well as writing materials, he had chosen circular stickers to represent a
quantity and cut out paper numerals for the number 37.

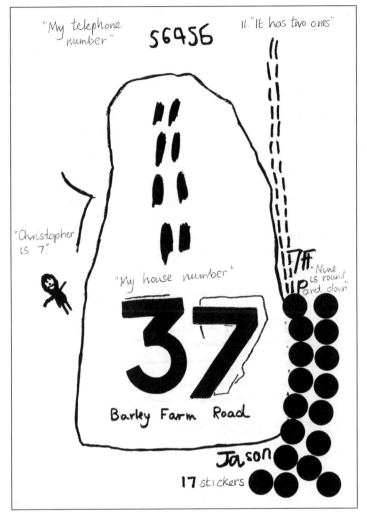

Figure 10.5 Jason's numbers

Name: Jason Green   Date: September 15   Age: 4 years 11 months.
Context: Whole-class assessment; put down anything you know about numbers.
What the child said: Jason was eager to tell me his telephone number; his brother's age; his house number and his address. He was also interested in the features of some numerals, 'Nine is round and down' 'Eleven has two ones' (this has also connections to his current schema, looking at parallel vertical lines).
What the child did: Jason selected materials he wanted to use. He stuck on 17 stickers and counted them and wrote 17 beside the 17 stickers. He used the cut-out numerals to make his door number, 37. The two parallel vertical lines seemed to fascinate him and he repeated these over and over again.
The mathematics: Counting beyond ten; representing numbers using standard symbols; linking quantity to a numeral accurately.

Parent/carer's comment: At home Jason's mum says he likes to draw and he is very interested in numbers. He likes to play number games like 'Snakes and Ladders'.

Assessment: Jason already knows that numbers can be represented in a variety of ways and that they have a purpose. He knows his personal numbers – his brother's age, and his own door number, address and telephone number. He can count beyond ten and represent this both pictorially and using standard symbols. He visually recognises numbers beyond 20 and can represent his door number. Jason has shown confidence and a willingness to communicate orally his representations of numerals on paper.

The next step: Jason may be willing to use operations on numbers and this will be presented to him in small group sessions. He is willing to use all sorts of materials and the writing and technology areas will interest him. Discussions focusing on using larger numbers will invite his interest. I will add some art straws in the construction area to support his interest in parallel vertical lines. I must look out a story about ladders, maybe one about fire engines.

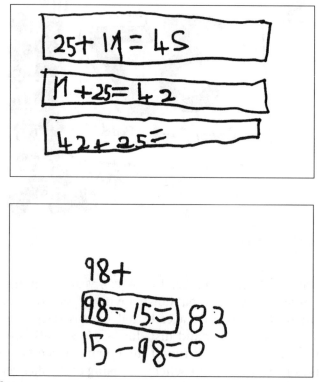

Figure 10.6 Super-zero

Name: Joel Nash   **Date:** 17 June   **Age:** 7 years 2 months
Context: whole class – mixed ages of 7 and 8 years. Joel has only been in our school for a few weeks and is very anxious about using writing of any sort, including mathematics, 'correct'. However, today he tackled the first question

and putting some of his working out on paper encouraged him to experiment.
What the child said: After he had worked out the answer to the first addition
question he reversed the calculation and compared the answers from both.
When he showed me he explained that he liked 'doing sums both ways' and
that he was going to do the same thing with a subtraction question. After
working out '98 −15 = ' he wrote '15 −98 = ' and paused, looking puzzled. I asked
him how he would work this out. He looked around and, pointing to the
number line on the table, said that he would use this. Joel began by counting
down from fifteen and then stopped at nought. Moving his finger beyond the
zero he said excitedly, 'Super-zero! Zero, zero, zero!'
What the child did: Joel tried to reverse the subtraction calculation in the same
way that he had done with the addition sum. His idea of using the number line
to count down led him into the area of negative numbers.
The mathematics: addition and subtraction; commutativity; negative numbers.
Parent/carer's comment: Joel's dad said that he often gives the family calculations to work out during supper and shows his own mental calculation skills
through doing this. Number bonds are his current favourite. He also spends a lot
of his spare time with a puzzle book he was given for his birthday, which includes
many number puzzles. Joel's family recognises that he had been anxious in his
previous school where the emphasis had been on correct spelling and right
answers rather than his thinking. They are pleased that he has begun to explore
mathematical ideas in his new class – he appears to feel happier at school now.
Assessment: trying to reverse the subtraction calculation led to the area of negative numbers and his description of 'super-zero' was quite an insight of the move
below zero. Joel has not worked with negative numbers. We discussed what he
had done at the end of the lesson and many of the children were so intrigued by
his term for moving into negative numbers that they burst into applause.
The next step: put up both a vertical and horizontal number line with negative
numbers – this will provide a useful resource for Joel to explore some more subtraction sums in reverse. I will also borrow a fridge thermometer when we make
some ice in the fridge in science next week and make sure Joel's group do this.

Having a dialogue with a child is not always easy, yet it is crucial in helping children discuss their mathematics. To find out about children's representations one
needs to ask them about it. If the atmosphere and culture of the classroom and
the school is a listening one, children will get more articulate about their mathematics. The importance of thinking and language is well documented (Brissenden, 1988; Durkin and Shire, 1991).

Modelling mathematics

One of the problems is that the language used in official documents is not
explicit about the difference between the terms 'modelling' and 'examples'. In
discussion with teachers we have found that modelling is usually interpreted as

'giving direct examples'. Teachers certainly need to introduce a variety of symbols and ways of recording as children grow and develop their understanding, but our evidence is that young children treat examples as something that we expect them to use. Lee proposes that examples 'show learners a way ... that frequently would be referred to as *the* way' (Lee, 2000. p. 28).

An example of 'an example'
In the nursery, a teacher provided paper for the children to represent the number of (sweet) eggs they had each put on the cakes they'd made. The children were hesitant and the teacher drew her own example of a bird's nest (cake) on a sheet of paper. She then counted four eggs on one of the cakes on the plate and drew four ovals in her drawing of a nest.

Following her example, every child in the group drew a nest, counted the eggs on their cake and drew some eggs on their drawing of a nest.

The children had all represented the number of eggs in exactly the same way in which the teacher had done. Clearly the teacher intended to support the children by providing an example of recording. However, as Lee (2000) has argued, examples are also 'restrictive'. The message that the children took from the teacher's example was that this was *the* way they should represent the number of eggs on their cake. Alternative ways they might have chosen (dots, other marks, numerals or their own approximations of numerals) were not used.

This had been our experience in our own classrooms and was a difficulty we recognised. We knew that we needed gradually to introduce children to standard symbols and various layouts but when we provided an example at the beginning of a lesson – intending to offer one possible way – the children copied exactly what we had done with limited understanding. It could be argued that this is a positive outcome since the children incorporated standard symbols and ways of working into what they did. However, rather than helping them, we were repeatedly confronted with children who were confused and could not apply what they had been introduced to in other contexts.

Examples or modelling?

To illustrate the ways in which children use teachers' examples and learn from teacher-modelling, one of us explored this question in a class we were visiting. The children were 5 years old and in their second term at school.

I divided the class into two, splitting each of the four ability groups so that the two halves of the class were balanced:

- Group 1: teacher providing explicit examples of ways of calculating on whiteboard. I then asked to 'put down on paper' what they had found out.

- Group 2: discussion of possible ways of representing calculation; children offering their own suggestions, some based on previous teacher-modelling and some children's original ideas. The children's different suggestions were valued and they were asked to 'put something down on paper' to show what they had found out.

For the purpose of our research, I taught each group in turn whilst the other group was engaged in choices of their own in the class writing area. The numbers I used were identical for both groups and I explained what I was doing using identical language. Whilst the first group watched as I drew teddies and wrote a standard horizontal calculation, I made sure that none of the children in the second group heard what we discussed or saw what I put on the whiteboard. The main part of the lesson focused on adding small quantities.

Group 1 – teacher example

Taking three teddies from the bag I put them beneath the whiteboard in a row and subsequently took two more teddies from the bag. We talked about what I had done and then I drew three teddies on the flip chart followed by the word 'and', then drew two more teddies. I used the words 'three bears and two more bears' and 'how many bears are there altogether?' I asked several children how we might find out and all chose to count the bears in the two sets continuously, counting five in response to my question.

Beneath my drawing of the bears I wrote the standard '3 + 2 = 5' calculation and explained this was another way of putting down 'three bears and five bears' and showing 'how many altogether'. I then asked two of the children to choose a small number of toys. Taking the four bears chosen by one child and the two chosen by the other, I asked them to 'find out how many bears there are altogether and put something down on paper' to show what they'd found out.

Outcome of Group 1

The children all drew bears and wrote a standard calculation beneath their drawing. Of the nine children I'd worked with, two had represented the question in the same way I had and arrived at the correct answer. James was the only child who had not copied my example. He had been more independent and had combined drawings of bears, words and the addition sign: he clearly understood what he had done and had arrived at a total of six bears.

The remaining six children experienced a range of difficulties – with their interpretation of the symbols, with what they were doing or why they had written certain numbers. Three children who had written the 'right' answer of '6' were confused by their use of standard symbols.

Leo read '4 + 2 = 6' as '4 plus 2 is 6': he was unable to explain what 'plus' meant and said that that the '=' symbol meant 'equals – or plus – I think'.

Marie explained that to arrive at her answer she 'guessed'. She said that the '=' sign meant 'adds' but then looking at where she'd written '2 + 4 = 6' she said 'Oh! But 4 plus 6 doesn't add!' Seeing another abstract sign (=) she guessed that this also meant add. Marie knew that '+' could mean add, explaining 'plusses – it's another of bears, more bears'.

Although the four bears and two bears were sitting in front of the children, Peter had drawn only four bears. Beneath his drawing he had written '3 + 2 = 5' (copied from my example on the flip chart). I asked 'Can you tell me what you found out?' but he looked very puzzled. Although he read '3 + 2 is 5' he was unable to say what the '=' sign might mean and could not relate his drawings to his standard calculation or to the six toys sitting in front of him. Clearly, using my example had really confused Peter.

The examples in Figure 10.7 show Louisa, John and Emily's confusion:

Figure 10.7 Louisa, John and Emily (example of adding teddies – following teacher modelling)

Louisa started as I had done in my example, by drawing the bears. She had written '5 + 6 = 10' and when I asked her to tell me what she had found out, she quickly crossed out the '= 10' and wrote '7' by the 6' then looking at the bears she'd drawn, she counted them all and wrote '6' at the end. Her written calculation had not matched her drawing so she altered the total to match the drawing that she trusted (Figure 10.7a).

John read 'one and' and then turned to me, looking confused. We counted the two bears and the four bears in front of him together but he was unable to relate what he had done to the bears he saw (Figure 10.7b).

Emily had drawn the correct number of bears but had also copied my example of '3 + 2 = 5' (Figure 10.7c). She was not able to explain the calculation and did not know what they symbols '+' and '=' meant, explaining 'I saw them on the board'. She read the string of numbers but had no idea what they related to other than saying 'you have to count'.

The problems experienced by these children illustrate some of the difficulties children experience when they use examples – including standard symbols – shown by their teacher and which they do not understand. They want to comply and interpret the request to 'put something down to show' as meaning 'do what I have just shown you'. This leads to compliance and conformity without understanding.

It is clear that following the teacher's example without understanding leads to confusion: if children continue in this way, even when they sometimes get 'right' answers, their difficulties are compounded. They also learn that they should not attempt to work things out in ways which might make sense to them since the teacher is looking for them to all use the same written method. If they use the teacher's method, formula or layout without understanding, many children come to learn that mathematics often does not make sense. A chasm has then been created between their informal mathematical understanding and standard 'school' mathematics that will be very difficult to bridge.

Group 2 – children's ideas based on previous modelling

I asked if any of the children had an idea of how they might 'put their ideas down on paper'. Responses included suggestions of 'drawing how many bears', 'putting tallies', 'numbers', 'shapes', 'letters' (words) and 'numbers'. The child who suggested 'shapes' explained she might put a square for each bear (iconic representation).

All of the eight children in this group understood what they had done, could explain their marks and all had the correct answer. Because they had chosen their own written method what they had done made sense to them. Only one child had made use of the standard '+' symbol but he was able to explain 'and – you count them all together', which as a method of addition is common at this stage. No child had used the standard equals sign.

Darrel used tallies to represent the bears, writing 'll lll and tez zixs all to gev'(' 2 3 and there's six all together').

William had worked it out mentally, writing '2 add 4 is 6'

Connor and Jake had drawn the bears. Connor used the word 'and' between the two sets then wrote '6 all together' beneath his drawing. Jake used the '+' symbol between the two sets of bears and then wrote the numbers '2' and '4' beneath each set, finally writing '6' beneath his drawing.

Catherine had referred to 'shapes' when we'd discussed what might be helpful. She drew six squares and separated them with a vertical line into two sets of two and four to represent the bears she was adding.

10.8a Brendon

10.8b Scarlett

10.8c Alice

Figure 10.8 Scarlett, Brendon and Alice (following teacher-modelling)

Scarlett also used shapes to represent the bears but to indicate the two different sets, she drew two circles and four squares (Figure 10.8b). Counting continuously, she then wrote the total of '6' beneath and finally she added to her circles and squares, turning them into balls and presents (using icons to stand for the bears).

Brendon was clear that he needed to count all the bears in front of him. Beginning in the centre of the paper and moving to the left, he wrote a number for each bear as he counted. Although not yet very secure in his knowledge of standard written numerals, he was able to self-correct and read what he had done as '1, 2, 3, 4, 5, 6 bears' (Figure 10.8a).

Alice drew the six bears and then counted them, adding a numeral to each in turn to arrive at her total (Figure 10.8c).

Outcome of Group 2

Looking at the written methods these eight children chose and talking to them, it is clear how much they understood about what they were doing and that this early addition made personal sense. The methods chosen by the children in the second group contrast sharply with those from the group which copied my example.

These findings point to the value of teacher-modelling in real contexts throughout the week, rather than at the beginning of a mathematics lesson or group session. When we model written mathematics, we try to ensure that the mathematics we use is for real purposes and real people – because someone needs to know the outcome. In the models we provide, we focus on aspects we wanted to introduce to the children such as use of a particular symbol or a clear way of setting out some data. In this way the children have access to a growing bank of written methods, ways of representing, layout and meaning of symbols and can select those that are most appropriate for their current stage of development.

In the following section we explore our research into the effects of teacher-modelling in a class of 5- and 6-year-olds that one of us visited on several occasions.

Modelling: children develop their mathematical representations

In another study I focused on modelling different aspects of data handling during short fortnightly visits to the school. I modelled a number of aspects including layout, and analysing data. Following my final visit we compared the children's first pieces of data handling with their final one to assess any gains. Of the 12 children who were present for both lessons, ten showed that they had used aspects that I had modelled with them. During the final lesson I had not referred to any of the features I had modelled in the previous two months. When comparing the two samples, 25 per cent of the children had included all three significant aspects I had modelled in their own data handling; a further 25 per cent had improved on two aspects and the remaining children had included one aspect. The two examples below from Ashley illustrate this development (Figure 10.9a and b).

In the first, Ashley collected responses from his friends and used tallies to mark their choices: the writing in this example is an account of three things he likes to do. In the second example Ashley's work shows that he incorporated some features that I had modelled during the term.

Lee (2000, p. 29) suggests that in contrast 'one feature of the modelling process is that it is intended to give an idea of the *quality of a way of working*, rather than a royal road to follow' (italics added). Modelling can be summarised with the following key points (based on Lee, 2000):

- When an adult models a way of representing some mathematics on paper, she can also model her thinking processes.
- The quality or way of representing the mathematics needs to be one that the children *themselves* can use if they choose.
- A model need not necessarily be finished or 'perfect'. This will allow children to reflect on difficult aspects.
- It must be able to be changed by learners to suit their own purposes.

Using models therefore allows children to take ownership of their mathematics whilst still offering them support. It is a way of introducing specific use of symbols within contexts that are real to the children that they may use if they understand them. It permits children to choose ways of representing that match their current ways of thinking and development, and their visual imagery. As Wray, Bloom and Hall suggest, children need to see others using literacies to 'demonstrate when it is used, how it is used, where it is used and what it is' (Wray, Bloom and Hall, 1989, p. 66).

Modelling in literacy – and mathematics

Modelling allows children to move from what they can achieve alone to what they can achieve with a more 'knowledgeable other' as Vygotsky identified in his 'zone of proximal development' (Vygotsky, 1978).

Barratt-Pugh and Rohl also emphasise the way in which modelling allows adults a means of introducing a variety of genres (Barratt-Pugh and Rohl, 2000). Different genres of mathematics in the Early Years can include lists, representing data, recipes (quantities and measures) or a means of totalling money spent for

Figure 10.9 Data handling (following examples)

a picnic (addition). Modelling these can extend children's repertoire and support their understanding since what they choose to do is something they understand. Discussing children's different mathematical graphics at the end of either a group or class lesson means that peer-modelling extends what the teacher modelled: for the children it may also help to reinforce the fact that there are many ways of representing mathematics. Significantly, it will also confirm that the teacher really does value the personal sense individuals make through their chosen ways of mathematical graphics.

Modelling mathematical symbols and signs

Graves argues that modelling opportunities 'are infinite' and that into the teacher's modelling, concepts are built (Graves, 1983). In mathematics modelling ways of recording will include specific symbols used in context and allow for discussion about alternative ways of representing the same meaning. We have shown how modelling mathematics allows children to choose from a variety of ways of representing meaning: these may include standard, abstract symbols when appropriate. By doing this the teacher can help children make links between their own (non-standard) marks and symbols (their first mathematical language) and the standard mathematics (or second language).

The examples of the subtraction (of beans) in Chapter 6 show the range of representation within a group of children and the different levels of symbol-use that the children appropriated. As we have seen, a positive classroom culture can encourage them to draw on a range of models for their own purposes so that children will do this with confidence. Heuvel-Panhuizen proposes that to help children move between their informal and formal levels, 'models have to shift from a "model of" a particular situation to a "model for" all kinds of other, but equivalent situations' (Heuvel-Panhuizen, 2001, p. 52).

In terms of writing stories, Graves argues that modelling is especially useful to explore *what* you have chosen to do and *why* (Graves, 1983). When a teacher models the use of the standard sign for 'take away' or subtraction, it is helpful if the children can see not only *what* is being written as in the example '–', but also *why*. Provided the classroom culture supports co-construction of meaning, those who are ready to relate the abstract symbol to their own ways of representing 'take away' will be moving towards the use of more standard forms.

Modelling has a role in what is termed 'progressive mathematisation' which distinguishes the Dutch 'Realistic Mathematics' or REM approach. This, Beishuizen argues, is important 'in the development of abstract thinking on different levels' (Beishuizen, 2001, p. 130). Whilst we do not claim to be using the REM approach, supporting children's mathematics through their early marks and own written methods may share some similarities in its process with Freudenthal's principles. We argue that co-constructing and negotiating meaning together is supported by a range of increasingly abstract models. These provide children with 'guided' opportunities 'to "reinvent" mathematics by doing it within a process of "progressive mathematisation"' (Anghileri, 2001, p. 34).

In the next chapter we consider a variety of ways in which teachers can involve parents and families in their young children's developing mathematics and share their children's excitement of learning.

11

Involving Parents and Families

Children's first and continuing educators

*Take an inquisitive three year old who needs to help you with every-
thing you do. He enjoys emptying your cupboards and likes to stack
pots and pans. He lines up the cutlery as you lay the table and when
out shopping he likes to put items in the trolley and then takes them
out again. When hanging out washing he insists that he is in charge
of the pegs and only gives them to you one at a time.*

*At four years he is in charge of the balance scales when you are
trying to weigh out ingredients to bake a cake. He has to dial the
numbers for all your phone calls and takes full responsibility for
sharing out the sweets. And he counts everything from the cars in the
street to the peas on his plate.*

*These everyday experiences are the foundation stones of children's
early numeracy and as parents we are our children's first and continuing educators. (Mills, 2002, p. 1)*

Introduction

During our long careers as teachers we have worked alongside parents as much
as constraints of external factors beyond our control could permit. As teachers
we value true collaboration with parents. Throughout this book we refer to
parents, carers and families: the relevance of the home and the family is richly
and finely threaded throughout. As Mills reminds us, no one knows the child
like his or her family (Mills, 2002). We, therefore, do not see this chapter as a
discrete section but as building on what we have already written.

In this chapter we draw on four studies we have made:

1 'The Sovay study': a case study of a child's number development from 22 to
  42 months.
2 A study of 'mathematics at home' based on questionnaires and diaries over
  seven days, completed by 31 mothers and fathers of children aged 4–6 years
  in one class.
3 A collaborative 'parents' mathematics group' during which we explored
  mathematical schemas together. Some parents in this group kept diaries of
  their 4–6-year-old children's mathematical schemas.

4 A 'holiday study' that involved parents of a class of 7–8-year-olds keeping
   diaries of their children's mathematical interests outside school.

These four pieces of research provided evidence of children's mathematical
interests, family mathematical 'events' (and parents' perceptions about children's mathematics (Barton, 1994).

The home is a rich learning environment

Before the child enters her first Early Years setting, her home has provided a meaningful environment where mathematics is used in real contexts. Children have
seen the purpose of mathematics woven through the day. They know the importance adults attach to mathematical areas such as time. 'I am going to be late, it is
nearly seven o'clock and I am not ready yet.' In each home there may be different
cultural considerations about the areas of mathematics that are used. In Chapter
2 we discussed some examples of these cultural differences. Children will see
mathematics written down for different purposes. This written mathematics is not
usually the formal abstract symbolism of school traditional approaches but there
will be elements of this. Resnick states that 'school cultivates symbolic thinking
whereas mental activity outside school engages directly with objects and situations' (Resnick, 1987, p. 16). For example, symbols will be used in shopping lists:
'2 cartons of juice' and on addresses such as '105, Brewland Street'.
   One of the central themes of this book is that there is a gap between home
informal mathematics that children bring to school and the school mathematics that seems detached from the outside world. The most difficult concepts children face are when they have to read or write the formal standard symbolisation
of mathematics at school. We argue that the gap can be bridged by encouraging
children to continue the informal home mathematics that they understand, as
they gradually assimilate the standard symbolisation of mathematics into their
own methods. In Chapters 6 and 7 we have shown how children's early numbers
and calculations develop from their informal marks.
   Tizard and Hughes in their study concluded that the home provides a 'very
powerful learning environment' (Tizard and Hughes, 1984, p. 249). Their study
included families from varied socio-economic backgrounds. It revealed that
there were no vast differences in learning opportunities whatever the background of the child. The differences appeared in content and values: all mothers
in the study were keen to give their children literacy and numeracy experiences.
'But the most frequent learning context was that of everyday living. Simply by
being around their mothers, talking, arguing and endlessly asking questions, the
children were being provided with large amounts of information relevant to
growing up in our culture' (Tizard and Hughes, 1984, p. 249).
   The home provides a real and purposeful learning situation with an immense
range of events that occur as a result of everyday living. The situations that children are exposed to are with people who know them, who share their back-

grounds and common experiences. This is important when the adults in the home are interacting with the children since it is easier to understand what the children are saying and to help them in their learning.

Nurseries and school settings cannot match the home as a learning environment. The Tizard and Hughes study in England also highlighted the differences between nursery settings and home and found that the home, in many ways, provided a more enabling learning environment.

Since the home is such a strong learning environment then Early Years settings need to continue to make connections with families to support and understand the child's home experience: in this way they will help the children make the connections necessary to understand their school mathematics. Through two case studies, one of a child at home (Carruthers, 1997c) and the other of a group of parents of a 4–6-year-old class we are going to analyse the following questions.

- What mathematics do young children do at home?
- What is their knowledge of mathematics?
- What is the role of parents in their children's mathematics?
- How do we work together with parents to support children's mathematics?
- Does the home continue to be supportive of children's mathematics?
- What mathematics do parents notice at home?
- What mathematical writing do young children see their parents and older siblings engaged in?
- What mathematical writing (marks) do parents observe their young children do?

What mathematics do young children do at home?

In a study of my own child I followed her own self-initiated numeracy-related actions on the world from the time she was 20 months to 40 months old (Carruthers, 1997c). Most of my findings of her development came from her number language. From this I observed that she developed an understanding of numbers and how they worked in a variety of meaningful, mathematical contexts. Before Sovay entered nursery school at 3 years 6 months she had, through her own chosen actions on the world, used mathematics in nearly every area of the subject. She had also tuned in to mathematics and had, in similar terms to Holdaway's literacy set, a mathematical set: the ability to tune in with appropriate action (Holdaway, 1979). Children who have developed a mathematical set (Carruthers, 1996) have the following abilities: they

- are aware that numbers have meaning in all mathematical areas and engage with numbers in a meaningful way
- use numbers to talk in the context of their own lives
- know that numbers can be written down and in some cases use their own written symbols

- play with numbers sometimes making up their own idiosyncratic games
- know that numbers have written symbols but may not know what they are
- know that numbers can be used in different ways, e.g. when counting you use a string of numbers and when you talk about time you use one single number
- have started to develop their own number system with notable conventions of number, e.g. some children count 1, 2, 6, 7, 8, 9, 11. They have used the numbers and they know some conventional strings.

I think it is important to note here that this knowledge can come before the child is observed counting with one-to-one correspondence, as was the case in Sovay's study. This also dispels the myth of the concept of 'pre-number' or 'readiness' activities. Children are always ready for numbers. The Durham Project (1994) also questioned this concept because, from the evidence of their research, children learn about number by counting objects in a variety of ways and not by traditional pre-number activities such as sorting and matching. Children also learn about numbers beyond counting in real life and purposeful contexts, as Sovay did.

As we have already emphasised, young children develop understandings about mathematics long before they enter school. Often when they start school their abilities are not always recognised by their teachers who pitch activities at a much lower level than that at which the children are functioning. Aubrey's (1994b) study highlighted this mismatch between teachers' expectations and the children's actual ability in mathematics. Wells (1986) found in his study of home and school that the home provides a rich learning environment where children ask questions, reflect, argue and therefore construct knowledge. Sovay in her mathematical development was observed reasoning, hypothesising and synthesising information. The following example of her engagement with number language emphasises the kind of learning and conversation that goes on at home. This conversation between Sovay and her mother happened the day before Sovay's third birthday. There had been much discussion about her party and her age.

Mum	How old will you be tomorrow?
Sovay	One.
Mum	No.
Sovay	One.
Mum	No.
Sovay	Two.
Mum	No.
Sovay	Four.
Mum	No.
Sovay	Yes, you said four.
Mum	I didn't.
Sovay	Eighteen.

Mum	No.
Sovay	What?
Mum	Three.
Sovay	Thirteen.
Mum	No, three.
Sovay	Fourteen.

Parents do ask questions of the testing type as well as teachers. This nearly 3-year-old did not give the adult the required response. If you study this closely you can see that Sovay did indeed know that she was going to be three. The wrong answer to Sovay appeared more stimulating than the right answer. She likes to play tricks. She probably knew that I would find her answers funny as I caught on to her joke, but at least at the beginning of the conversation I wanted to achieve my goal. I gave up in the end and I played along with her joke. Dunn (1988) studied children's humour and found that 2-year-olds explore and exploit the possible distortions of what is accepted in different ways with their siblings and their mothers. They are frequently amused by violation of rules.

Sovay actually gave me a richer indication of what she knew than if she had played along with my expectations and given the standard answer of 'three'. The evidence indicates that Sovay was playing with numbers in a most sophisticated way.

- She jumped around the number three, moving from two to four. This may have indicated that she was aware of the numbers before and after three.
- She used higher numbers, e.g. eighteen.
- She indicated an awareness of the relationship between three and thirteen. She made out she had heard me say thirteen instead of three perhaps because it sounds similar but she knows there is a difference.
- Following thirteen she said fourteen. Again she may be indicating that she knows the relationship between thirteen and fourteen as next to each other in the counting sequence.
- She used all these numbers with ease and confidence and was bold enough to use them to tease an adult.

Sovay constructed her mathematical knowledge with her family. The influence of her elder sister whom she loved to copy was valuable in aiding her growth. They went about their childhood world comparing, examining and playing. A favourite game was hide and seek and, even though Sovay could not count in the conventional manner to be a 'seeker', she was permitted to do so by her sister and her friends. The democratic atmosphere of the home allowed her to experiment and become a mathematician.

Sovay also started to take an interest in writing down mathematics. I noted when she was 3 years old that she wrote a dinner money envelope for her sister: she talked about money and wrote her own symbols down. She also wrote her own symbols at 4 years 3 months, explicitly naming numerals. However, these were the only two incidents in two years that I noted Sovay engaging with this kind of mathematical mark-making. Her number talk and social interaction was much more dominant.

We believe that children are learning complex meanings and understandings of their world at home and we argue throughout this book that they can construct their own meanings of mathematics on paper at home and continue to build on this, provided it is recognised in school. Children have been observed to struggle with a formally presented mathematical concept at school, yet have worked out their own way of solving the calculations, outside school (Carraher, Carraher and Schleimann, 1985).

What mathematics do parents notice at home?

As part of our research into young children's mathematical understanding and marks, we wanted to explore the home sociocultural influence of children in school. One of us made this study whilst teaching a class of 4–6-year-olds. This builds on the study of Sovay in the home (Carruthers, 1997c). Clearly such a study with a group of parents has the potential to provide a variety of information: this can help teachers build on children's understanding.

The most positive outcome was the rich information it provided from the children's families, in terms of their mathematics experiences at home and their parents' perspectives. The children attended a small village school with about 70 pupils from 4 to 8 years who came from all social backgrounds, with a mix of children living in the village and others from the nearby city. Fathers and mothers were invited to participate and 31 separate questionnaires were returned completed. Some of the data collected is explored below.

Awareness of early understanding of mathematics

At what age do parents believe that children begin to learn mathematics? This questionnaire revealed that a common perspective was that counting and numbers – the visible evidence of mathematical knowledge – were signs that children had begun to show an awareness or knowledge of mathematics. For example, one parent commented that her child's early number development began when she did 'basic counting such as counting stairs and fingers and knowing how many sweets she had'.

Above all, counting and numbers were identified as evidence of early mathematical development. Whilst a few parents believed that children started to learn mathematics from birth – a fact supported by research (e.g. Karmiloff-Smith, 1994) – the majority had identified signs of early mathematical development as beginning between the ages of 2–3 years of age: this is a time when children are very vocal and physically active. A few parents suggested that mathematical understanding began as late as 4 years. The audible language of counting as children climbed stairs or the visible actions of sharing combined with talk 'one for you, one for me' appeared to confirm that their child was developing mathematical understanding. An example of this is given on p. 204 when Sovay was talking with her mother about her age.

Mathematics events within one family

What is viewed as mathematics in early childhood behaviour and activities at home? I invited parents to make a note of the children's involvement in anything that involved mathematics, or anything mathematical their child saw or heard other family members do, during one week. Some parents noticed a great deal of mathematics in everyday experiences such as birthdays, sharing food and counting pocket money.

Talking mathematics

High levels of talk about numbers in the home through everyday language has been documented by Durkin and Shire (1986). Adults also help children focus on specific numerical goals and these help them understand basic quantitative tasks (Saxe, Guberman and Gearhart, 1987). The data collected of Sovay's mathematical development was largely through her talk (Carruthers, 1997c).

In this study most of the mathematical events that Rose and Ben's father noted, included adults talking. This has the effect of alerting the children to the mathematics in what they are doing and of scaffolding their learning (Bruner, 1971). In many of the families in this study, talk was a significant feature:

- 'Jack is always asking "how many minutes before we get there?" when we're in the car.'
- 'Talked about changing the clocks.'
- 'We discussed the price of a scooter as Daniel would like one'.

In some families parents also capitalised on incidental opportunities to help their children explore mathematics at a deeper level, within contexts that were meaningful to their child. 'James said he could "eat a hundred roast dinners in a week" and we talked about how long between meals he would need and how long it would take to eat one hundred dinners.'

In the 'mathematics at home' study a great deal of informal mathematics talk occurred in their families. Most parents also played mathematics games and sang number songs and rhymes. Television programmes with a mathematical focus and, for a few children, mathematical computer software provided additional opportunities for mathematical talk. Only three parents referred to any direct teaching: 'I'm trying to teach Jack how to tell the time on his watch', 'we're learning the numbers on the new music organ', 'adding numbers together; 2 + 2 etc.'. These can sometimes be valid activities on which to focus, but lack the real contexts and purpose for mathematical understanding.

Shopping, cooking and household tasks

Family activities provided many opportunities for mathematics: I noted, for example, that parents listed 17 responses referring to these types of activities. These included 'using a tape measure to check length of knitting' and 'discussing the choice of sandwich – 4 squares = 1 round of bread. Adam spread two squares with 'Marmite' and two with jam'.

The examples noted by the parents in this study indicate the rich sociocultural themes that influence and guide young schoolchildren's understanding and knowledge of mathematics within their families. Similar rich themes are highlighted in the study of Sovay long before she started school. When adult family members and older siblings use mathematics for real purposes such as 'measuring a curtain rail and estimating how many hooks to buy for curtains' they are helping children make the links between their own talk and play about mathematics. Ben also did this when he decided to measure the bathroom and hall with toilet paper. Our two studies point to the continuities of sociocultural themes that begin in infancy and continue to provide rich contexts for learning through meaningful interactions (Carruthers, 1997c).

The children experienced a full range of mathematics including a variety of calculations, all aspects of measurements, probability and money. Sometimes they used specific resources such as a measuring jug for milk or a foot gauge in a shoe shop, and money counted was always real. These incidents occurred either because:

- they were necessary
- they were initiated by the child
- they were fun
- they were part of the normal family routine.

Child-initiated play

In this study parents seldom noted children's self-initiated play as mathematical and there were only five recorded incidents of their play. As experienced Early Years educators and parents we might find this surprising. The growing body of research on the early development of the brain (Carnegie Corporation of New York, 1994; Greenfield, 1997; Nash, 1997) schemas (Athey, 1990) and infants' understanding of mathematics (e.g. Karmiloff-Smith, 1994) point to rapid development of mathematical understanding from birth. Recent research suggests links between early marks and emerging literacies. Sheridan proposes that children's early scribbling:

> ... serves four critical purposes: to train the brain to pay attention and to sustain attention; to stimulate individual cells and clusters of cells in the visual cortex for line and shape; to practise and organise the shapes and pattern of thought; and through an increasing affinity for marks, to prepare the human mind for its determining behaviour: literacy. This literacy is multiple: visual and verbal, artistic and scientific, mathematical, musical and literary (Sheridan, 2003, p. 2).

Yet these research findings are in contrast to the outcome of our 'Mathematics at Home' study in which parents appeared unaware of the mathematics within their children's play, unless it was a specific game such as playing shops. This suggests then that adults generally have difficulty recognising mathematics within play unless it is couched in specific mathematical language – usually of counting – or uses specific mathematical resources such as money.

Becoming alert to written mathematics

As their child's first and continuing educators, it is clear that parents are very keen to support and extend their child's understanding (Athey, 1990; Hannon, 1995). However, very few of the children in this study saw their parents write mathematics for their own interests or work, activities that help establish the sociocultural contexts of mathematics and the variety of marks and written methods. The few comments noted by parents during the seven days included:

- studying the football league tables and cricket score cards
- converting rent paid per calendar month to weekly amount and vice versa – using a ready reckoner, calculator and head
- Amy asked me what I was writing on my timesheet for work. I explained that I was writing the number of hours I worked each day and that this would be used to calculate how much money I earned.

Whilst some of their parents' work may have seemed a little remote, other children were regularly involved in what their parents did. Rose attended the 'After-School' Club that her mother ran. Her mother commented that 'at home, Rose looked on as I wrote out the bills for After-School Club'.

It is significant that no parents mentioned any marks their children made (print, symbols, drawing, numbers) on paper. This suggest that it is likely that such children's behaviours were not seen as 'mathematics'. In Sovay's study it was found that she did not use a prolific amount of mathematical representation: most of her representations after the age of 4 years were connected with her current schema. As Bottle has observed, 'parents may not always be aware of, or be able to identify their own contribution to the development of their child' (Bottle, 1999, p. 56). Yet it is the very fact that they have learnt mathematics at home in real contexts that provides young children with the rich, informal knowledge that they bring to school.

When teachers and parents are able to share their knowledge, then parents' awareness of play and mark-making can increase – and so, of course, can teachers'. For example, in a study of parents' observations of their 7-year-olds' mathematical schemas, one of us had shared her knowledge of schemas with the parents. The parents could then easily identify their children's interests in this area when they realised the possibilities.

The literacy events into which children are socialised also help children 'to survive, to consume, to act in the world' (Barton, quoted in Barratt-Pugh and

Rohl, 2000, p. 32). Barton arranged family literacy events into categories. We have developed this theme below for written mathematics based on responses from our questionnaires in this study.

Mathematical literacy events within families

The comments below are taken directly from the parents' questionnaires.

There were what Barton terms 'private events' which, in my study of 'Mathematics at Home' included comments such as 'read a book about planets – counted and compared sizes and distances' and 'learning the numbers on the new music organ'. Other events involved instructions and consumable goods, for example 'we measured washing powder (how many scoops)'. Most parents recognised the mathematics of television and videos and some helped their children understand when they 'talked about the way the hands go round the clock' or 'checked on Teletext'. Numbers occurred in different contexts when the family organised their lives including 'paying money in to bank' or filling the petrol tank of the car. A high proportion of comments related to social and community activities such as 'adding snooker scores' and 'changing the hymn numbers at church'. Finally, from their replies it was clear that some children saw their parents engaged in mathematics related to their work, including 'doing the accounts' and 'writing number of hours I worked each day, on timesheet'.

This shows something of the considerable range of mathematical literacy events in children's homes which include written aspects of mathematics and which may often not be recognised by parents. Hill et al. argue that in fact there is a considerable range of literacy learning in children's homes before they enter Early Years settings and that early childhood professionals need to understand and build on this (Hill et al., 1998).

Parents observe a wealth of mathematics

In two shorter studies we explored children's mathematical interests with parents. The first was with a group of parents of the class of 4–6-year-olds and the second with a class of 7- and 8-year-olds: we were both their class teachers at the time. Both studies followed meetings in which we had shared information about their children's schemas. One parent of a 5-year-old chose to keep a diary and noted:

> Sam has been interested in shapes that are produced when shadows are cast. He is becoming aware of when you place one shape together or beside another shape, how this produces yet another shape. He also can often name the shape created.

In my class of 7- and 8-year-olds, I asked the parents to keep a diary of their children's interests over the summer holidays. On several occasions I had discussed schemas and the link to mathematics, with the parents. The parents' notes reflected the breadth of the mathematics in which the children were engaged and that they were able to identify. We were also able to celebrate the children's focus and reflect on how we could all support the children's interests.

Parent's diary, 25 July – Julian age 7 years:

> Drew maps with contour lines, mountains, ship-wrecks, compass points, roads, bridges and rivers. Made 'collections' of stones, foreign money, stamps and buttons.

Helping parents recognise children's mathematical marks

McNaughton argues that 'there is a need for educators to be clearer about supporting complementary activities at home … (and) develop shared goals and activities with parents' in order that practice is shared across the home and education setting (McNaughton, 1995, p. 192). Open communication and collaboration between early years settings and families appear to be the key to developing shared practice and understandings about the children's mathematical development.

When teachers and parents do share their understandings such as the parents exploring their children's schemas and mathematical interests, teachers, children and families gain in understanding. 'Parents can be effective only if professionals take notice of what they say and how they express their needs and treat their contributions as intrinsically important' (Warnock Report, 1978, cited in Whalley, 1994, p. 64). This, we believe, is true for the parents of all children.

Many schools send home reading books, but there is scant evidence of a collaboration between parents and Early Years settings in terms of children's early writing, drawing or mathematical marks. We are certainly not arguing for an early emphasis on formal drawing, reading, writing and mathematics. However, we do believe that there is enormous potential in teachers and parents communicating about young children's early mark-making, meaning and development.

As Pahl suggests, 'perhaps the current enthusiasm for reading to five year olds for twenty minutes a night should be extended to encouraging twenty minutes of making a den or biscuits or mud pies' (Pahl, 1999a, p. 106). It is in such multimodal forms of representing meaning that the seeds of mathematics grow.

Parents' questions about children's mathematical graphics

When do they start doing sums?

A: Although your child might not be writing sums in the traditional way, she is often engaged in a variety of addition and subtraction. Much of the mathematics we directly teach to 4- and 5-year-olds is through talking, games and problem-solving. She is given opportunities to write down her mathematics. Look in her folder and you will see her mathematics. We are giving her opportunities to explore her own ways of writing down her addition and subtraction, as well as showing her the standard models and signs. Would you like me to talk through some of the mathematics she has done on paper?

In my day we had to use squared paper – that really helped us get it neat– why do you use blank paper?

A: Good question. We use blank paper so that children can make their own decisions about layout. Sometimes children want to draw pictures, arrows or numbers. We discuss with the children what they have written or drawn. Later we will introduce a variety of jottings to help the children work out calculations with larger numbers.

My son keeps on getting his numbers the wrong way round. We've shown him the right way but he can't remember – can you tell him?

A: We do talk about writing numerals and we practise this in a variety of ways. For example the children draw numerals on the carpet with their fingers. They also use the chalk board when they're thinking about the numbers that are really difficult for them, such as '5', '2' and '8'. Many children reverse numerals. This is common until the children are about 7 years of age. Your child is very good at mental mathematics and solving problems, and his handwriting skills will develop to match his mental ability as he sometimes works out his ideas about mathematics, on paper.

When do they get on to real maths?

A: I noticed when your child came to school, she was already very interested in mathematics. She has really developed this and now her interest is in money. She is also very interested in capacity which she often explores outside through filling containers and climbing inside large cardboard boxes. In our mathematics lessons I focus on specific mathematical topics; this week we are exploring space and shape, and the children are inventing their own three-dimensional shapes with the blocks.

This is all real mathematics and links with what they will be learning in the next class. We are having a parents' discussion about the children's mathematics next week. Would you like to come? It will be a small, informal group.

I know they like play but my child is ready for proper maths

A: Play is part of the children's learning and their mathematics. Your child particularly likes the office play area and last week she used the calculator to experiment with '99 + 6' and '99 + 7'. She predicted the answer each time and then checked it on the calculator. The other children were very interested and copied her, testing out their own calculations. Of course, as her teacher I teach the class specific aspects of mathematics every day. We also make frequent observations of the children's play and plan ways of supporting individuals. We keep records of their mathematical progress throughout the year.

I don't understand all those scribbles in their maths folders – it doesn't look like maths

A: Yes. It can be difficult for adults to understand but there is a lot of meaning in your child's marks. I have written what your child said about her marks in pencil at the bottom of each page. We are having an exhibition of children's mathematics, from nursery through to 8-year-olds. If you are free to come you will see what it is all about. Children's written mathematics is also only a part of their mathematics but it does help their thinking and mental methods.

Conclusion

Developing a genuine partnership with parents and carers can enrich all our lives. When teachers and parents share their knowledge about what they have seen and heard children do and say, they gain more than new knowledge: together they share a little of the child's inner world of meanings and possibilities.

12

Children, Teachers and Possibilities

Grown-ups love figures. When you tell them that you have made a new friend, they never ask you any questions about essential matters. They never say to you, 'What does his voice sound like? What games does he love best? Does he collect butterflies?' Instead they demand: 'How old is he? How many brothers has he? How much does he weigh? How much money does his father make?' Only from these figures do they think they have learned anything about him. (Saint-Exupéry, 1958, p. 15)

Inclusion

We wrote this book in the understanding that we have written for all children. Throughout the book the examples we have used cross a range of children, some of them have been categorised as children with special needs. We prefer not to label these children since it seems neither relevant nor important to do so. All the children with whom we have worked have been able to express their mathematics on paper. The diversity of the responses confirmed our own past experiences, that children think in a diversity of ways. We have discussed the children's marks and written methods with them and 'labelling' the children did not cross our minds. We both believe that it has actually freed the children who have been labelled as having 'special needs', to have opportunities to put their own mathematical marks on paper. Robins states that 'the mathematical experiences of many children with learning difficulties have centred around worksheets' and continues by proposing that such materials may be overused (Robbins, 2002, p. 133). In Chapter 10 we outlined the disadvantage of using worksheets. For children who may have a particular special need, using their own thinking about layout and making other decisions for themselves has helped them towards independence. There has been much stress on understanding in mathematics and a move away from hurrying children through standardised procedures. When children use their own ways of recording it is easier to assess what they understand and the nature of any difficulties. Anghileri supports this view, reasoning that 'errors and misconceptions may be identified more readily through informal and idiosyncratic working' (Anghileri, 2001b, p. 18).

Newman argues that 'activities that involve fragments of language, that discourage children taking chances, that don't permit the exchanging of idea, can only serve to make reading and writing more difficult' (Newman, 1984, p. 72). This is true for all young children learning mathematics but, we argue, it is even more so for children who may have learning difficulties.

The need to work from where the child is, can help us know where to start supporting the children's own methods. Their own ways make sense to them. In discussing children's own mathematics with them we can quite often be excitedly surprised by what they do know. Children's own mathematics provide adults with a 'discussion paper': for many children with special needs worksheets are a recipe for failure. They perpetuate a right/wrong culture. Cockburn believes that when children enter school they often learn to 'play the (mathematics) game' where the emphasis is on finding the right answer – which is always the teacher's answer (Cockburn, 1999, p. 9). Additionally, when children record in their own way, because they have to think carefully about what they do and consider a range of possibilities, they will learn more about the mathematics. It is because of this struggle that occurs within their minds that 'they will do better than their perceived best' (Brighouse and Woods, 1999, cited in Robbins, 2002, p. 5).

Children's questions

Listening to children, not only to what they have to say about their marks but what they have to say in general, can instigate a change in your teaching. I remember when I asked the children in my class what questions they had when we were discussing Holland. One child asked, how many cows are there in Holland? I was not expecting that kind of question but it has been in my mind ever since. It is an interesting question and I believe only a child would ask it. The questions below are from children in our own classes and from other classes in which we have taught. We have included questions and comments from children in classes where teachers had just started to support their own mathematical graphics.

Lia, 7:0	**Are you allowed to show your working?**
Response:	If writing down your mathematics helps your thinking, then of course. Sometimes just putting something down helps your memory when you have a lot of calculations to do – otherwise you may forget. However, if you can do the mathematics in your head, well, just write the answer down.
Jason, 8:2	**Can I use a rubber?**
Response:	It is better not to use rubbers, because you may want to look back at the strategies you have used. I like to see what you have written as it shows all your thinking. All good mathematicians keep all of their written work, even if it did not work out: they can go over it again and see where they might have worked in a different way. They don't use rubbers – every mark is important.

Sophie, 5:5   **Can I colour it in?**
                    I would like to listen to what you have to say about these inter-
                    esting marks you have made, then we can discuss whether you
                    still want to colour it in and if it will help your thinking.

Neil, 7:3   **My mum does it a different way.**
                    We have looked at several different ways to do subtraction.
                    Come and show us what your mum does and perhaps some of us
                    would like to try that way.

Stella, 5:1   **He's doing it wrong, miss!**
                    There is no one, right way to work this calculation out. When
                    he's finished, Larry might like to explain what he did and you
                    can show him your way.

Ralph, 6:9   **But I know the answer already!**
                    That's great Ralph! Put your answer down and we can discuss
                    ways that you could check it.

Genevieve, 6:6 **Do I have to do it?**
                    Can you think of another way you could show your thinking?
                    Perhaps there is something else in the room you would like to
                    use rather than paper and pencil?

Charlotte, 6:0   **But I have only just started and it's dinner time.**
                    Yes Charlotte, you have been thinking very carefully – try to
                    make quick notes of your thinking up until now and you can
                    continue after lunch. You have some good ideas and I'd like to
                    know more about them.

Silence as a question: occasionally teachers are met with silence when they
have invited children to 'put something down on paper' to show their thinking.
This may be because they have been worksheet dependent and are new to the
idea of making their own marks or choosing their own written methods. We find
it is helpful to suggest that they work from what they know, perhaps visualising
aspects of the problem or calculation in their heads. They might also find it
helpful to discuss ideas with a partner and just jot down a few ideas that they
can then discuss together with their teacher.

Teachers' questions

But surely nursery children shouldn't be doing written maths?

Writing, numbers, symbols and pictures are everywhere around us – outside and
in children's homes. Providing opportunities to make marks helps young children understand that their marks can carry meaning: this helps them relate their
marks to what they see in the world. Some of their early marks will carry mathematical meaning. When young children have an opportunity to do this, it
helps them develop their understanding, provided their teacher understands

how she might support and extend their understanding. In the nursery children may choose to use their own personal marks, scribbles, numbers and drawings (see nursery examples in chapters 2, 6, 8 and 9). Writing sums is not appropriate for nursery children.

Would you expect to see written mathematics develop in the same way as their writing?

We can see many similarities in children's development of their marks for writing and for mathematics. Children's earliest mathematical graphics develop from early marks which they do not talk about, through to standard numerals that they use in appropriate contexts (see Chapter 6). In all their graphical languages (drawing, writing and mathematics) whilst developmental pathways have been identified this does not mean that all children move through all the stages, or do so in the same order. Understanding the development of children's writing and of their mathematical graphics is very helpful for teachers. It means that teachers can then understand how to support children, based on what they have observed children do.

What I don't understand, is when you stop doing emergent writing and start doing real writing

The terms emergent (or early) writing and mathematical graphics refer to children's development of writing and 'written' mathematics. They are very real to the children at the moment they make their marks. It is essential that children's growing understanding is supported by teachers, since without our support they will be unable to make essential links with their standard written language (such as English or Greek) or the standard symbolism of mathematics. The 'journey' from their earliest marks to standard forms needs to be a smooth transition, therefore we never 'stop' supporting their early marks and 'start' expecting only standard letters and symbols.

It doesn't look like the mathematics they usually do – what do I say to my headteacher?

Begin in a small way, perhaps with a few children. Keep, date and annotate what they do, writing down what each child says about her marks. In this way you will be able to build up a profile of the children's mathematical graphics in your class. Doing this will help you to assess what the children really know and can do. This way of working is recommended (in England) in both the *Curriculum Guidance for the Foundation Stage* and the *National Numeracy Strategy*. Your headteacher is likely to be supportive when she understands that you are planning your teaching and support based on what you know about the children. The examples in this book do not look like mathematical worksheets or standard sums because they are the children's own, rather than an adult's. They make very real sense to the children and help their understanding.

I do support children's own methods but when the children move on to another class, this doesn't continue

We think it is really important that children continue using their own methods throughout the school. In many schools staff have developed a policy on written methods that supports a whole-school approach. Such a document provides examples of children's written mathematics from nursery through to 11 years of age. It is the product of a series of meetings in which the staff agree teaching approaches and how to respond to children's marks. A good way to start is to look at your policy on supporting children's writing and see if your setting is giving the same messages in mathematics.

What do I say to the parents?

We found several positive ways of communicating what we were doing, with parents. We have used pieces of children's mathematical graphics in displays and supported this by including our written comments, pointing out what the children had shown that they understood. Some parents will need reassurance that a 4-year-old's scribbles will develop into standard numerals and sums. When we had a lot of examples we put on a small exhibition in the hall and this allowed us to show the development of their mathematics on paper, during the year.

We also invited parents to meet together to discuss ways of supporting their children's mathematics and the subject of their written mathematics arose at this time. It may reassure parents to know that (in England) this is what is recommended practice in the *National Numeracy Strategy* and the *Curriculum Guidance for the Foundation Stage.*

How can I tell if they're making progress?

We find that making informal observations (formative assessment) really tells us a great deal about what children can do. Observing and really listening to what children say about what they are doing, is a very positive way of assessing children's understanding. In order to know if children are progressing from what you observe them do today, you will need to date and keep their mathematical graphics, and occasionally annotate them when time allows. In this way you will have first-hand evidence of each child's development during the course of the year. It may be possible for this to be continued for several years, to build up a profile during their time in the nursery or infant school.

How can we keep track of all the bits of paper?

Some teachers find a cardboard 'envelope' folder for each child is an easy way to store all they do. Just make sure each piece is dated, if you are able. Children may want to take some pieces home or you may use them in a display – then the photocopier will allow you to keep a copy for the child's folder too.

How do I convince teachers of older pupils – they have been rather sceptical in my school?

Make changes slowly. If you are keeping children's mathematical graphics you will be able to show their development over time. Using children's own marks (rather than copied numbers or sums) is an invaluable means of assessment. Change can be threatening for us all but it will reassure colleagues to know that (in England) this is what is recommended, and that research shows that this really does help children understand standard written mathematics at a deep level. The children who are now in your class and making their own early marks will have moved on to many of the standard forms with understanding, when they are older.

I put columns and boxes in the children's work books because they don't know how to organise their own work

There is evidence to show that children need to experiment with ways of setting out a page and make their own decisions about whether to put a box around some figures, or how to organise data they have collected. At first it will not look like the standard forms of layout, but doing this will help them understand why some layouts work better than others for particular aspect of mathematics.

We don't keep any of the children's own mathematical marks from their play – we like to let them take it home

Young children especially like to take things home. However, it is important that you build up a profile of their understanding through their mathematical graphics and photocopies will do just as well.

Where do I start?

You have already begun, by reading some of this book. You may like to reflect on what you have deliberately done, that has already helped children's early writing development. Perhaps adding writing tools and paper to the role play area generated marks within the context of children's play roles. It may be that creating a graphics area or putting up a noticeboard generated different writing 'genres'. These may be useful places to begin (see Chapter 8). You will also benefit if you are able to discuss what is happening in your nursery or class with an interested colleague.

It's all very well – but what about test scores?

When children try to show their own methods on paper in national tests for mathematics, it helps them think through the question and often leads to a correct answer. For example, in the Key Stage 1 SATS in England, some children tackled the more difficult problem-solving questions by using their own methods. One question in recent years asked children to work out how many packs – of four cartons of juice in each pack – would be needed for a party which 26 children would attend (Figure 12.1).

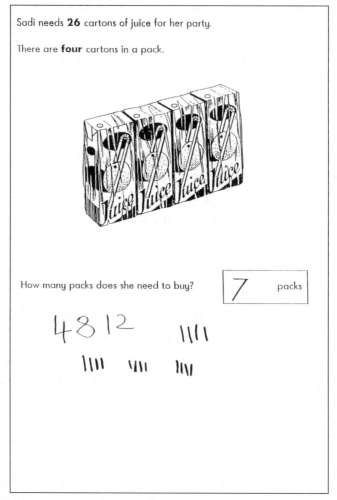

Figure 12.1 Using own written methods

Jenny, 7:3, thought this through by counting in multiples of four – 4, 8, 12. When she had exhausted her knowledge of that she reverted to tallies (or an iconic method of representation). Perhaps if she had not been used to using her own methods she would not have answered this question.

Out of three schools we surveyed we found that in their SATS, children who had used their own written methods to solve the problems were successful in achieving the correct answers for those questions. Price also reported that, when using a developmental approach to mathematics and allowing children to record in their own way, their SATS scores increased (Price, 1994). We therefore believe that supporting children's own methods and chosen ways of representing their mathematical thinking will help children's performance in national tests.

Reflections

Throughout time and now throughout a greater part of the world, print – and other marks that humans make in order to reflect on and communicate their ideas – have been a significant and powerful feature of our development. In many countries, still, literacy has the capacity to lift people out of poverty. The potency of the written word which is, in essence, the power of peoples' thoughts, has at different times in our history been both seen as a threat and as a strength. Written words and other graphical languages hold significance in the lives of millions of people today more than at any time in our history.

Perhaps it is now time to recognise the huge potential of children's early mathematical marks in helping them understand the abstract symbolism of mathematics.

As we have argued throughout this book, children need to become bi-numerate to understand the abstract symbolism of mathematics. Leone Burton stresses that the individual strengths, interests and cultures of the children provide them with a familiar basis from which the mathematics can emerge, this: 'encourages curiosity and excitement because the learner begins with a feeling of comfort' (Burton, 1992, p. 19).

We have based this book on our mathematical research in the home and classroom. Combining the two has been essential to find the translation pathways that loop between informal and abstract mathematics. As a parent, Heidi Mills reflects that the process that has remained a consistent feature and driving force in her children's growth, is the constant search for connections between higher experiences and their current ones.

Teachers have a vital role in the process of bi-numeracy since it is they who can help the children make connections. The flame of mathematical intuition is within the children but teachers need to be aware of the interactive networks within the children's brains, to keep the flame burning. Wilkinson emphasises the importance of teachers' views of the nature of mathematics and of knowledge, society and the future. She argues that 'officially and effectively, teachers are the formers of the nation's mind': 'if teachers are too narrow, too limited in their view of themselves as educators, too confined in their views of mathematics then we shall produce a generation of adders and dividers rather than pupils who are seekers and solvers of problems and makers of new mathematical meanings' (Wilkinson, 1998, p. 23).

It is not easy to teach mathematics well, some teachers call it a minefield (Desforges and Cockburn, 1987). For many teachers the struggle is like understanding the picture of the boa constrictor at the beginning of this book. Some may choose to ignore the children's own mathematics; others will find it hard to accept that the children's own mathematical marks are the foundations of their learning the abstract symbolism of mathematics and written methods. Developing good teaching has no simple answers, but in the chapters of this book we hope you hear the children's mathematical voices shining through:

> and he laughed again. 'You are not fair, little prince,' I said. 'I don't know how to draw anything except boa constrictors from the outside and boa constrictors from the inside.'
>
> 'Oh, that will be alright,' he said, 'children understand.' (Saint-Exupéry, 1958, p. 77–78)

Appendix: Our Research

We have drawn on 13 separate pieces of our own research. These studies have not previously been published.

- *Analysis of 700 samples of mathematical graphics, collected from children 3–8 years*. The examples of children's graphics included throughout this book are all drawn from this collection. We collected and analysed almost 700 examples of children's mathematical marks and own written methods, from the 3–8-year age range. Examples are from children at home, from a variety of nursery settings and from children in schools during a period of 12 years. Analysis of these provided information on the development of the children's marks that led to the categories in Chapters 6 and 7.
- *Teachers' questionnaires*. Two hundred and seventy-three teachers of children 3–8 years old completed questionnaires about children's recording in mathematics. The teachers came from four areas of England – three cities and one rural county: our findings from their responses are referred to in Chapter 1 and in Chapter 5.
- *Telephone interviews*. We conducted telephone interviews with a sample of teachers who had completed the questionnaires and who offered to help us. Some of the findings from these are included in Chapter 1, Chapter 5 and Chapter 12,
- *Parents' schema diaries (children 4–6 years)*. We have drawn on observations from parents of children in a class of 4–6-year-olds, of their children's schema interest at home. This 'Parents' Group' met regularly during one term to share ideas of ways of supporting their children's mathematics, from infancy to 8 years: see Chapter 3 and Chapter 11.
- *Nine-month observational study – patterns of children's schemas*. Informal observations of children's self-initiated play in the same class provided rich insights into their mathematical schemas. These led to the 'map' tracing Aaron's pattern of schemas' that is reproduced in Chapter 3. It also provided evidence for the section on children's schemas and their early writing in Chapter 4.
- *Holiday mathematical interest diaries – children 7–8 years*. Diaries kept during one summer vacation by parents of older children provided insights into their mathematical interests at home: see Chapter 11.
- *MEd dissertation – unpublished This* was a *study of assessment of levels of cognitive challenge in a class of children 4–6 years*. We draw on some outcomes from

this study in Chapter 3.

- *MEd dissertation, 'the Sovay study'.* This is a parent–child study of a young child's developing mathematical understanding between the ages of 22 months and 42 months. We have drawn on this study in Chapters 2, 3 and 11.

- *Group Parents' Study.* Thirty-one parents (mothers and fathers) of children aged 4–6 years completed questionnaires of their children's mathematics at home and of their own experiences of learning mathematics. Some of the findings from these questionnaires are included in Chapter 11.

- *Nursery study – India.* This study was conducted in nursery schools in rural south India and focused on teaching and learning. We draw on this in Chapter 1, when we consider the international perspective.

- We carried out a *study of mathematics SATs papers* in four schools. In this study we focused on the extent to which children used their own written methods – see Chapter 12.

- *Study to compare outcomes of teacher-modelling and teacher-given examples.* The implications of this small-scale study in a class of 5-year-olds are explored in Chapter 10.

- *Assessing the contribution of teacher-modelling on children's developing mathematics graphics.* The effects of teacher-modelling mathematics in a class of 6-year-olds were assessed during the course of one term – also referred to in Chapter 10.

- *Observations of children's self-initiated writing behaviours (marks relating to writing and mathematics)*: these observations were made during two three-week periods following the addition of resources to support writing in the first instance and then additional resources to support mathematical behaviour and mark-making. We refer to the outcome of these observations in Chapter 8.

- *Research: 2003–04. Teachers share children's mathematics online – an elearning approach*: an action research project: 'Building a community of practice: a mentoring programme on e-facilitation'. Supported by the Institute of Education, University of London and Mirandanet. Research funded by the General Teaching Council and the DfES.

Glossary

Below we provide definitions for some of the important terms which we use in this book: these definitions refer to their use within the context of this study.

algorithm	A step-by-step procedure that produces an answer to a particular problem (a standard algorithm is a set procedure for a problem which has been generally recognised as the most efficient way to solve an addition, subtraction, division or multiplication problem). Standard algorithms are part of the established arithmetic culture in many countries.
bi-numerate	Through using their own mathematical graphics children translate between their own informal understanding and abstract mathematical symbolism, in an infinite feedback loop. We originated the term 'bi-numerate' to describe the translation between these two systems. This allows children to exploit their own informal marks and use this knowledge to gradually construct deep personal meaning of standard mathematical symbols and subsequent standard written calculations.
code switching	Switching from informal representation to include some standard symbols within a piece of mathematical graphics or calculation.
dimensions of mathematical graphics	These represent the development of children's mathematical graphics (see p. 126).
dynamic	Marks that are lively and suggestive of action – full of energy and new ideas.
example	When a teacher provides a direct example and then children follow the teacher's example when representing their mathematics: this usually results in all children copying what the teacher has done.
iconic	Marks based on one-to-one counting. These may include tallies or other marks and symbols of the children's own devising (Hughes, 1986).
implicit symbols	Symbols that are implied within the child's marks or layout, but are not represented: this is a significant stage in children's developing understanding of the abstract language of mathematics.
jottings	Informal, quick marks that are made to aid memory when working out mental calculations.
marks	In the context of this study, we use this term to refer generally to children's marks on paper: children also make graphical marks on other surfaces such as sand, paths and windows.
mark-making	Children's own, self-initiated marks which may be explored through their actions or forms of symbolic languages such as drawing, writing or mathematics.
mathematical graphics	Children's own choice of marks that may include scribbles, drawing, writing, tallies, invented and standard symbols.

modelling	Teachers (or children) using chosen ways to represent some mathematics, usually for a real need and which they show to other children. Modelling is not followed by children copying what has been shown, but over time provides a 'tool box' of ideas and possible marks, symbols, ways of representing and of layout.
multi-modal	Children create their meanings by using the representational resources available to them at the time (Kress, 1997).
narrative	When children represent their calculations as narratives, with a sense of relating a story: e.g. 'first I did this, then I added two more, then I had 5 altogether'.
narrative action	Children include some means of showing the action of (often) addition or subtraction by, for example, drawing a hand removing some items or arrows pointing to some numerals – more often found in representations of subtraction.
number	Numbers are ways of expressing and recording quantities and measurements.
numeral	A numeral is a digit, which is a single symbol: for example, 45 is a number but within that number there are two numerals, 4 and 5.
operator	This is a symbol to show which operation is to be used, i.e. +, -, ×, ÷.
operation	An operation is a rule that is used to process one or more numbers, e.g. subtraction, addition, multiplication or division. Algebraic forms of mathematics use more complex operations.
pictographic	A drawing giving something of the appearance of what was in front of the child; actually representing something the child was looking at (Hughes, 1986).
recording	When children use practical equipment and then they record what they have done.
representation	This refers to children's own mathematical thinking on paper. It may also be used to refer to children's interest in representing their ideas through, for example, using blocks, paper cut-outs, play or construction.
schemas	Patterns of children's own repeated behaviour that gives us a window on their thinking (cognition) (Athey, 1990).
socioculturalism	Children learn about the world and construct mathematical understanding through the sociocultural practices in which children and adults are involved (see Barratt-Pugh and Rohl, 2002).
symbolic	This stage arises out of all previous stages. 'Standard symbolic' refers to the use of standard forms of numerals and some standard signs such as + and = (Hughes, 1986).
symbols	Mathematical symbols such as = and +. Children may also use their own intuitive or invented symbols as they move towards understanding the standard forms.
transitional forms	When children move between one graphical form and another, for example, from pictographic to iconic.
written (form)	Using words or letter-like marks in a calculation, which are read as words and sentences.
written methods	These are forms of mathematics that children write down to answer a problem, i.e. written calculations.

References

Alexander, R. (2000) *Culture and Pedagogy: International Comparisons in Primary Education.* Oxford: Blackwell.

Allardice, B. (1997) 'The development of written representations for some mathematical concepts', *Journal of Children's Mathematical Behaviour,* **1** (4), 135–48.

Anghileri, J. (2000) *Teaching Number Sense.* London: Continuum.

Anghileri, J. (ed.) (2001a) *Principles and Practice in Arithmetic Teaching: Innovative Approaches for the Primary Classroom.* Buckingham: Open University Press.

Anghileri, J. (2001b) 'A study of progression in written calculations and division', *Support for Learning,* **16** (1), 17–22.

Anning, A. (2000) *The Influence of the Socio-Cultural Context on Young Children's Meaning Making through Mark-Making, Drawing, Modelling and Playing with Objects.* Working Paper 22. Leeds: Centre for Research on Family, Kinship and Childhood.

Anstey, M. and Bull, G. (1996) *The Literacy Labyrinth.* Sydney: Prentice Hall.

Arnold, C. (1997) *Child Development and Learning 2–5 Years: Georgia's Story.* London: Hodder and Stoughton.

Ashton-Warner, S. (1965) *Teacher.* New York: Simon and Schuster.

Askew, M. (1998) *Teaching Primary Mathematics.* London: Hodder and Stoughton.

Askew, M. (2001) 'A response to Girling and Zarzycki', *Mathematics Teaching,* **174**, 13–14 March.

Askew, M. and Wiliam, D. (1995) *Recent Research in Mathematics Education 5–16.* OFSTED Reviews of Research. London: School of Education: King's College.

Askew, M., Brown, M., Rhodes, C. and Wiliam, D. (1997) *Effective Teachers of Numeracy: Final Report.* London: Hodder and Stoughton.

Athey, C. (1990) *Extending Thought in Young Children: A Parent–Teacher Partnership.* London: Paul Chapman Publishing

Atkinson, S. (1992) *Maths with Reason.* London. Hodder and Stoughton.

Aubrey, C. (1994a) *The Role of Subject Knowledge in the Early Years of Schooling.* London: Falmer Press.

Aubrey, C. (1994b) 'An investigation of children's knowledge of mathematics at school entry and the knowledge their teachers hold about teaching and learning mathematics, about young learners, and mathematical subject knowledge', *British Educational Research Journal,* **20** (1), 105–20.

Aubrey, C. (1997a) 'Children's early learning of number in school and out', in I. Thompson (ed.) *Teaching and learning Early Number.* Buckingham: Open University Press.

Aubrey, C. (1997b) *Mathematics Teaching in the Early Years: An Investigation into the Role of Teachers' Subject Knowledge.* London: Falmer Press.

Bakhtin, M. M. (1981) *The Dialogic Imagination: Four Essays.* Austin, TX: University of Texas Press.

Bakhtin, M. M. (1986) *Speech Genre and Other Late Essays.* C. Emerson and M. Holquist (eds), Austin, TX: University of Texas Press.

Baroody, A. (1987) 'The development of counting strategies for single-digit addition', *Journal for Research in Mathematics Education,* **18** (2), 141–57.

Barratt-Pugh, C. (2000) 'The socio-cultural context of literacy learning', in C. Barratt-

Pugh and M. Rohl (eds), *Literacy Learning in the Early Years*. Buckingham: Open University Press.

Barratt-Pugh, C. and Rohl, M. (Eds) (2000) *Literacy Learning in the Early Years*. Buckingham: Open University Press.

Barratta-Lorton, M. (1976) *Mathematics their Way*. Menlo Park, CA: Addison Wesley.

Barton, D. (1994) *Literacy: An Introduction to the Ecology of Written Language*. Oxford: Blackwell.

Beishuizen, M. (2001) 'Different approaches to mastering mental calculation strategies', in J. Anghileri (ed.), *Principles and Practices in Arithmetic Teaching*. Buckingham: Open University Press.

Bennett, N., Wood, E. and Rogers, S. (1997) *Teaching through Play*. Buckingham: Open University Press.

Bissex, G. (1980) *GNYS AT WRK: A Child Learns to Read and Write*. Cambridge, MA: Harvard University Press.

Bottle, G. (1999) 'A study of children's mathematical experiences in the home', *Early Years*, **20** (1), Autumn pp. 53–64.

Bourdieu, P. (1977) *Outline of a Theory of Practice*. Cambridge: Cambridge University Press.

Bourdieu, P. (1991) *Language and Symbolic Power*. Cambridge, CA: Stanford University Press.

Brighouse, T. and Woods, D. (1999) *How to Improve your School*. London: Falmer Press.

Brissenden, T. (1988) *Talking about Mathematics*. Oxford: Blackwell.

Bruce, T. (1991) *Time to Play in Early Childhood Education*. London: Hodder and Stoughton.

Bruce, T. (1997) *Early Childhood Education*. London: Hodder and Stoughton.

Bruner, J. S. (1971) *Towards a Theory of Instruction*. Cambridge, MA: Harvard University Press.

Bruner, J. (1996) 'What we have learned about learning', *European Early Childhood Education Research Journal*, **4** (1), 5–16.

Burt, C., cited in D. Selleck, 'Baby Art: art is me', in P. Gura (ed.) (1997) 'Reflections on early education and care', *Early Education Papers 1–11*. London: British Association for Early Childhood Education.

Burton, L. (1992) 'Working together', *Mathematics Teacher*, **140** pp. 16–19.

Burton, L. (1994) 'Evaluating an "entitlement curriculum": mathematics for all?', in M. Selinger, (ed.), *Teaching Mathematics*. London: Routledge.

Buys, K. (2001) 'Progressive mathematization: sketch of a learning strand', in J. Anghileri (ed.), *Principles and Practices in Arithmetic Teaching*. Buckingham: Open University Press.

Cambourne, B. (1988) *The Whole Story: Natural Learning and the Acquisition of Literacy in the Classroom*. Auckland: Ashton Scholastic.

Carnegie Corporation of New York (1994) *Starting Points for Young Children*. New York: Carnegie Corporation of New York.

Carpenter, T. and Moser, J. (1984) 'The acquisition of addition and subtraction concepts in grades one through three', *Journal for Research in Mathematics Education*, **15** (3), 179–202.

Carr, M. (2001) *Assessment in Early Childhood Settings*. London: Paul Chapman Publishing.

Carraher, T., Carraher, D. and Schleimann, A. (1985) 'Mathematics in the streets and in school', *British Journal of Developmental Psychology*, **3**, 21–9.

Carruthers, E. (1996) 'A pattern of children's learning in number: a developmental theory', *Primary Practice*. (5), June, 14–16.

Carruthers, E. (1997a) 'A number line in the nursery classroom: a vehicle for understanding children's number knowledge', *Early Years*, **18** (1), Autumn, 9–14

Carruthers, E. (1997b) 'Talking numbers: a developmental link between literacy and numeracy', *Early Education*, Summer, 5–6.

Carruthers, E. (1997c) 'Number: a developmental theory. A case study of a child from twenty to forty-four months', unpublished MEd dissertation, University of Plymouth.

Centre for Literacy of Quebec (1999) at literacycyntr@dawsoncollege.qc.ca

Chiazzari, S. (1998) *The Healing Home*. London: Ebury Press.

Chomsky, M. (1965) *Aspects of the Theory of Syntax*, Cambridge, MA: MIT Press.

Claxton, G. (1997) *Hare Brain and Tortoise Mind*. London: Fourth Estate.

Clay, M. (1975) *What Did I Write?* London: Heinemann.

Cockburn, A. (1999) *Teaching Mathematics with Insight*. London: Falmer Press.

Cockcroft, W. (1982) *Mathematics Counts*. London: HMSO.

Coltheart, M. (1979) 'When can children learn to read – and when can they be taught?', in T. Wallerr and G. Mackinnon (eds), *Reading Research: Advances in Theory and Practice*, vol. 1. New York: Academic Press.

Cook, V. (1992) 'Evidence for Multi-competence', in *Language Learning*. 42 (4), p. 557–91.

Cook, V. (2001) *Second Language Learning and Language Teaching*. London: Arnold, Hodder Headline Group.

Court, S. (1925) 'Numbers, time and space in the first five years of a child's life', *Pedagogical Seminary*, 27, 71–89.

Crawford, P. (1995) 'Early literacy: emerging perspectives', *Journal of Research in Childhood Education*, 10 (1), 71–86.

Cullen, J. and St George, A. (1996) 'Scripts for learning: reflecting dynamics of classroom life', *Journal for Australian Research in Early Childhood Education*, 1, 10–19.

David, T. (1999) *Teaching Young Children*. London: Paul Chapman Publishing.

Davis, A. and Pettitt, D. (eds) (1994) *Developing Understanding in Primary Mathematics: Key Stages 1 & 2*, London: Falmer Press.

DeLoache, J. (1991) 'Symbolic functioning in very young children: understanding of pictures and models', *Child Development*, 62, 736–52.

Deloache, J., Uttal, D. and Pierroutsakos, S. (1998) 'The development of early symbolisation: educational implications', *Learning and Instruction*, 8 (4), 1325–39.

Desforges, C. and Cockburn, A. (1987) *Understanding the Mathematics Teacher: a study of practice in First Schools*. London: Falmer Press.

DfEE (1999) *The National Numeracy Strategy*. London: Department for Education and Employment.

Donaldson, M. (1978) *Children's Minds*. Glasgow: Fontana.

Driver, R., Guesne, E. and Tiberghien, A. (1985) *Children's Ideas in Science*. Buckingham: Open University Press.

Drummond. M. J. (1993) *Assessing Children's Learning*. London: David Fulton.

Drury, R. (2000) 'Bi-lingual children in the nursery: a case study of Samia at home and at school', in *European Early Childhood Research Journal*. 8 (1), pp.43–59.

Dunn, J. (1988) *The Beginnings of Social Understanding*. Oxford: Blackwell.

Durkin, K. and Shire, B. (1991) *Language in Mathematical Education: Research and Practice*. Buckingham: Open University Press.

Egan, K. (1988) *Primary Understanding*. London: Routledge.

Eng, H. (1999) *The Psychology of Children's Drawings from the First Stroke to the Coloured Drawing*. London: Routledge.

Engel, B. (1995) *Considering Children's Art: Why and How to Value their Works*. Washington, DC: National Association for the Education of Young Children.

Ernest, P. (1991) *The Philosophy of Mathematics Education*. London: Falmer Press.

Ewers-Rogers, J. and Cowan, R. (1996) 'Children as apprentices to number', *Early Childhood Development and Care*, 125, 15.15–17.

Fein, S. (1997) cited in D. Selleck, 'Baby Art: art is me', in P. Gura, (ed.), Reflections on Early Education and Care, *Early Education Papers 1–11*. London: British Association for Early Childhood Education.

Ferreiro, E. and Teberosky, A. (1979) *Literacy before Schooling*. London: Heinemann.

Fisher, J. (1996) *Starting from the Child?* Buckingham: Open University Press.

Freudenthal, H. (1968) Why? To teach mathematics so as to be useful', *Educational Studies in Mathematics*, **1**, 3–8.

Fuson, K. (1988) *Children's Counting Concepts and Concepts of Number*. New York: Springer-Verlag.

Fuson, K. and Hall, J. (1983) 'The acquisition of early number word meanings', in H. Ginsberg (ed.), *The Development of Children's Mathematical Thinking*. New York: Academic Press.

Gardner, H. (1980) *Artful Scribbles: The Significance of Children's Drawings*. New York: Basic Books.

Gardner, H. (1993) *The Unschooled Mind: How Children Think and How Schools Should Teach*. London: Fontana.

Gardner, H. (1997) *Extraordinary Minds*. London: Weidenfeld and Nicolson.

Gelman, R. (1991) 'Epigenetic foundations of knowledge structures: initial and transcendant conditions', in S. Carey and R. Gelman (eds), *The Epigenesis of Mind: Essays on Biology and Cognition*. Hillsdale, NJ: Erlbaum.

Gelman, R. and Gallistel, C. R. (1978) *The Child's Understanding of Number*. Cambridge, MA: Harvard University Press.

Gelman, R. and Tucker, M. F. (1975) 'Further investigations of the young child's conception of number', *Child Development*, **46**, 167–75.

Gifford, S. (1990) 'Young children's representations of number operations', *Mathematics Teaching*, **132**, 64–71, September.

Gifford, S. (1997) 'When should they start doing sums? A critical consideration of the emergent mathematics approach', in I. Thompson (ed.), *Teaching and Learning Early Number*. Buckingham: Open University Press.

Gifford, S. (2003) 'A new mathematics pedagogy for the Early Years?' Paper presented to members of the Early Childhood Mathematics Group. Institute of Education, University of London.

Ginsburg, H. (1977) *Children's Arithmetic*. New York: Van Nostrand.

Ginsberg, H. (1989) *Children's Arithmetic*. Second edition. Austin, TX: Pro-ed.

Glaser, B. and Strauss, A. (1967) *The Discovery of Grounded Theory*, Chicago, IL: Aldine.

Goleman, D. (1996) *Emotional Intelligence*. Reading: Cox and Wyman.

Goodman, K. (1986) *What's Whole in Whole Language?* London: Scholastic.

Graves, D. (1983) *Writing: Teachers and Children at Work*. London: Heinemann.

Greenfield, S. (1997) *The Human Brain: A Guided Tour*. London: Weidenfeld and Nicolson.

Groen, G. and Resnick, L. B. (1977) 'Can preschool children invent addition algorithms?', *Journal of Educational Psychology*, **69**, 645–52.

Gulliver, J. (1992) Key speech at the first Emergent Mathematics Teachers' Conference, University of Exeter.

Gura, P. (ed.) (1992) *Exploring Learning: Young Children and Blockplay*. London: Paul Chapman Publishing.

Hall, N. (1987) *The Emergence of Literacy*. London: Hodder and Stoughton.

Hall, N. (ed) (1989) *Writing with Reason*. London: Hodder and Stoughton.

Hall, N. (1998) 'Concrete representations and the procedural analogy theory', *Journal of Mathematical Behaviour*, **17** (1), 33–51.

Hall, N. and Robinson, A. (1995) *Exploring Writing and Play in Early Years*. London: David Fulton.

Halliday, M. (1975) *Learning How to Mean*. London: Arnold.

Hannon, P. (1995) *Literacy, Home and School*. London: Falmer Press.

Harries, T. and Spooner, M. (2000) *Mental Mathematics for the Numeracy Hour*. London: David Fulton.

Harste, J., Woodward, V. and Burke, C. (1984) *Child Research and Development.* New York: Casey.

Hebbeler, K. (1981) 'Young children's addition', in A. Floyd (ed.), *Developing Mathematical Thinking.* Wokingham: Addison Wesley.

Heuvel-Panhuizen, M. van den. (2001) 'Realistic mathematics education in the Nether-lands', in J. Anghileri (ed.), *Principles and Practices in Arithmetic Teaching.* Buckingham: Open University Press.

Hiebert J. (1984) 'Children's mathematical learning', *Elementary School Journal,* **84** (5), 497–513.

Hill, S., Comber, B., Louden., W., Rivilland, J. and Reid, J. (1998) *100 Children go to School: Connections and Disconnections in Literacy development in the Year Prior to School and the First year at School.* Australian Language and Literacy National Literacy project report, Department of Education, Training and Youth Affairs (SETYA), South Australia.

Holdaway, D. (1979) *The Foundations of Literacy.* Sydney: Scholastic.

Holloway K. (1997) 'Exploring mental arithmetic', *Mathematics Teaching,* **160**, 26–28.

Hopkins, C., Gifford, S. and Pepperell, S. (1999) *Mathematics in the Primary School.* London: David Fulton.

Hughes, M. (1986) *Children and Number: Difficulties in Learning Mathematics.* Oxford: Blackwell.

Hughes, M., Desforges, C. and Mitchell, C. (2000) *Numeracy and Beyond.* Buckingham: Open University Press.

John-Steiner, V. (1985) 'The road to competence in an alien land: a Vygotskian perspec-tive on bilingualism', in J. Wertsch (ed.), *Culture, Communication and Cognition: Vygot-skian perspectives.* Cambridge: Cambridge University Press.

Johnson, D. (ed.) (1989) *Children's Mathematical Frameworks 8–13: A Study of Classroom Teaching.* Windsor: NFER (cited in Askew and Wiliam, 1995, p. 10).

Karmiloff-Smith, A. (1994) *Baby It's You.* London: Ebury Press.

Kellog, R. (1969) *Analysing Children's Art.* Palo Alto, CA: National Press Books.

Kress, G. (1997) *Before Writing: Re-thinking the Paths to Literacy.* London: Routledge.

Lave, J. and Wenger, E. (1991) *Situated Learning.* Cambridge: Cambridge University Press.

Leder, G. (1989) 'Number concepts of pre-school children', *Perceptual and Motor Skills,* **69**, 1048–50.

Lee, C. (2000) 'Modelling in the mathematics classroom', *Mathematics Teaching,* June, 28–31.

Lewis, A. (1996) *Discovering Mathematics with 4–7 Year Olds.* London: Hodder and Stoughton.

Litherand, B. (1997) 'Reflections on the assessment of mathematics', in *Mathematics Teaching,* 159, June.

Luke, A. (1993) 'The social construction of literacy in the primary school', in L. Unsworth, *Literacy, Learning and Teaching: language as a social practice in the primary School.* Melbourne: Macmillan.

Luria, A. (1983) 'The development of writing in the child', in M. Martlew (ed.), *The Psy-chology of Written Language.* Chichester: John Wiley.

Maclellan, E. (2001) 'Representing addition and subtraction: learning the formal con-ventions', *European Early Childhood Education Research Journal,* **9** (1), 73–84.

MacNamara, A. (1992) 'How many are there?', *Early Years,* **3** (1).

Malaguzzi, L. (1996) in T. Filippini and V. Vecchi (eds), *The Hundred Languages of Children.* p. 3. Reggio Emila: Reggio Children.

Malchiodi, C. (1998) *Understanding Children's Drawings.* London: Jessica Kingsley.

Manning, B. and Payne, D. (1993) 'A Vygotskian-based theory of teacher cognition towards the acquisition of mental reflection and self-regulation', *Teaching and Teacher Education,* **9** (4), 361–71.

Markman, E. (1990) 'Constraints children place on word meanings', *Cognitive Science*, **14**, 55–7.

Matthews, J. (1999) *The Art of Childhood and Adolescence: The Construction of Meaning*. London: Falmer Press.

McNaughton, S. (1995) *Patterns of Emergent Literacy*. Oxford: Oxford University Press.

Meade, A., with Cubey, P. (1995) *Thinking Children*, Wellington: NZCER.

Merttens, R. and Brown T. (1997) 'Number operations and procedures', in R. Merttens (ed.), *Teaching Numeracy*. Leamington Spa: Scholastic.

Millet, A. and Johnson, D. (1996) 'Solving teachers' problems; the role of the commercial mathematics scheme', in D. Johnson and A. Millett (eds), *Implementing the Mathematics National Curriculum*. London: Paul Chapman Publishing.

Mills, H. (1995) 'Follow our children's thinking', *Dimensions of Early Childhood*. Summer. 24–25.

Mills, J. (2002) 'Early numeracy: children's self-initiated recordings (3–5 years)', unpublished PG Diploma Assignment, Swift Masters Programme, College of St Mark and St John. Plymouth.

Montague-Smith A. (1997) *Mathematics in the Nursery Education*. London: David Fulton.

Mor-Sommerfield, A. (2002) 'Language Mosaic. Developing literacy in a second-new language: a new perspective', in *Reading: literacy and language*. Oxford: UKRA. Blackwell Publishers. **36** (3), pp. 99–105. November.

Munn, P. (1994) 'The early development of literacy and numeracy skills', *European Early Childhood Research Journal*, **2** (1), 5–18.

Munn, P. (1997) 'Children's beliefs about counting', in I. Thompson (ed.), *Teaching and Learning Early Number*. Buckingham: Open University Press.

Munn, P. and Schaffer, H. (1993) 'Literacy and numeracy events in social inter-active contexts', *International Journal of Early Years education*, **1** (3), 61–80.

Munn, P., Gifford, S. and Barber, P. (1997) 'Gimme sum loving', *Times Educational Supplement*, 6 June, 14.

Murshad, A-H. (2002) 'Tools for talking: the purposeful and inventive use of languages by bi-lingual children in primary classrooms', in *Reading: literacy and language*. Oxford: UKRA. Blackwell Publishers 36 (3), pp. 106–112). November.

Nash, J. (1997) 'Fertile minds', *Time*, **149**, 48–56.

National Writing Project. (1989) *Becoming a Writer*. Walton-on-Thames: Thomas Nelson.

Newman, J. (1984) *The Craft of Children's Writing*. New York: Scholastic Book Services.

Nunes, T. and Bryant, P. (1996) *Children Doing Mathematics*. Oxford. Blackwell.

Nutbrown, C. (1994) *Threads of Thinking: Young Children Learning and the Role of Early Education*. London: Paul Chapman Publishing.

Oers, B. van (1994) 'Semiotic activity of young children in play: the construction and use of schematic representations', *European Early Childhood Education Research Journal*, **2** (1) 19–33.

Oers, B. van (1997) 'The narrative nature of young children's iconic representations: some evidence and implications', *International Journal of Early Years Education*, **5** (3), 237–45.

Opie, I. and Opie, P. (1969) *Children's Games in Street and Playground*. Oxford: Open University Press

Orton, A. (1992) *Learning Mathematics*. London: Cassell.

Pahl, K. (1999a) *Transformations: Meaning Making in Nursery Education*, Stoke-on-Trent: Trentham Books.

Pahl, K. (1999b) 'Making models as a communicative practice – observing meaning making in the nursery', *Reading* UKRA, November.

Paley, V. (1981) *Wally's Stories*. Cambridge, MA: Harvard University Press.

Pascal, C. (1990) *Under-Fives in the Infant Classroom*. Stoke-on-Trent: Trentham Books.

Pascal, C. and Bertram, T. (eds) (1997) *Effective Early Learning*. London: Hodder and Stoughton.

Pearsall, J. (ed.) (1999) *Concise Oxford Dictionary*. Oxford: Oxford University Press.

Pengelly, H. (1986) 'Learning to write mathematics by writing mathematics', unpublished article.

Pettitt, D. and Davis, A. (1994) 'Mathematics beyond the school and a summing up', in D. Pettitt and A. Davis, *Developing Understanding in Primary Mathematics*. London: Falmer Press.

Piaget, J. (1958) *The Child's Construction of Reality*. London: Routledge and Kegan Paul.

Pimm, D. (1981) 'Mathematics? I speak it fluently', in A. Floyd (ed.), *Developing Mathematical Thinking*. Wokingham: Addison Wesley.

Pound, L. (1998) 'Noses to the worksheets', *Nursery World*, 12 March, 12–13.

Pound, L. (1999) *Supporting Mathematical Development in the Early Years*. Buckingham: Open University Press.

Price, A. (1994) 'Developing a concept of number at Key Stage 1 – can the principles of developmental writing help?', paper presented at BERA conference, Oxford.

QCA (1999) *Teaching Written Calculations*. National Numeracy Strategy. London: Qualifications and Curriculum Authority.

QCA (2000) *Curriculum Guidance for the Foundation Stage*. London: Qualifications and Curriculum Authority.

Resnick, L. (1987) *Education and Learning to Think*. Washington, DC: National Academic Press.

Robbins, B. (2002) *Inclusive Mathematics*. New York: Continuuim.

Saint-Exupéry, A. de (1958) *Le Petit Prince*. London. Heinemann Educational.

Saxe, G., Guberman, S. and Gearhart, M. (1987) 'Social processes in early number development', *Monographs of the Society for Research in Child Development*, 29 (2), serial no. 216.

Selinger, M. (1994) *Teaching Mathematics*. London: Routledge in association with the Open University.

Selinker, L. (1972) 'Interlanguage', *International Review of Applied Linguistics*, 10 (3), 209–31.

Selleck, D. (1997) 'Baby art: art is me' in P. Gura (ed.), *Reflections on Early Education and Care*. London: British Association for Early Childhood Education.

Sharpe, R. (2000a) 'Mathematics: aims and practices', in K. Ashcroft and J. Lee. (eds), *Improving Teaching and Learning in the Core Curriculum*. London: Falmer Press.

Sharpe, R. (2000b) 'New approaches: the National Numeracy Project, the "Numeracy Hour" and the teaching of mathematics', in K. Ashcroft and J. Lee. (eds), *Improving Teaching and Learning in the Core Curriculum*. London: Falmer Press.

Shearer, J. (1989) 'How much do children notice?', in N. Hall (ed.), *Writing with Reason*. London: Hodder and Stoughton.

Sheridan, S. R. (2003) *Very Young Children's Drawings and Human Consciousness: The Scribble Hypothesis. A plea for brain-compatible teaching and learning* (Abstract) on: www.drawingwriting.com/scribReQ.html pp.2–6.

Sinclair, A. (1988) 'La notation numérique chez l'enfant', in A. Sinclair (ed.), *La Production de Notation chez le Jeune Enfant: langue, nombres, rythmes et melodies*. Paris: Presses Universitaires de Frances.

Skemp, R. (1971) *The Psychology of Learning Mathematics*. London: Penguin Books.

Smith, F. (1978) *Reading*. Cambridge: Cambridge University Press.

Smith, F. (1982) *Writing and the Writer*. London: Heinemann Educational.

Smith, J. and Elley, W. (1997) *How Children Learn to Write*. London: Paul Chapman Publishing.

Sophian, C. (1995) *Children's Numbers*. Dubuoue, Iowa, Madison, Wisconsin: Brown and Benchmark.

Steffe, L. (1983) 'Children's algorithms as schemes', *Educational Studies in Mathematics*, **14** (2), 109–25.

Stoessinger, R. and Edmunds, J. (1992) *Natural Learning and Mathematics*. Melbourne: Thomas Nelson.

Stoessinger, R. and Wilkinson, M. (1991) 'Emergent mathematics', *Education 3–13*, **19** (1), 3–11.

Sutton, E. (1984) *My Cat Likes to Hide in Boxes*. Barnstaple: Spindlewood.

Sylva, K., Roy, C. and Painter, M. (1986) *Childwatching at Playgroup and Nursery School*. Oxford: Blackwell.

Threfall, J. (1992) 'No sums please, we're infants.' *Education 3–13*, **20** (2), 15–17.

Thompson, I. (1995) 'The role of counting in the idiosyncratic mental calculation algorithms of young children', *European Early Childhood Research Journal*, **3** (1), 5–16.

Thompson, I. (ed.) (1997) *Teaching and Learning Early Number*. Buckingham: Open University Press.

Thrumpston, G. (1994) 'Mathematics in the National Curriculum: implications for learning in the Early Years', in G. Blenkin and A. Kelly, (eds), *The National Curriculum and Early Learning*. London: Paul Chapman Publishing.

Tizard, B. and Hughes, M. (1984) *Young Children Learning: Talking and Thinking at Home and at School*. London: Fontana.

Torrance, H. (2001) 'Assessing for learning: developing formative assessment in the classroom', *Education 3–13*, October. **29** (3), 26–42.

Treffers, A. (1978) *Wiskobas doelgericht* (Wiskobas goal-directed). Utrecht: IOWO.

Trevarthen, C. (1980 and 1988) in J. Matthews (1990) *The Art of Childhood and Adolescence: The Construction of Meaning*. London: Falmer Press.

Vergnaud, G. (1982) 'Cognitive and developmental psychology and research in mathematics education: some theoretical and methodological issues', *For the learning of Mathematics*, **3** (2), 31–41.

Vygotsky, L. S. (1978) *Mind in Society: The Development of Higher Psychological Thought Processes*, eds M. Cole, V. John-Steiner, S. Scribner and E. Souberman. Cambridge, MA: Harvard University Press.

Vygotsky, L. S. (1983) 'The pre-history of written language', in M. Martlew (ed.), *The Psychology of Written Language*. Chichester: John Wiley.

Vygotsky, L. S. (1986). *Thought and Language*. New York: John Wiley.

Walkerdine, V. (1988) *The Mastery of Reason: Cognitive Development and the Production of Reality*. London: Routledge.

Warnock Report (1978) *Report of the Committee of Enquiry into the Education of Handicapped Children and Young People*. London: HMSO.

Weinberger, J. (1996) 'Young children's literacy experiences within the fabric of daily life', in R. Campbell (ed.), *Facilitating Pre-School Literacy*. Delaware: Interactive Reading Association.

Wells, G. (1986) *The Meaning Makers: Children Learning Languages and Using Language to Learn*. Portsmouth, NH: Heinemann Educational.

Wertsch, J. (1990) 'The voice of rationality in a socio-cultural approach to mind', in L. Moll (ed.), *Vygotsky and Education: instructional implications and applications of socio-cultural psychology*. Cambridge: Cambridge University Press.

Whalley, M. (1994) *Learning to be Strong*. London: Hodder and Stoughton.

White, L. (1949) *The Science of Culture*. New York: Farrar and Straus.

Whitebread, D. (1995) 'Emergent mathematics or how to help young children become confident mathematicians', in J. Anghileri (ed.), *Children's Mathematical Thinking in the Primary Years*. London: Cassell.

Whitin, D., Mills, H. and O'Keefe, T. (1990) *Living and Learning mathematics: stories and strategies for supporting mathematical literacy*. Portsmouth, NH: Heinemann.

Wilkinson, M. (1998) 'Mathematics ... and does it matter?', *Mathematics Teaching*, March. 3–11.

Williams H. (1997) 'Developing numeracy in the Early Years', in R. Merttens (ed.), *Teaching Numeracy*. Leamington Spa: Scholastic.

Woods, D. (1988) *How Children Think and Learn*. Oxford: Blackwell.

Worthington, M. (submitted as Hayton) (1995) University of Exeter: Unpublished MEd dissertation entitled 'High/Scope in the Reception Class: a Domain of Cognitive Challenge. Awarded 1996.

Worthington, M. (published as Hayton) (1996a) 'Emergent and developmentally appropriate learning: the relationship to personal views of learning', *Primary Practice* (5), June, 16–17.

Worthington, M. (published as Hayton) (1998) 'Solving problems together: emerging understanding', *Mathematics Teaching*, **162**, March, 18–21.

Worthington, M. (published as Hayton) and Carruthers, E. (1998) 'A collaborative approach', *Mathematics Teaching*, **162**, March, 11–15.

Worthington, M. (published as Hayton) and Murchison, P. (1997) *Mathslines: A Mathematical Framework for Four Year Olds*. Devon: Devon Curriculum Advice.

Wray, D., Bloom, W. and Hall, N. (1989) *Literacy in Action: The Development of Literacy in the Primary Years*. Lewes: Falmer Press.

Zarzycki. P. (2001) 'In the clutches of algorithms: a view from Poland', *Mathematics Teaching*, **174**, March.

Zevenbergen, R. (2002) Using mental computations for developing number sense at http://gamt.cqu.edu.au/QAMTAC2000/mental_comp.rtf p.4.

Author Index

Subject Index

Teaching Number

Advancing Children's Skills and Strategies

Robert J Wright *Southern Cross University, Australia*,
Jim Martland *University of Liverpool*,
Ann K Stafford *Mathematics Recovery, South Carolina* and **Garry Stanger** *New South Wales Department of Education & Training, Australia*

'This is a highly detailed and well-structured text to support the teaching of number skills at the primary phase with particular emphasis given to the 4-8 years age range' - **Mathematics in Schools**

This book provides a structured approach to the teaching of early numeracy, which has been extensively developed through the *Mathematics Recovery* and *Count Me In Too Projects* in Australia, the United Kingdom and the United States.

The book lets teachers identify where their students are in terms of number skills, and sets out a strategy for developing their knowledge. This book will be useful to primary teachers, especially in the early years, mathematics co-ordinators, heads of school, mathematics advisers, learning support personnel, lecturers and educational psychologists.

Abridged Contents
Introduction \ Advancing Children's Strategies and Knowledge in Early Numbers \ Individualized Teaching in Mathematics Recovery \ Whole Class Teaching \ General Introduction to Chapters 4 to 8 \ Teaching the Emergent Child \ Teaching the Perceptual Child \ Teaching the Figurative Child \ Teaching the Counting-On Child \ Teaching the Facile Child

P·C·P
Paul Chapman
Publishing

2002 • 242 pages
Cloth (0-7619-7050-9) • Paper (0-7619-7051-7)

ALSO AVAILABLE

Early Numeracy

Assessment for Teaching and Intervention

Robert J Wright *Southern Cross University, Australia,*
Jim Martland *University of Liverpool* and
Ann K Stafford *Mathematics Recovery, South Carolina*

'The book would be particularly useful for anyone wanting to know more of MRP, and to maths co-ordinators/SEN teachers, trainers and numeracy consultants' - *Primary Mathematics*

'An ambitious book about an ambitious project. It offers a detailed description of some aspects of Mathematics Recovery' - *Times Educational Supplement*

Early Numeracy offers schools an assessment instrument to identify and deal with children who underachieve in early numeracy. It will enable teachers, trainers and numeracy consultants to learn a distinctive and comprehensive approach to assessment and teaching.

Based on extensive long-term research, the authors' *Mathematics Recovery Programme* has been successfully applied by teachers in Australia, the United Kingdom and the United States, in specialist interventions and general classroom settings.

Abridged Contents

Children, Numeracy and Mathematics Recovery \ The Learning Framework in Number \ Mathematics Recovery Assessment \ The Stages of Early Arithmetical Learning \ Identifying the Stages of Early Arithmetical Learning \ Preparing for the Assessment Interview \ Coding and Analyzing the Assessment Interview \ Learning from Mathematics Recovery \ Extending the Learning Framework to Multiplication and Division

P·CP
Paul Chapman Publishing

2000 • 208 pages
Paper (0-7619-6529-7)